Mastering Sales

CAROLINA ACADEMIC PRESS MASTERING SERIES
RUSSELL WEAVER, SERIES EDITOR

For other titles, please go to caplaw.com.

Mastering Administrative Law, Second Edition
Linda D. Jellum

Mastering Adoption Law and Policy
Cynthia Hawkins DeBose

Mastering Alternative Dispute Resolution
Kelly M. Feeley, James A. Sheehan

Mastering American Indian Law
Angelique Wambdi EagleWoman, Stacy L. Leeds

Mastering Appellate Advocacy and Process, Revised Printing
Donna C. Looper, George W. Kuney

Mastering Art Law
Herbert Lazerow

Mastering Bankruptcy
George W. Kuney

Mastering Civil Procedure, Third Edition
David Charles Hricik

Mastering Constitutional Law, Second Edition
John C. Knechtle, Christopher J. Roederer

Mastering Contract Law
Irma S. Russell, Barbara K. Bucholtz

Mastering Corporate Tax, Second Edition
Gail Levin Richmond, Reginald Mombrun, Felicia Branch

Mastering Corporations and Other Business Entities, Second Edition
Lee Harris

Mastering Criminal Law, Second Edition
Ellen S. Podgor, Peter J. Henning, Neil P. Cohen

**Mastering Criminal Procedure, Volume 1:
The Investigative Stage, Second Edition**
Peter J. Henning, Andrew Taslitz, Margaret L. Paris, Cynthia E. Jones, Ellen S. Podgor

**Mastering Criminal Procedure, Volume 2:
The Adjudicatory Stage, Second Edition**
Peter J. Henning, Andrew Taslitz, Margaret L. Paris, Cynthia E. Jones, Ellen S. Podgor

Mastering Elder Law, Second Edition
Ralph C. Brashier

Mastering Employment Discrimination Law, Second Edition
Paul M. Secunda, Jeffrey M. Hirsch, Joseph A. Seiner

Mastering First Amendment Law
John C. Knechtle

Mastering Income Tax
Christopher M. Pietruszkiewicz, Gail Levin Richmond

Mastering Intellectual Property
George W. Kuney, Donna C. Looper

Mastering Labor Law
Paul M. Secunda, Anne Marie Lofaso, Joseph E. Slater, Jeffrey M. Hirsch

Mastering Legal Analysis and Communication
David T. Ritchie

Mastering Legal Analysis and Drafting
George W. Kuney, Donna C. Looper

Mastering Negotiable Instruments (UCC Articles 3 and 4)
and Other Payment Systems, Second Edition
Michael D. Floyd

Mastering Negotiation
Michael R. Fowler

Mastering Partnership Taxation
Stuart Lazar

Mastering Professional Responsibility, Second Edition
Grace M. Giesel

Mastering Property Law, Revised Printing
Darryl C. Wilson, Cynthia Hawkins DeBose

Mastering Sales
Colin P. Marks, Jeremy Kidd

Mastering Secured Transactions: UCC Article 9, Second Edition
Richard H. Nowka

Mastering Statutory Interpretation, Second Edition
Linda D. Jellum

Mastering Tort Law, Second Edition
Russell L. Weaver, Edward C. Martin, Andrew R. Klein,
Paul J. Zwier, II, John H. Bauman

Mastering Trademark and Unfair Competition Law
Lars S. Smith, Llewellyn Joseph Gibbons

Mastering Trusts and Estates
Gail Levin Richmond, Don Castleman

For other titles, please go to caplaw.com.

Mastering Sales

Colin P. Marks
ERNEST W. CLEMENS PROFESSOR OF LAW
ST. MARY'S UNIVERSITY SCHOOL OF LAW

Jeremy Kidd
ASSOCIATE PROFESSOR OF LAW
MERCER UNIVERSITY SCHOOL OF LAW

CAROLINA ACADEMIC PRESS
Durham, North Carolina

Library of Congress Cataloging-in-Publication Data

Names: Marks, Colin P., author. | Kidd, Jeremy, author.
Title: Mastering sales / Colin P. Marks and Jeremy Kidd.
Description: Durham, North Carolina : Carolina Academic Press, LLC,
  [2018] |
Series: Carolina Academic Press Mastering Series
Identifiers: LCCN 2018010985 | ISBN 9781611638523 (alk. paper)
Subjects: LCSH: Uniform commercial code. Sales. | Sales--United
  States--States. | Contracts--United States--States. | Breach of
  contract--United States--States. | Warranty--United States--States. |
  Damages--United States--States.
Classification: LCC KF915 .M39 2018 | DDC 346.7307/2--dc23
LC record available at https://lccn.loc.gov/2018010985

eISBN 978-1-61163-990-2

Carolina Academic Press, LLC
700 Kent Street
Durham, North Carolina 27701
Telephone (919) 489-7486
Fax (919) 493-5668
www.cap-press.com

Printed in the United States of America

Dedication

To my mother and father,
who have always supported me in all my endeavors, and
to my wife Jill and children Savy-Jo and George,
who make me happy every day–CM

To my wife, Heather, whose patience and
love makes it all worthwhile–JK

Contents

Preface   xvii

Series Editor's Foreword   xix

Chapter 1 · The Scope of Article 2   3
  Roadmap   3
  A. Introduction to Commercial Law   3
  B. The Scope of Article 2   4
      1. "Transactions"   5
      2. "Goods"   6
      3. Hybrid transactions   7
      4. Software   9
  C. Merchant Status   11
  Checkpoints   14

Chapter 2 · Distinguishing Sales from Leases   15
  Roadmap   15
  A. How a Sale Can Resemble a Lease   15
  B. Why the Sale/Lease Distinction Matters   16
  C. Resolving the Sale/Lease Distinction Under § 1-203(b):
      The "Bright-Line" Test   18
  D. The "Economic Realities" Test   20
  Checkpoints   22

Chapter 3 · Contract Formation Under the U.C.C.   23
  Roadmap   23
  A. The U.C.C.'s Broad Conception of Contract Formation   23
  B. Distinguishing Advertisements from Offers   25
  C. Acceptance and How It Differs from the Common Law   26
  D. Consideration in Requirements and Exclusive Dealings
      Contracts   28

E. Firm Offers   30
F. Contract Formation in the Electronic Age   32
Checkpoints   34

Chapter 4 · Battle of the Forms—Offer and Acceptance   35
Roadmap   35
A. Two Situations Covered by U.C.C. § 2-207   35
B. Contract Formation with a Written Offer and Acceptance
    Under U.C.C. § 2-207(1)   37
C. What Terms Control When an Acceptance Adds Terms to
    the Offer   38
    1. Additional terms when a non-merchant is involved   39
    2. Treatment of additional terms as between merchants   39
D. What Terms Control When an Acceptance Changes Terms
    in the Offer   41
    1. Treat as additional approach   42
    2. Ignore the proposed change approach   42
    3. The "knock-out rule"   43
E. Contract Formation Under U.C.C. § 2-207(3) When the
    Writings Fail to Form a Contract   44
Checkpoints   46

Chapter 5 · Battle of the Forms—Confirmations   47
Roadmap   47
A. How Confirmations Arise   47
B. What Terms Control When a Confirmation Adds to or
    Changes the Terms of an Oral Agreement   48
C. The Rolling Contract Approach to Contract Formation   49
    1. ProCD, Inc. v. Zeidenberg and establishment of
        the rolling contract approach   49
    2. Limitations on the rolling contract approach   51
D. The Intersection of Rolling Contracts with U.C.C. § 2-207   52
Checkpoints   53

Chapter 6 · Statute of Frauds   55
Roadmap   55
A. An Introduction to the Statute of Frauds   55
B. The Threshold Requirements of § 2-201(1)   56

C. The "Between Merchants" Exception 57
D. The Part Performance Exceptions 59
    1. Specially manufactured goods exception 59
    2. Payment/acceptance exception 60
E. Admission Exception 61
F. Interaction of § 2-201 with §§ 2-207 and 2-209 62
Checkpoints 64

Chapter 7 · Contract Interpretation and the Parol Evidence Rule 65
Roadmap 65
A. Interpretive and Constructive Tools Under the U.C.C. 65
B. Judicial Approaches to Ambiguity and Contract Interpretation 67
C. Introduction to the Parol Evidence Rule Under the U.C.C. 69
    1. Application of the parol evidence rule to partially
       integrated contracts 69
    2. Application of the parol evidence rule to fully integrated
       contracts 71
D. Avoiding Application of the Parol
Evidence Rule 71
Checkpoints 73

Chapter 8 · Express Warranties 75
Roadmap 75
A. How Express Warranties Arise 75
    1. Affirmations of fact, promises, and descriptions 76
    2. Sample or model 79
B. The Basis of the Bargain 79
C. The Role of Puffery 81
Checkpoints 83

Chapter 9 · Implied Warranties 85
Roadmap 85
A. Introduction to Implied Warranties 85
B. The Implied Warranty of Merchantability 86
    1. When does the implied warranty of merchantability
       arise? 87
    2. What does it mean to be merchantable? 88

   C. Implied Warranty of Fitness for a Particular Purpose   89
   Checkpoints   92

Chapter 10 · Disclaiming and Limiting Warranties   93
   Roadmap   93
   A. The Use of Contract to Disclaim or Limit Warranty   93
   B. Disclaiming Express Warranties   94
   C. Disclaiming Implied Warranties   95
      1. Disclaiming implied warranties under § 2-316(2)   95
      2. Disclaiming implied warranties: the easy way   97
      3. Disclaiming implied warranties by inspection   98
      4. Disclaiming implied warranties under § 2-316(3)(c)   99
   D. Limiting Remedies   100
   Checkpoints   102

Chapter 11 · Warranty of Title   103
   Roadmap   103
   A. How Title Is Transferred   103
      1. Void versus voidable title   104
      2. Entrustment   106
   B. The Implied Warranty of Title   107
   C. Disclaiming the Implied Warranty of Title   108
   D. The Warranty Against Infringement   109
   Checkpoints   111

Chapter 12 · Breach and Cure   113
   Roadmap   113
   A. Perfect Tender Rule   113
      1. Reject the whole   116
      2. Accept non-conforming goods   119
      3. Accept commercial units and reject the rest   120
   B. Duty to Mitigate   121
   C. Opportunity to Cure   124
   D. Installment Contracts   125
   Checkpoints   128

Chapter 13 · Anticipatory Repudiation and Adequate Assurances   129
   Roadmap   129
   A. Repudiation of a Contract   129

B. Walking the Mitigation/Breach Tightrope 131
C. Demanding Adequate Assurance 132
Checkpoints 135

Chapter 14 · Impracticability 137
Roadmap 137
A. Excuse by Impracticability 137
    1. Unexpected contingency 138
    2. Unallocated risk 139
    3. Performance is impracticable 140
    4. When identified goods are harmed 141
B. Effect on the Parties' Responsibilities 142
Checkpoints 144

Chapter 15 · Unconscionability 145
Roadmap 145
A. Unconscionability 145
B. Procedural Unconscionability 146
    1. Absence of meaningful choice 147
    2. Unequal bargaining power 148
    3. Contracts of adhesion 148
C. Substantive Unconscionability 149
D. Unconscionability Is Rarely a Successful Claim 150
Checkpoints 151

Chapter 16 · Rejection and Revocation 153
Roadmap 153
A. Rejecting Non-Conforming Goods 153
    1. Must reject in a reasonable time 154
    2. Must give seasonable notice 155
B. Revoking Acceptance 155
    1. Nonconformity must substantially impair the value 157
    2. No substantial change in condition 157
    3. Burden of proof shifts 158
Checkpoints 159

Chapter 17 · Privity 161
Roadmap 161
A. Who Has Privity? 161

B. Intended Beneficiaries   162
    1. Creditor beneficiaries   162
    2. Donee beneficiaries   164
    3. Other intended beneficiaries   164
C. Incidental Beneficiaries   165
D. Privity and Warranties Under the U.C.C.   165
Checkpoints   167

Chapter 18 · Risk of Loss   169
Roadmap   169
A. Why Risk of Loss Is Important   169
B. When Does It Pass?   169
    1. When goods are shipped   170
    2. The case of breach   175
C. Least Cost Avoider   176
Checkpoints   177

Chapter 19 · Seller's Remedies   179
Roadmap   179
A. Wrongful Rejection of Goods   179
B. Cover   181
C. Hypothetical Cover   182
D. Lost Volume Sellers   183
E. Recover Price   185
F. Scrap and Salvage or Finish?   186
Checkpoints   188

Chapter 20 · Buyer's Remedies   189
Roadmap   189
A. Rejection of Imperfect Tender   189
B. Cover   190
C. Hypothetical Cover   191
D. Specific Performance   192
E. Damages After Acceptance   192
F. Scrap and Salvage   194
G. Incidental and Consequential Damages   195
H. Limitations on Damages   197
Checkpoints   199

Chapter 21 · Specific Performance and Liquidated Damages   201
  Roadmap   201
  A. Specific Performance   201
    1. Default is no specific performance   202
    2. Unique goods   202
    3. "Other circumstances"   203
    4. Replevin   204
  B. Liquidated Damages   204
    1. Reasonableness   205
    2. No penalties   206
  Checkpoints   207

Mastering Sales Checklist   209

Index   227

Preface

You have in your hands a comprehensive overview of Article 2 of the Uniform Commercial Code. Whether you are a first-year law student being introduced to contract law for the first time, a more advanced law student seeking to enhance your understanding of sales, a practitioner who wants a refresher, or even a non-lawyer who just wants an educated peek into the world of contract law, this book will help you on your way.

We have been teaching contracts for many years, and we know that the doctrines contained in Article 2 can be confusing if not placed in the proper context. Of particular importance is understanding how all the parts of Article 2 fit together. With that in mind, we have endeavored in this book to break down the legal doctrines into clear, easy-to-understand language. It is our hope that this book will make your journey through Article 2 clearer and easier, and that you will emerge on the other side having a working mastery of these important contract principles.

As you use this book to enhance your studies, it will navigate you through the various provisions of the Code, walking you through contract formation, performance, breach, and remedies. We have taken great care to break down and explain complicated concepts, such as the notorious Battle of the Forms and the parol evidence rule, in plain English, but without losing any of the nuances of rules.

If you are familiar with the Mastering Series, you'll recognize the familiar roadmap at the beginning of each chapter and a checkpoint of important rules (and their exceptions) at the end. These will help you organize your thinking as you begin learning the legal doctrines and before you move on to the next chapter.

Colin P. Marks
Jeremy Kidd

Series Editor's Foreword

The Carolina Academic Press Mastering Series is designed to provide you with a tool that will enable you to easily and efficiently "master" the substance and content of law school courses. Throughout the series, the focus is on quality writing that makes legal concepts understandable. As a result, the series is designed to be easy to read and is not unduly cluttered with footnotes or cites to secondary sources.

In order to facilitate student mastery of topics, the Mastering Series includes a number of pedagogical features designed to improve learning and retention. At the beginning of each chapter, you will find a "Roadmap" that tells you about the chapter and provides you with a sense of the material that you will cover. A "Checkpoint" at the end of each chapter encourages you to stop and review the key concepts, reiterating what you have learned. Throughout the book, key terms are explained and emphasized. Finally, a "Master Checklist" at the end of each book reinforces what you have learned and helps you identify any areas that need review or further study.

We hope that you will enjoy studying with, and learning from, the Mastering Series.

Russell L. Weaver
Professor of Law & Distinguished University Scholar
University of Louisville, Louis D. Brandeis School of Law

Mastering Sales

Chapter 1

The Scope of Article 2

Roadmap

- Introduction to commercial law
- The Scope of Article 2
- Transactions
- Goods
- Hybrid transactions
- Software
- Merchant status

A. Introduction to Commercial Law

Commercial law is a broad topic that covers a number of aspects of American business and consumer lives, from buying goods, to writing checks, to collateralizing loans, and everything in-between. Out of a concern that various state laws would create confusion and inefficiency, state legislatures sponsored the National Conference of Commissioners on Uniform State Laws (NCCUSL) to draft uniform model statutes governing commercial law to be proposed to the state legislatures for adoption. The NCCUSL, working in conjunction with the American Law Institute (ALI), draft and update the Uniform Commercial Code (U.C.C.). It should be stressed that the U.C.C. is a model code, but its provisions have been adopted nearly verbatim in almost every state. Along with promulgating the U.C.C. provisions, the drafters also included comments to the code provisions to help explain the various provisions and sometimes to provide examples. Though not all of the states explicitly incorporate these comments, courts find them highly persuasive and helpful in interpreting the U.C.C. (and you should too).

The U.C.C. is divided into a number of articles, each of which governs a particular aspect of commercial law. For instance, Articles 3 and 4 govern negotiable instruments and bank deposits, Article 8 governs investment securities, and Article 9 governs secured transactions. Of particular interest to this text is Article 2, which governs sales of goods, and to a lesser extent Article 2A, which governs leases of goods.

Before delving into the scope of Article 2, however, a word about the role the U.C.C. plays in the broader context of the common law is in order. Article 1, which contains general provisions pertaining to all of the articles, sets forth the purpose of the U.C.C. Section 1-103(a) states the purpose of the U.C.C. is to "simplify, clarify, and modernize the law," and to promote uniformity among the various jurisdictions. Section 1-103(b) then explains the role the U.C.C. plays with regard to the common law, stating: "Unless displaced by the particular provisions of the Uniform Commercial Code, the principles of law and equity, including the law merchant and the law relative to capacity to contract, principal and agent, estoppel, fraud, misrepresentation, duress, coercion, mistake, bankruptcy, and other validating or invalidating cause supplement its provisions." This provision is of particular importance to sales, as a number of doctrines developed through the common law are not mentioned in Article 2, while others are altered or displaced. What subsection (b) is saying, in simple terms, is that if Article 2 addresses a matter in a different way than the common law, then the common law is displaced in favor of the U.C.C. provisions. But if a matter is not addressed in the U.C.C., then the common law steps in. For instance, Article 2 does not have a stand-alone provision on the voidability defense of duress. Nonetheless, if a contract governed by Article 2 is entered into under duress, it would still be voidable under common law principles, which supplement the U.C.C. You may have noticed that duress is, in fact, specifically mentioned in § 1-103(b), along with a number of other principles. This list, however, is not exhaustive or exclusive, but is merely "illustrative." U.C.C. § 1-103, cmt. 4.

B. The Scope of Article 2

Section 2-102 sets forth the basic scope of Article 2, stating that "[u]nless the context otherwise requires, this Article applies to *transactions in goods. . . .*" (emphasis added). Seems straight-forward enough, right? It is, so long as you feel confident that you know what a "transaction" is, and what "goods" are — two topics covered below. But even before exploring those terms, the first clause of section 2-102, "[u]nless the context otherwise requires," needs some explanation. As mentioned above, the U.C.C. has a number of articles governing various aspects of commercial transactions. Sometimes these sections intersect with the sale of goods. The most obvious place where this occurs is in the area of secured transactions, which are governed by Article 9.

To understand this interaction, it is worth taking a moment to explain what a secured transaction actually is. Though the topic is complex, and the subject of its own Mastering Series book, a simple example can illustrate the basics. Anyone who has bought a car on credit has probably been involved in a secured transaction. A secured transaction is one in which a creditor retains an interest in a piece of the debtor's collateral. The process need not involve a sale of goods, but often does. Therefore, if buyer, Betty, purchases a car on credit from the dealership, and if the dealership takes the correct steps, it can retain an interest in Betty's car and repossess should she default on the loan. The formalities of how to create an enforceable security interest are governed by Article 9, but obviously a sale of goods has also occurred. Section 2-102 simply recognizes that as to the sales aspect of the transaction, Article 2 applies, but as to the secured transactions aspect, Article 2 gives way to the provisions of Article 9. Section 2-102 also recognizes, however, that sometimes parties may try to structure a transaction or structure transactions to avoid the formalities of Article 9, and thus makes clear that "[Article 2] does not apply to any transaction which although in the form of an unconditional contract to sell or present sale is intended to operate only as a security transaction." This prevents parties from structuring a transaction as a "sale" when, in fact, a debtor has merely granted a security interest in goods that the debtor already owns—an interaction in which no sale is involved.

If you look at section 2-102, you may have noticed a further caveat on the scope of Article 2: "nor does this Article impair or repeal any statute regulating sales to consumers, farmers or other specified classes of buyers." This clause is simply meant to make clear that Article 2 does not displace other specific legislative enactments, such as consumer protection statutes. But Article 2 is generally not displaced by these statutes either. To understand this, think of all of the numerous types of goods that are also subject to other legislative enactments: pharmaceuticals (subject to the Food, Drug, and Cosmetic Act), sales of automobiles (subject to state certificate of title regulations), sales of meat (subject to regulation by the United States Department of Agriculture), sales of cashmere sweaters (did you know there is a Wool Products Labeling Act?), etc. Generally, these regulations co-exist peacefully, with Article 2 controlling the sales aspects.

1. "Transactions"

Typically, Article 2 is described as applying to sales of goods. Indeed, section 2-101 states Article 2 "shall be known . . . as Uniform Commercial Code—Sales." The word "sale" is defined in section 2-106 as "the passing of title from the seller to the buyer for a price." As the definition includes the passing of title, a sale necessarily excludes transactions in which title does not pass, i.e., leases.

However, as noted above, section 2-102 states Article 2 applies to "*transactions* in goods," not sales (emphasis added). Unfortunately, the U.C.C. does not define the term "transactions." Black's Law Dictionary offers the following definition: "1. The act or an instance of conducting business or other dealings; esp., the formation, performance, or discharge of a contract." Note that this would appear to encompass a larger number of transactions than just sales. At one time, there was some controversy over whether this meant that Article 2 applied also to leases, as leases would appear to be "transactions in goods." However, with the promulgation of Article 2A, which specifically governs the leasing of goods, the controversy has become moot. Article 2 *does not* apply to leases. But not all sales are clearly labeled as such, and some leases are in fact disguised sales—a subject explored in the next Chapter. Another murky area involves software, which raises questions as to both the nature of the transaction—is it a sale or a license—and whether software even qualifies as a good. We defer this discussion for now until subsection B.4. below.

2. "Goods"

Unlike the term "transactions," the U.C.C. does define "goods." Section 2-105(1) defines "Goods" as "all things (including specially manufactured goods) which are movable at the time of identification to the contract for sale other than the money in which the price is to be paid, investment securities (Article 8) and things in action." From this definition, two clear categories are excluded: money and securities. "Money" is defined in section 1-201(24) as "a medium of exchange currently authorized or adopted by a domestic or foreign government." The comments to section 2-105 clarify, however, that money is not a good only in so far as it is being used as a method of payment. If the money at issue is being treated as a commodity (perhaps a rare coin), then it does qualify as a good. It is worth noting that bitcoin, or other cyber currencies, are treated as a commodity, but they do not qualify as "money" under this definition as they are not currently authorized by any government. The second clearly excluded category is investment securities, such as stocks. There is a third excluded category that may seem mysterious—the "things in action" category. This category is meant to reach certain intangibles, such as the buying and selling of debts or rights to sue.

Generally, what qualifies as a good would seem to be straight-forward. So long as something is identifiable and moveable at the time of contracting, it is a good. Your car is undoubtedly a good. Real estate is not (it is not moveable). Gray areas do exist, however, such as with utilities. Courts have generally had no problem identifying natural gas as a good, but have reached mixed results with regard to electricity. Section 2-105(1) adds to the list of what are goods, stating "'[g]oods' also includes the unborn young of animals and growing crops and other identified things attached to realty as described in the section on goods to be severed from realty (Section 2-107)." Section 2-107 specifically describes minerals such as oil and gas, crops, and timber to be cut as "goods" so long as they are to be removed or severed from the land.

3. Hybrid transactions

Recall that Article 2 displaces the common law, including that of contracts, when a transaction in goods takes place. For many transactions, it will be apparent what law to apply. For instance, if you go to the local hardware store to buy tile and grout for the purpose of remodeling your bathroom, these sales would be considered sales of goods governed by Article 2. If, upon returning home, you decide the job is too much for you and hire a handyman to use your pre-purchased tile and grout to re-tile the bathroom, this would be a service contract. But what if you simply hired your handyman to re-tile the bathroom, with the understanding that the price paid would include him purchasing all of the necessary materials, including tile and grout? Should Article 2 apply to such a mixed transaction, as goods are involved, or should the common law control, as your handyman is also providing a service? Such mixed contracts are referred to as "hybrid" transactions, and courts generally adopt one of two methods to resolve the matter.

The majority approach to dealing with hybrid transactions is the **predominant purpose test.** Under this test, the court will ask, "What is the primary purpose for which the parties have entered into the contract?" If it is to obtain a service, with goods incidentally involved, then the common law will apply. If, instead, it is to obtain goods with services incidental to the transaction, then Article 2 will apply. In resolving this question, courts typically consider a number of factors, such as the language of the contract, the nature of the business or businesses involved (for instance, whether the seller is primarily in the business of selling goods), and the relative costs of the goods in the transactions versus the service aspect.

Returning to our tile job hypothetical, suppose the total cost is $1,000, but the tile only costs the handyman $200, and the handyman is primarily in the business of making repairs and fixing things (a service). Under these facts, a court may very well determine the contract is not primarily for goods, but instead, is predominantly for a service, and the tiles are incidental to the main purpose of the contract. If, however, the court determines the contract is predominantly for the sale of goods, then Article 2 will apply to the entire transaction. This is no small matter, as Article 2 has certain implied warranties (to be explored later) that are implied in every transaction, and which are not implied under the common law. Of particular importance to our hypothetical, the implied warranty of merchantability would apply to the entire contract were Article 2 to apply, but not if the common law applied.

A complicating factor to the predominant purpose test is that the definition of goods specifically includes "specially manufactured goods." However, when one pays for specially manufactured goods, there is surely a prominent service aspect to the sale. If you were to commission an artist to paint a portrait of you based upon the artist's skill and reputation, would the sale of the portrait be primarily for the service of painting or for the final specially manufactured good (consistent with section 2-105)? Alas, there is no consistent answer, but courts tend to consider relevant the importance of the provider's skill to the transaction and whether the manufacture was from a pre-fabricated design, with the former leaning toward service and the latter leaning toward goods.

The minority approach to hybrid transactions is the **gravamen test**. This approach separates contracts into their service and goods components and applies the law that forms the gravamen of the complaint. If what is complained of concerns a faulty service, then the common law applies, but if a faulty good is at issue, then the U.C.C. applies.

To demonstrate how the gravamen test might come out differently than the predominant purpose test, consider the following hypothetical. Doug walks into Robert's Barber Shop for a haircut. At the end of the haircut, Rob applies a styling gel to Doug's hair. Unfortunately, the gel is defective and burns Doug's scalp. Assuming Doug wished to sue Robert in contract, under the predominant purpose test, Robert and Doug's contract would likely be governed by the common law as the provision of the good at issue, the gel, was incidental to the overall purpose of the contract, i.e., for Doug to receive the service of a haircut. But under the gravamen test, the court would look to what was at the heart of the complaint. Here, it is a faulty good and so the U.C.C., with its implied warranty of merchantability, would apply.

Courts that utilize the gravamen test often cite to the rather arbitrary result that would occur under the predominant purpose test. After all, had Doug purchased the gel himself at a store, surely the U.C.C. would apply. So why should there be a different result simply due to the fortuitous way in which he came into contact with the product? But that is not to say the gravamen test is not without its own faults. Splitting a contract into its component parts can be messy, sometimes requiring different statutes of limitations to the common law parts of the contract as to the U.C.C. portions, or various applications of the Statute of Frauds. Also, many courts find merchants should be able to have some degree of predictability in what law will apply to them, and the gravamen test inserts uncertainty into this forecast. As a result, despite the drawbacks to the predominant purpose test, it remains the majority approach.

4. Software

As previously noted, though many contracts will clearly involve "transactions in goods," many gray areas persist. Perhaps no area involves a greater illustration of this than the "sale" of software. First off, it may be that there is, in fact, no "sale" at all, but just a non-exclusive license to use the software, which brings up the question of whether licensing something should qualify as a "transaction." Second, whether software should qualify as a "good" is also highly questionable. Though software can be recorded to a tangible medium, such as a CD-ROM, it can also simply be downloaded directly. And, even if software does qualify as a "transaction in goods," is the sale of software predominantly for the service required to write the software, or is it predominantly for the end "good"?

Unfortunately, no clear majority approach has emerged. A revision to Article 2 that was proposed in 2003 would have excluded "information" from the definition of "goods," but the amended Article 2 was not adopted by any states and was eventually withdrawn in 2011 by the Uniform Law Commission and the ALI. Some courts have chosen to apply Article 2 to software in order to fill the legislative void. Others have taken a more ad hoc approach, considering various aspects of the transaction at issue. For instance, some courts have found the fact that software is pre-packaged and mass-marketed as indicating that the sale involves a good. If software is developed for a particular client, however, then this indicates the contract is for services. This examination of how the software is acquired bears much in common with the predominant purpose test, and indeed, some courts have explicitly applied the predominant purpose test to resolve the issue. This approach has some common-sense appeal in a number of situations that, in truth, had raised similar issues long before the advent of software.

For instance, though there is undoubtedly intellectual property wrapped-up in a sale of a music CD (or vinyl record for those of you who remember such things or are simply retro) and a book, most courts would not have given it a second thought to apply Article 2 to the sale of such items. But even these examples are not as clear cut as they may first appear. If a CD is scratched or a book's binding is warped, surely a court would have no problem applying Article 2; but what if the suit is based on the information contained in the physical item? What if the book contains faulty information? Should Article 2's implied warranties apply to such a situation?

In *Winter v. G.P. Putnam's Sons*, 938 F.2d 1033 (9th Cir. 1991), just such a situation arose. In *Winter*, some mushroom enthusiasts became severely ill after picking and eating mushrooms they selected by relying on information in a book on mushrooms. They brought suit against the book's publisher, but the district court granted summary judgment to the book's publisher. On appeal, the Ninth Circuit held the plaintiffs could not recover against the book's publisher under a products liability theory, and that the book's publisher had no duty to investigate the accuracy of the book. Though the case involved a tort claim, the court made the distinction between the book itself, which is a product, and the information in the book, which is not, stating "[a] book containing Shakespeare's sonnets consists of two parts, the material and print therein, and the ideas and expression thereof. The first may be a product, but the second is not."

In the Florida state court case of *Cardozo v. True*, 342 So. 2d 1053 (Fla. App. 1977), a similar issue arose, and the issue of Article 2's application was put squarely before the court. The question before the court was whether a retail book dealer was liable to a purchaser of a cookbook for injuries caused by a lack of adequate warnings as to poisonous ingredients used in a recipe in the book. The court of appeals answered that the retail book dealer was not liable under U.C.C. Article 2 for injuries and damages caused by improper instructions or lack of adequate warnings as to poisonous ingredients used in the recipe. After reviewing other decisions, the court concluded,

> The common theme running through these decisions is that ideas hold a privileged position in our society. They are not equivalent to commercial products. Those who are in the business of distributing the ideas of other people perform a unique and essential function. To hold those who perform this essential function liable, regardless of fault, when an injury results would severely restrict the flow of the ideas they distribute. We think that holding [the retail book dealer] liable under the doctrine of implied warranty would, based upon the facts as certified to us, have the effect of imposing a liability without fault not intended by the Uniform Commercial Code.

The court held that the implied warranty of merchantability was limited to the *physical properties* of such books and did not extend to material communicated by the book's author or publisher. Thus, interestingly, the court appeared to adopt a gravamen approach to such transactions. However, it should be noted that in both of the above decisions, there were also First Amendment concerns lurking in the background, and a fear that applying such warranties could chill free speech may have played a role, even if only in the background.

Given that software is essentially information that can be reduced to a physical medium, the analogy to the above cases seems apt. Furthermore, software can just as easily be downloaded directly onto a computer or other electronic device with no need to reduce the software to a physical medium first. Thus, if a downloaded piece of software with a "bug" caused harm to a purchasing consumer, it would seem to make little sense to apply Article 2 only if the software had first been reduced to a physical medium, but not if it was downloaded directly.

While all of the above makes for fascinating dinner conversation (well, it does for members of the ABA subcommittees on the U.C.C.), none of this brings us closer to a resolution to the question of "does Article 2 apply to software"? Perhaps the best that can been said on the topic is that it is still evolving, but courts still find Article 2 to apply to software in a number of situations, especially when the software is akin to a mass-marketed good.

C. Merchant Status

The term "merchant" has a particular meaning under the U.C.C., and merchant status can affect the rights and obligations of parties under Article 2. But before delving any deeper into the topic, a large warning is in order: **Article 2 applies to merchants and non-merchants alike.** While merchant status has a special meaning, and the U.C.C. was clearly written with merchants in mind, it would be a mistake to think that Article 2's provisions are irrelevant to non-merchants. In fact, Article 2 is clear when applying a different rule to merchants, so you should presume that all rules are applicable to merchants and non-merchants alike, unless you see language expressly limiting the rule's application to merchants. You may, at this point, be wondering why there are separate provisions just for merchants. The whole purpose of treating merchants differently, under some provisions, is to hold them accountable for the greater sophistication and knowledge they possess, especially where it might give them an unfair edge in a transaction.

With that brief matter out of the way, let's move on to the U.C.C.'s definition of merchant. Section 2-104 defines a merchant as:

> [A] person who deals in goods of the kind or otherwise by his occupation holds himself out as having knowledge or skill peculiar to the practices or goods involved in the transaction or to whom such knowledge or skill may be attributed by his employment of an agent or broker or other intermediary who by his occupation holds himself out as having such knowledge or skill.*

From this definition, you should see that one can become a merchant both by being one, and by employing one. The last phrase, "or to whom such knowledge or skill may be attributed by his employment of an agent or broker," encompasses this latter situation and is meant to bring large organizations that use purchasing agents or have specialized business personnel into the definition.

We still need to flesh out what the first phrase means, however, if we are to understand when to apply the special merchant provisions of Article 2. The opening phrase is almost stunningly broad in its potential reach, "a person who deals in goods of the kind or otherwise by his occupation holds himself out as having knowledge or skill peculiar to the practices or goods involved in the transaction." This cannot be taken at face value. To understand why, simply think of all of the transactions in which you yourself "deal in goods of the kind"—for instance, you probably regularly shop at the grocery store. Perhaps you buy bananas on every trip. Wouldn't this be dealing in bananas? And as such, should you be deemed a banana merchant? Surely not, and the comments confirm this by noting "[t]he term 'merchant' as defined here roots in the 'law merchant' concept of a professional in business." It goes on to require specialized knowledge of either the goods, business practices, or both.

However, that is not the end of the matter. The comments then go on to divide merchant status further, depending on the provisions at issue. We will call these the broad and narrow definitions of merchant. Under the broad definition of merchant, one qualifies simply by being knowledgeable of general business practices, such as the import of receiving a mailed confirmation. Article 2's provisions dealing with the Statute of Frauds (section 2-201), firm

---

offers (2-205), the battle of the forms (2-207) and post-contract modifications (2-209) all contain special merchant provisions that use the broad definition of merchant. Therefore, for purposes of these sections, almost every
person in business would qualify as a "merchant." But this is only when the
business is acting in its business capacity. In other words, the simple fact that
you are a lawyer that represents businesses does not mean you are a merchant
when you go buy a car for your own use, even under the broad definition of
merchant.

The narrower definition of merchant requires that the person actually
deal in goods of the kind at issue. This narrower definition applies to three
particular provisions: the implied warranty of merchantability (section 2-314),
a special exception to a creditor's rights to void a sale when a merchant-seller
retains possession in good faith (2-402(2)), and the ability of a merchant-
seller to pass good title on goods with which he has been entrusted (2-403(2)).
The definition of merchant for these provisions is meant to reach a much
smaller group than the broader definition, as these provisions contemplate
merchants who have more extensive knowledge of the goods at issue.

The two major categories of merchant status are detailed above, but the
comments to section 2-104 also lay out a third that relates to the definition of
"good faith." However, due to a revision to Article 1, this third category is
now completely moot. To understand why, you must read the definition of
good faith found in Article 1 under section 1-201(2), which provides that
"good faith . . . means honesty in fact and the observance of reasonable commercial standards of fair dealing." This standard applies both a subjective
and an objective standard and makes no special provisions for merchant status. This was not always the case. Once upon a time, this definition only
applied to merchants, while non-merchants had a looser standard that only
applied the subjective "honesty in fact" aspect of the definition. This changed
in 2001 when, like Article 2, Article 1 underwent a revision. Unlike the Article 2 revision, however, Article 1's revision *has* been uniformly adopted. Thus,
under this new definition of good faith, everyone, merchants and non-
merchants alike, are governed by the two-part good faith standard, which, per
section 1-304, applies to every contract or duty under the U.C.C. As there is
no longer a division in how good faith is defined, these comments regarding
merchant status are no longer relevant.

Checkpoints

- Article 2 of the U.C.C. displaces the common law for contracts.
- Where Article 2 does not address a matter, it is supplemented by the common law.
- Article 2 covers "transactions in goods," which includes sales.
- Though the term "transactions" is broader than just sales, it does not include leases.
- "Goods" are all things that are movable and identifiable.
- The term "Goods" does not include money used to buy things or securities.
- "Hybrid" or "mixed" transactions involve services and goods.
- The majority approach to "hybrid" transactions is the predominant purpose test.
- The minority approach to "hybrid" transactions is the gravamen test.
- Software is a gray area, and application of Article 2 may depend on the manner in which the software is marketed.
- Article 2 applies to merchants and non-merchants alike, but there are special provisions for merchants.
- The term merchant applies more broadly to some provisions, such as the statute of frauds, but narrowly to others, such as the implied warranty of merchantability.

Chapter 2

Distinguishing Sales from Leases

Roadmap

- How a sale can resemble a lease
- Why the sale/lease distinction matters
- Resolving the sale/lease distinction under § 1-203(b): the "bright-line" test
- The "economic realities" test

A. How a Sale Can Resemble a Lease

As noted in the previous chapter, Article 2 applies to "transactions in goods," but its scope does not include leases of goods. Leases are governed by Article 2A, which on many topics mirrors the provisions of Article 2. In many cases, it may be obvious that the transaction at issue is a true lease, but sometimes a transaction that is in fact a sale may be disguised as a lease.

For instance, assume that ScafCo sells scaffolding for large construction projects. Build Inc. wishes to buy certain scaffolding for $24,000, but does not have cash on hand to pay. ScafCo could sell to Build Inc. on credit with an agreement that Build Inc. will make monthly payments for 2 years of $1,000 plus $120 in interest per month for a monthly bill of $1,120. If ScafCo retains an interest in the scaffolding sold on credit, then the transaction would be a secured transaction and ScafCo would have a security interest in the scaffolding.[1] Alternatively, ScafCo could "lease" the same scaffolding to Build Inc. for $1,120 per month for two years, with an option that Build Inc. buy the scaffolding for $100 at the end of the two years. If we ignore the $100 as nominal, these two transactions will likely have the same result—at the end of the two

---

1. U.C.C. § 1-201(35) states a "'Security interest' means an interest in personal property or fixtures which secures payment or performance of an obligation."

years, Build Inc. will own the scaffolding outright, having paid the same price for the "lease" as it would have had it simply bought the scaffolding on credit.

Though the parties may have cleverly re-labeled the transaction a "lease," the courts may not do so. Article 1 of the U.C.C. states that "[w]hether a transaction in the form of a lease creates a lease or security interest is determined by the facts of each case." U.C.C. §1-203(a). Similarly, Article 9 states that "this article applies to: (1) a transaction, regardless of its form, that creates a security interest in personal property or fixtures by contract." U.C.C. §9-109(1)(a). The implication of these sections is that courts should look to the substance of the transaction over the form or what it is labelled. The remainder of this chapter will discuss how courts distinguish between a lease and a disguised sale with a security interest; but first, it is useful to explore why the distinction even matters.

B. Why the Sale/Lease Distinction Matters

Looking at our scaffolding hypothetical, as the amount paid at the end is nearly the same whether it is structured as a sale or a lease, it is natural to wonder why the form may matter. There are two primary reasons this matters. The first is that leases are governed by different laws than sales accompanied by a security interest. This distinction has implications for the rights of the parties, and can become of great importance should the buyer/lessee enter into bankruptcy. The second reason this distinction matters is that the transaction's label has tax implications.

The most obvious difference between a lease and a sale is that a lease will be governed by Article 2A rather than Article 2. But given that Article 2A is very similar to Article 2, this distinction alone would not warrant much attention to the matter. The larger issue is with regard to Article 9, which governs secured transactions. A full review of the provisions of Article 9 is beyond the purview of this text, but should a transaction be labelled a sale with a secured transaction (a secured sale), the lessor may be surprised to find that his or her rights to repossess the collateral and resell it have statutory limitations that might not otherwise apply. Furthermore, if the transaction is labelled a secured sale, then the seller often must take certain steps to put other parties on notice that it has retained a security interest (a process known as "perfection" under Article 9). A failure to do so could prejudice the seller's rights to repossess the collateral later on if another party takes a security interest in the same collateral.

This failure to "perfect" becomes especially important should the lessee/ buyer enter into bankruptcy. Once a bankruptcy petition has been filed, a trustee is named (frequently this is the debtor themselves in a business reorganization), and a bankruptcy estate is created consisting of the bankrupt's assets. To dramatically oversimplify the process of bankruptcy, the idea is to create a big pile of assets that belong to the bankruptcy estate, and that can be sold to pay off the bankrupt's creditors. Once the assets have been sold, the trustee usually divides the resulting pile of cash on a pro rata basis among general creditors (those that are just owed money, and that don't have a security interest). In the end, general creditors are often lucky to get any money at all. Secured creditors are much better off, at least those that have perfected their security interests, because they have the right to take possession of certain assets from the pile before the trustee begins selling them. However, secured creditors who have failed to perfect their interest may have their security interests avoided and get lumped in with the general creditors to take on a pro rata basis.

Using the hypothetical from section A will help illustrate how the sale/lease distinction and the failure to "perfect" may affect a lessor/seller. In that hypo, ScafCo "leased" scaffolding to Build Inc. under a 2-year term with payment terms that mirrored the terms of a sale. Assume that one year into the lease, Build Inc. entered into bankruptcy. If the transaction was labelled a "lease," then ScafCo may be a general creditor for any amounts owed to it under the lease, but its ownership of the scaffolding would not be affected. Should Build Inc. choose to avoid the leasing contract, ScafCo would get its scaffolding back. Conversely, if the transaction were recast as a secured sale, the result would be very different. The scaffolding would belong to Build Inc. and thus would be a part of the bankruptcy estate. Additionally, ScafCo would have a claim for the outstanding amount owed to it under the sale, and if ScafCo has perfected its interest, it can retain an interest in the scaffolding (meaning it is at least entitled to the value of the scaffolding to pay off the outstanding amount owed). However, if ScafCo truly thought it had entered into a lease, it may not have bothered to perfect its interest, meaning that its interest in the scaffolding could be avoided by the bankruptcy trustee, thus relegating ScafCo to a general creditor. Note the effect on how the transaction is labelled: if it is a lease, ScafCo may not get paid, but it at least can get back its scaffolding; however, if it is a secured sale and ScafCo has not perfected, it is out both the money and the scaffolding. It should come as no surprise that many legal battles have been fought over this distinction.

Characterization of the lease as a secured sale also can have important tax consequences. If characterized as a lease, the owner-lessor would remain the tax owner of the property and would be entitled to claim depreciation deductions and possible tax credits related to the property. The owner-lessor will also have to recognize the rental income payments it receives on its taxes. The lessee making the payments will be entitled to deductions for payments of rent to the owner-lessor, provided that the equipment rental is a business expense. If the lease is characterized as a secured sale, however, the seller cannot claim the depreciation or tax credits (as it is not the owner anymore), but it does not have to recognize the entire monthly payments as income—only the interest. Meanwhile, the buyer would not get to deduct the entire payment as a business expense—only the interest portion.

C. Resolving the Sale/Lease Distinction Under § 1-203(b): The "Bright-Line" Test

With a firm understanding of why the parties may wish to re-characterize the form of the transaction as a lease or secured sale, we can now proceed to explain how courts resolve the issue. The process involves a two-step inquiry, beginning with section 1-203(b). Embodied in this section is the so-called "bright-line" test for whether a lease is in fact a disguised secured sale. This section provides:

> A transaction in the form of a lease creates a security interest if the consideration that the lessee is to pay the lessor for the right to possession and use of the goods is an obligation for the term of the lease and is not subject to termination by the lessee, and:
>
> (1) the original term of the lease is equal to or greater than the remaining economic life of the goods;
>
> (2) the lessee is bound to renew the lease for the remaining economic life of the goods or is bound to become the owner of the goods;
>
> (3) the lessee has an option to renew the lease for the remaining economic life of the goods for no additional consideration or for nominal additional consideration upon compliance with the lease agreement; or
>
> (4) the lessee has an option to become the owner of the goods for no additional consideration or for nominal additional consideration upon compliance with the lease agreement.

U.C.C. § 1-203(b).* This section is a two-part test. The first part of the test asks whether the "lease" permits the lessee to terminate the lease before the

---

* Uniform Commercial Code, copyright © by the American Law Institute and the National Conference of Commissioners on Uniform State Laws. Reproduced with the

end of the term of the lease. While this may be explicit in some cases, not all leases will be so obvious. For instance, if ScafCo inserts a provision that Build Inc. can terminate the lease at any time, but must make all remaining payments under the lease to do so, this would not truly be terminable by the lessee. The inquiry focuses on whether the lessee is bound to pre-agreed repayment terms that make it highly unlikely it will terminate the lease.

If this first part of the test is met, then the court looks to see if one of the subsections (1)–(4) are met. These subsections all look to see if the "lessor" is retaining any residual value at the end of the purported lease. The subsections are separated by an "or," so any of these "residual value" factors will do so long as it is in combination with the first condition that the lease is not terminable by the lessee. For instance, the first two factors look to whether the lessee will use up the economic value of the goods during the mandated lease-term, thus leaving the lessor with nothing at the end. The last two factors look to the lessee's ability to either purchase or re-lease the goods for the remaining economic life of the goods for nominal or no consideration. Again, under these factors, it is unlikely the lessor will have anything of value at the end of the lease.

Under the bright-line test, if the lease is not terminable, and one of the "residual value" factors are met, then the "lease" is in fact a sale, and not a lease. But the bright-line test still has areas which may draw further inquiry from a court, particularly with regard to the terms "economic life of the goods" and "nominal value." Defining "economic life of the goods" is complicated due to the fact that many goods can have their life extended if money is invested in them. For instance, a car's remaining economic life may be very short due to a faulty transmission and cracked engine block, but the economic life of the car could be extended if money was invested in the car, and a new engine was installed. So if the car was leased for one year (its expected remaining life), could the lessor argue that through an infusion of money, the car in fact has many years left and the lease is a true lease? A court likely would not side with the lessor in such a situation, as the salvage value at the end of the lease is likely higher than the use value. Though money could be spent to extend the life, the cost of repair is likely too high when compared to the remaining usefulness of the car. That being said, close cases will arise, and a case-by-case analysis is required (indeed, U.C.C. § 1-203(e) explicitly states the inquiry should be based on the time the transaction was entered into).

The issue of "nominal value" can also be a close one. Assume in our hypothetical, ScafCo had included a term in its lease with Build Inc. that it could buy the scaffolding at the end of the lease for $5 when the fair market value of the scaffolding is $10,000. Clearly this would be nominal, but what if the purchase option was $5,000? This is still a bargain, but does that make it nominal? Section 1-203(d) provides some guidance, stating that if the renewal lease term or purchase price is equivalent to the fair market value, then the price is not nominal. But what about prices that fall below fair market value, but are not obviously nominal (such as our $5,000 example)? The comments to the U.C.C. offer some guidance, stating, "[t]here is a set of purchase options whose fixed price is less than fair market value but greater than nominal that must be determined on the facts of each case to ascertain whether the transaction in which the option is included creates a lease or a security interest." U.C.C. § 1-203, cmt. 2.

D. The "Economic Realities" Test

The above bright-line test helps resolve whether a lease is in fact a disguised secured sale. But a determination that a lease does not meet the bright-line test is not the end of the inquiry. Should a lease not meet the bright-line test, courts will then analyze the lease under the "economic substance" or "economic realities" test. This test does not come from the Code, however, as the only further guidance the Code offers is to examine the "facts of each case." U.C.C. 1-203. Section 1-203 does provide a list of factors that alone are not sufficient to determine that a security interest has been created (though a court may consider them in the balance under the economic realities test):

> (c) A transaction in the form of a lease does not create a security interest merely because:
> (1) the present value of the consideration the lessee is obligated to pay the lessor for the right to possession and use of the goods is substantially equal to or is greater than the fair market value of the goods at the time the lease is entered into;
> (2) the lessee assumes risk of loss of the goods;
> (3) the lessee agrees to pay, with respect to the goods, taxes, insurance, filing, recording, or registration fees, or service or maintenance costs;
> (4) the lessee has an option to renew the lease or to become the owner of the goods;
> (5) the lessee has an option to renew the lease for a fixed rent that is equal to or greater than the reasonably predictable fair market rent

for the use of the goods for the term of the renewal at the time the option is to be performed; or

(6) the lessee has an option to become the owner of the goods for a fixed price that is equal to or greater than the reasonably predictable fair market value of the goods at the time the option is to be performed.

U.C.C. § 1-203(c).*

Under the "economic realities" test, the court looks at the facts and circumstances of each case to determine whether there has been a true lease or a financed secured sale. Much of the thrust of this test is focused on whether the lessor can reasonably expect to get anything of meaningful value back at the end of the lease term. This is sometimes referred to as the lessor retaining a meaningful reversionary interest in the goods.

To demonstrate, think back again to our hypothetical between ScafCo and Build Inc. Assume that under the lease, Build Inc. was free to terminate the lease at any time, but still retained the right at the end of the lease to purchase the scaffolding for $100. The ability to exit the lease at will means the bright-line test is not met, but that is not the end of the inquiry. Now we must ask whether ScafCo is likely going to get anything of value back at the end of the lease. Given that the $100 is likely nominal, and the scaffolding is worth much more, Build Inc. would have to be crazy to pass up the option to buy. Thus, it is very unlikely that ScafCo has retained a meaningful reversionary interest in the scaffolding and the lease will likely be deemed a secured sale under the economic realities test. However, assume that the fair market value of the scaffolding will be $10,000 at the end of the lease, and Build Inc. has an option to purchase the scaffolding at the end of the lease for that amount. Section 1-203(c)(6) tells us that this fact alone is not enough to find that the lease is a disguised secured sale, but further inquiry into the facts of the case may still be necessary.

Checkpoints

- A transaction involving a secured sale of goods can be structured to look like a lease.

- Leases of goods are governed by Article 2A, while secured sales are governed by Articles 2 and 9.

- Characterization of a lease as a sale can negatively affect the lessor/seller's rights under Article 9 and bankruptcy if the interest is not perfected.

- Characterization of a lease as a sale may also affect tax deductions.

- To determine whether a lease is a disguised secured sale, courts use two tests: the "bright-line" test and the "economic realities" test.

- The "bright-line" test has 2 elements: 1) lessee has no right to realistically terminate the lease; and 2) one of the "residual value" factors are met.

- If the "bright-line" test is not met, courts move on to the "economic realities" test, which looks to see if the lessor is retaining a meaningful reversionary interest in the goods.

Chapter 3

Contract Formation Under the U.C.C.

Roadmap

- The U.C.C.'s broad conception of contract formation
- Distinguishing advertisements from offers
- Acceptance and the special situation of offers for prompt shipment
- Consideration and its interaction with requirements and exclusive dealings contracts
- Firm offers as distinguished from an option contract
- Contract formation in the electronic age

A. The U.C.C.'s Broad Conception of Contract Formation

Article 2 of the U.C.C. was drafted to reflect the way sales transactions occur in real life. In keeping with this purpose, section 2-204 sets out contract formation in very broad terms, stating:

> (1) A contract for sale of goods may be made in any manner sufficient to show agreement, including conduct by both parties which recognizes the existence of such a contract.
> (2) An agreement sufficient to constitute a contract for sale may be found even though the moment of its making is undetermined.
> (3) Even though one or more terms are left open a contract for sale does not fail for indefiniteness if the parties have intended to make a contract and there is a reasonably certain basis for giving an appropriate remedy.[*]

---

[*] Uniform Commercial Code, copyright © by the American Law Institute and the National Conference of Commissioners on Uniform State Laws. Reproduced with the

Note that this provision does away with any need for a particular form that the offer or acceptance must conform to—so long as the parties intended there be a contract, Article 2 will try to give effect to that intention. This may be true even if some terms are missing. This is not to say that all attempts at contract formation will succeed. The lack of definite terms may still destroy contract formation if a court cannot determine there was an intent to be bound. Furthermore, some contracts must be in writing and certain terms, such as quantity, may be required under the Statute of Frauds (discussed in Chapter 6).

Perhaps in keeping with this broad conception of contract formation, Article 2 contains no specific provisions defining "offer." In the absence of a definition, the common law supplements the Code, and so we can look to the Restatement (Second) of Contracts section 24. Section 24 provides that an offer is the "manifestation of willingness to enter into a bargain, so made as to justify another person in understanding that his assent to that bargain is invited and will conclude it." The offer can usually be regarded as having two parts: a procedural part that concerns the manner in which acceptance to the offer may occur, and a substantive part that lays out what is actually being offered. For instance, if Charlie emails Baxter, "By this email, I offer to sell to you my 1964 red Camaro for $15,000 cash. You have until May 1 to accept my offer. The acceptance must be signed and in writing," we can easily see the substance of the offer is the Camaro for $15,000 cash. The procedural aspect is that the acceptance must be manifested in a signed writing and Baxter has until May 1 to do so.[1]

Though Article 2 does not have a provision governing offers, it does have a provision governing acceptance. Section 2-206 (1)(a) largely mirrors the common law, providing that if the offer addresses the procedural manner in which acceptance must occur, then that is how you accept. If the offer is silent on how to accept, then acceptance may be in any manner that is reasonable under the circumstances. Thus, if Charlie had simply emailed that he was

---

permission of the Permanent Editorial Board for the Uniform Commercial Code. All rights reserved.

1. The U.C.C. does not address the mailbox rule and thus, again, the common law would apply. Under the mailbox rule, so long as the mail is a reasonable method of acceptance under the circumstances, Baxter's acceptance will be effective on the date it is placed in the mail. Thus, so long as Baxter places his acceptance in the mail by May 1 (and it is in a signed writing), the acceptance is effective, despite the fact that Charlie won't receive the acceptance until sometime later. To avoid application of the mailbox rule, Charlie could use language that clearly displaces it, such as by writing into the offer "the acceptance will not be effective until received by me."

offering to sell his Camaro to Baxter for $15,000 cash, Baxter would be free to accept in any manner that would be reasonable under the circumstances. This may be simply emailing back "I accept" or showing up the next day with the cash. Though no time period is stated, at some point, the offer will lapse, but again, this would be after a "reasonable" period, which obviously leaves a lot of wiggle room.

B. Distinguishing Advertisements from Offers

One tricky area of offers involves distinguishing whether an advertisement is actually an offer. For instance, if you walk into an electronics store and see a price of $200 listed for a software program that is meant to assist you in learning another language, is the listed price an offer to sell you the software for $200, or is it simply a solicitation? If it is the former, then when you present your payment at the counter, you will likely be deemed to have accepted the offer. However, if the $200 is merely a solicitation, then it is you who has made the offer to buy the software at the advertised price of $200. At this point, the difference may not seem that important — after all, in both situations, the buyer walks away with the software for a price of $200. As we will see in Chapters 4 and 5, this distinction can affect whether additional terms found inside the software box are binding.[2]

As to the question of whether the listed price is an offer or a solicitation, the U.C.C. provides no guidance, but the comments to the Restatement (Second) of Contracts section 26 indicate that price listings and the like are presumptively *not* offers. These comments note:

> Advertisements of goods by display, sign, handbill, newspaper, radio or television are not ordinarily intended or understood as offers to sell. The same is true of catalogues, price lists and circulars, even though the terms of suggested bargains may be stated in some detail. It is of course possible to make an offer by an advertisement directed to the general public . . . , but there must ordinarily be some language

---

2. The difference could also matter if the display had a typo. For instance, if the advertised price said $20 but it was supposed to say $200, it matters very much whether it is an offer that can be accepted by slapping $20 down on the counter, or a solicitation that need not require the store to sell for $20. Such a hypothetical could also implicate consumer protection and false advertising statutes, however, that are beyond the scope of this text.

of commitment or some invitation to take action without further communication.*

But even though the presumption is that ads and the like are not offers, the comments indicate that ads *can* rise to the level of an offer. Though the comments are vague on how an ad becomes an offer, cases have often noted that an ad or solicitation that is clear and definite as to how to accept, and leaves nothing open for negotiation is, in fact, an offer.

C. Acceptance and How It Differs from the Common Law

As noted above, though Article 2 does not address "offer," it does address "acceptance." Section 2-206 provides:

(1) Unless otherwise unambiguously indicated by the language or circumstances

(a) an offer to make a contract shall be construed as inviting acceptance in any manner and by any medium reasonable in the circumstances;

(b) an order or other offer to buy goods for prompt or current shipment shall be construed as inviting acceptance either by a prompt promise to ship or by the prompt or current shipment of conforming or non-conforming goods, but such a shipment of non-conforming goods does not constitute an acceptance if the seller seasonably notifies the buyer that the shipment is offered only as an accommodation to the buyer.

(2) Where the beginning of a requested performance is a reasonable mode of acceptance an offeror who is not notified of acceptance within a reasonable time may treat the offer as having lapsed before acceptance.

Subsection (1)(a) largely mirrors the common law, noting that an acceptance must conform to the procedural aspects of the offer. If there are no procedural terms, then the offer can be accepted in any manner that is reasonable under the circumstances. This may be a written acceptance, an oral promise or even an action. For instance, if Bert offers to buy Sal's car on Friday for $5,000, and tells Sal to come by his house with the car on that day, then even if Sal says nothing in response, the act of showing up at Bert's house on Friday with the car will likely indicate his acceptance.

Subsection (1)(b) requires a little more explanation. First, note from the first line that we have a qualifier for the entire subsection — "an order or other offer to buy goods **for prompt or current shipment**." This means that the only time you need worry about subsection (b) is if the buyer indicates he or she needs the goods quickly. If the buyer so qualifies the order, and in response the seller simply ships the goods, the Code deems the act of shipping the goods as accepting the order. This would be a rather unremarkable provision, except the Code notes that it is an acceptance by the seller even if the goods are non-conforming. This is a departure from the common law that would have deemed the shipment of nonconforming goods as a counter-offer, but the provision makes sense if we put it into a commercial context and consider the effect such a rule has on remedies.

Imagine that on Monday, Gilda Gala, a wedding planner, is organizing an impromptu wedding for this coming Saturday. The happy couple insists that bottled Coca-Cola be available for the guests as it is their favorite beverage. There are many distributors to choose from, but Gilda contacts Sammy's Sodas, via email, and orders 100 cases of Coca-Cola to be delivered on Friday. Sammy looks at his inventory and realizes he is out of Coca-Cola and so, without warning or explanation, simply has 100 cases of Pepsi shipped to Gilda on Friday. Gilda is aghast when she sees the wrong soda and is forced to rush out to three different grocery stores to buy the necessary cola at a considerable increase in cost over the price she would have gotten from a distributor. Had the normal common law rule been in effect, Sammy's shipment of the Pepsi would have been deemed a counter-offer which Gilda would be free to reject, but how is that fair to poor Gilda, who now has spent numerous hours and extra money trying to get the product she thought she was getting all along?

Subsection (1)(b) remedies this situation by deeming Sammy's response not as a counter-offer, but as an acceptance of the offer to send Coca-Cola. Obviously, by sending Pepsi, Sammy is in breach of this sales contract. Thus, Gilda can now pursue contract remedies in the form of direct and indirect damages, i.e., any expenses in dealing with the breach, and the difference between what she would have paid under the Sammy contract and what she ended up paying to fix the error. You should take two points from this: 1) by responding to a request for prompt shipment by sending nonconforming goods, the seller has both accepted and breached the contract in the same act; and 2) this result allows the buyer to be made whole through contract damages.

So how does a seller like Sammy avoid such a result? The simple answer would be to call or alert Gilda immediately that he is out of Coca-Cola and doesn't accept the offer. But sellers want to sell their wares, and if a seller thinks the buyer may be just as happy with a substitute, the seller may just send the substitute hoping to consummate a sale. When time is not a factor, the seller may simply go back and forth with the buyer on a reasonable accommodation, but when the buyer requests prompt shipment, time is of the essence. Luckily for the Sammys of the world, the drafters realized this and inserted the final line of subsection (1)(b): "but such a shipment of non-conforming goods does not constitute an acceptance if the seller **seasonably notifies the buyer** that the shipment is offered only as an accommodation to the buyer." Thus, if Sammy wished to avoid the result described above, he could still ship the goods but email Gilda that same day something to the effect of "sorry, I'm out of Coca-Cola, so I sent Pepsi." By letting Gilda know the Pepsi is an accommodation, he has essentially made a counter-offer, which Gilda is free to reject. But unlike the above example, where no notification was given, Gilda now has time to find a different distributor. Note, however, that for this to work, Sammy must send the notification "seasonably"; sending a note with the Pepsi that Gilda doesn't see until the Pepsi arrives on Friday will put her in the same bind as before and should not qualify as "seasonable." Of course, what is or is not seasonable will vary from contract to contract, depending on the context of the situation, providing contract litigators reasons to justify their fees as they dispute the matter.

The last provision of section 2-206, subsection (2), is similar to the common law rule with regard to communication of an acceptance. Generally, an acceptance must be communicated before it is effective (subject to the common law mailbox rule). Under the circumstances of a particular contract, however, it may be reasonable to accept an offer in such a way that the offeror does not know the offeree has accepted. For instance, say while attending a family reunion, you offer to pay your cousin $400 to make a custom bicycle for you. Your cousin says he's interested but never commits to the endeavor. Nonetheless, the next day he begins to construct the bike. Under subsection (2), his acceptance through performance will not be effective unless he notifies you within a reasonable time that he has accepted.

D. Consideration in Requirements and Exclusive Dealings Contracts

Article 2 does not alter the basic common law requirement that for there to be a valid contract, there must be consideration. While most contracts for sales of goods involve money, Article 2 makes clear that payment can be in other forms, such as a barter transaction. When both sides to a transaction are providing goods, then the U.C.C. considers them both "sellers" in Article 2 parlance. *See* U.C.C. § 2-304. There are, however, three areas where the U.C.C. addresses circumstances involving consideration. The first involves contract modifications. Unlike the common law, the U.C.C. does away with the need for consideration to modify an existing contract. *See* U.C.C. § 2-209(1). As this U.C.C. provision implicates the Statute of Frauds as well as contract interpretation, we forgo further discussion until Chapter 6. The second area, firm offers, is addressed in the next section.

The final area in which consideration is addressed is in what are called output or requirements contracts. An output contract is one in which a seller promises to supply, and a buyer agrees to buy, all the goods the seller produces during a specified period, normally at a set price. A requirements contract is similar, but simply switches how to measure the quantity in that a buyer promises to buy, and a seller to supply, all the goods that a buyer needs during a specified period. Thus, the quantity term is measured by the buyer's requirements. In both scenarios, section 2-306 makes clear that the lack of a definite term does not destroy contract formation (consistent with section 2-204(3) discussed above), but obligates both parties to act in good faith, providing:

> (1) A term which measures the quantity by the output of the seller or the requirements of the buyer means such actual output or requirements as may occur in good faith, except that no quantity unreasonably disproportionate to any stated estimate or in the absence of a stated estimate to any normal or otherwise comparable prior output or requirements may be tendered or demanded.
> (2) A lawful agreement by either the seller or the buyer for exclusive dealing in the kind of goods concerned imposes unless otherwise agreed an obligation by the seller to use best efforts to supply the goods and by the buyer to use best efforts to promote their sale.

U.C.C. § 2-306.* To illustrate, assume that Jack owns a diner in a college town where he makes his own french fries and hash from locally grown potatoes. Rather than constantly trying to go out and find the lowest priced supplier every month, Jack simply enters into a five-year contract with Seamus that he

---

* Uniform Commercial Code, copyright © by the American Law Institute and the National Conference of Commissioners on Uniform State Laws. Reproduced with the permission of the Permanent Editorial Board for the Uniform Commercial Code. All rights reserved.

will buy all of his potatoes from Seamus at a favorable set price. Because his needs fluctuate from month-to-month, depending on factors such as if school is in session and whether there are many home football games that month (both of which increase his needs), he does not feel comfortable buying a set amount. Section 2-306 makes clear that he doesn't need to — he simply needs to provide Seamus with a good faith[3] estimate of his needs each month and Seamus to agree to supply those potatoes at the agreed price. The only way Seamus could escape his contractual obligation to supply Jack with his good faith needs is if something happened that disproportionately increased Jack's needs. So, if Jack expanded his business in a way that was not contemplated by the requirements contract, and his needs tripled from all prior needs, section 2-306 excuses Seamus from performing.

You might have noted section 2-306(2) addresses another aspect of this outputs/requirements contract relationship, i.e., exclusivity. For section 2-306(1) contracts to be valid, there must be a mutuality of obligation between the parties, otherwise they lack consideration. However, a 2-306(1) contract could be exclusive only up to a certain quantity, after which the buyer, for instance, would be free to buy elsewhere. Section 2-306(2) explicitly addresses the exclusivity agreement, but you should understand that exclusivity is required under either provision. To understand why, consider our diner owner, Jack. If Jack was free to buy potatoes from elsewhere, then the five-year contract would not be enforceable, as Jack has not obligated himself to do anything. To be enforceable, the contract must either explicitly, or implicitly, require Jack to get his potatoes only from Seamus (or some minimum amount from Seamus). Subsection (2) provides that in such an exclusive contract, the parties must use their best efforts to supply and promote the goods.

E. Firm Offers

Another area where Article 2 departs from the common law is in that it permits offerees to hold merchants to promises to keep offers open for a period of time without consideration under the concept of a "firm offer." But before delving into the nuances of the firm offer, it is necessary to distinguish this concept from the related concept of an option contract. An option contract is a contractual obligation to keep an offer open for a specified period, that the offeror cannot revoke because it is supported by consideration. For instance,

---

3. "'Good faith,' means honesty in fact and the observance of reasonable commercial standards of fair dealing." U.C.C. § 1-201(b)(2).

if Sal offered to sell his car to Bert for $5000, and Bert wished to think about the offer, he could pay Sal $10 to keep the offer open until the following Friday. Sal is now contractually obligated to keep the offer open until next Friday, and can no longer revoke the offer.[4]

Article 2 does not alter this result, but creates a method of holding sellers to their promises to keep offers open without any consideration. Section 2-205[*] provides:

> An offer by a merchant to buy or sell goods in a signed writing which by its terms give assurance that it will be held open is not revocable, for lack of consideration, during the time stated or if no time is stated for a reasonable time, but in no event may such period of irrevocability exceed three months; but any such term of assurance on a form supplied by the offeree must be separately signed by the offeror.

This Code provision does away with the need for consideration when certain circumstances are met. These circumstances can be broken down into three parts: 1) the offeror (be he the seller or buyer) MUST be a merchant; 2) the period that the offer is to be held open cannot be longer than three months; and 3) if the offeree is trying to hold the merchant offeror to a firm offer in a form he supplied, the offeror must separately sign off on that term.

So, in our Sal/Bert hypothetical, if Sal was a merchant and he promised Bert he would keep the offer open to Bert until next Friday, there would be no need for Bert to pay Sal, as § 2-205 would bind Sal without the need for consideration, so long as the firm offer is no longer than three months. What if Bert needs time to get the money together and he wants the offer to stay open longer than three months? Section 2-205 will be of no use to Bert, but he can still pay Sal the $10 to keep it open for more than three months under an option contract. Many people mistake the two concepts, thinking that section 2-205 replaces the common law's option contract principles. Not so. It is better to think of the firm offer as a distinct way of holding a contract offer open that exists coextensively with the option contract.

---

4. You may recall the general rule for offers is that they are freely revocable any time prior to acceptance. The option contract and firm offers affect this general rule.

F. Contract Formation in the Electronic Age

Many sales transactions take place online. While the internet has revolutionized the way we buy and sell goods, many of the contract formation principles remain unchanged. However, rather than have a formal offer and acceptance in-store, online contracts are usually assented to by clicking a button. Internet retailers have taken advantage of this ease by adding links to "terms of use" or "terms and conditions." In an online transaction, the vendor has the ability to make its terms and conditions available prior to the transaction being consummated. The duty to read assumes that parties to a contract have read and understood the terms and conditions in the contract. This is a bedrock principle of the objective theory of contract formation.

However, before the duty to read arises, the parties must be aware of the existence of the terms and conditions. This is not to say that the parties must actually read the terms, but only that they are made aware of them so as to be put on "inquiry notice." In the world of online contracting, the key question is whether the design of the website puts the purchaser on reasonable notice of the terms' existence. Though the ways in which savvy retailers are able to insert notice of their terms and conditions is constantly evolving, there appears to be four broad categories of online agreements: browsewrap agreements, clickwrap agreements, scrollwrap agreements, and sign-in wrap agreement.

Browsewrap agreements are the most typical way retailers make consumers aware of the terms and conditions. In a browsewrap agreement, the website will contain a notice somewhere on the page that by using the services of, obtaining information from, or initiating applications within the website, the user agrees to, and is bound by, the site's terms of service. Browsewrap agreements tend to be passive in nature, as there is no need to click separately to continue with a purchase. The links are not always easy to find, however, and many have been attacked as not giving consumers fair notice of their existence.

Clickwrap agreements necessitate an active role by the user of a website. The typical clickwrap agreement comes in the form of a box that must be checked by the user before proceeding. By checking the box, the user agrees that he or she has read the terms and conditions and is bound by them. By requiring a physical manifestation of assent, a user is said to be put on inquiry notice of the terms assented to.

Scrollwrap agreements are a variation of the clickwrap agreement, but where clickwrap agreements require the user to click a box, scrollwrap agreements force the user to view the terms and conditions as part of the website's construction and design. This could come in the form of a pop-up box containing the terms and conditions, with an "I agree" button that must be pressed to proceed. What clickwrap and scrollwrap have in common is that they both require an active step by the consumer, and are both generally viewed as more enforceable than browsewrap agreements. This is not to say that the mere use of clickwraps or scrollwraps will automatically shield vendors from arguments of reasonable notice; but case law seems to suggest these agreements are generally enforceable.

The fourth type[5] of online agreement that appears to be gaining popularity among online vendors is the sign-in wrap agreement. Sign-in wrap agreements share characteristics of both browsewrap and clickwrap agreements. Unlike clickwrap agreements, sign-in wrap agreements do not require the user to click on a box showing acceptance of the "terms of use" in order to continue. Instead, the website purposely notifies a user of the existence and applicability of the vendor's terms when proceeding through the website's sign-in or checkout process. By giving such notification, this form is more explicit than the pure browsewrap, but retains the efficiency of the browsewrap in that the user is not forced to take the extra step of clicking a box before proceeding, or navigating a pop-up screen. The sign-in wrap can come in a couple of forms. One such form forces a user to create an account and then sign in before shopping, such as Amazon.com requires. Alternatively, the sign-in wrap may simply have a notification next to the "check-out" or "submit" button informing the user that by proceeding, the user is binding themselves to the retailer's terms and conditions.

---

5. A fifth type that appears to be gaining popularity, and that doesn't fit neatly into the above four categories, involves a banner popping up at the top or bottom of the viewable page alerting the user of the terms of use. This "banner wrap" shares some characteristics with the browsewrap in that it is simply on the page and requires no active click, but unlike the browsewrap, it ensures it is visible on the page and calls the user's attention to its existence.

Checkpoints

- Article 2 endorses a broad approach to contract formation, looking to the intent of the parties to be bound.

- Ads are presumptively not offers but can become offers if clear and definite as to how to accept, and if they leave nothing open for negotiation.

- With regard to acceptance, Article 2 differs from the common law only when the offer calls for prompt shipment, in which case the offeree can accept by shipping nonconforming goods, thus accepting and breaching the contract.

- In output/requirements contracts, the U.C.C. excuses a definite quantity, obligating the parties to rely upon good faith needs.

- Output/requirements contracts must be exclusive-dealings contracts to be enforceable.

- Firm offers are distinct from option contracts in that there is no need for consideration, so long as the offeror is a merchant and the period is no longer than three months.

- Online terms and conditions are governed by the same rules as other contracts, but the key inquiry is whether the design of the website puts the purchaser on reasonable notice of the terms' existence.

Chapter 4

Battle of the Forms—Offer and Acceptance

Roadmap

- Two situations covered by U.C.C. §2-207
- Contract formation with a written offer and acceptance under U.C.C. §2-207(1)
- What terms control when an acceptance adds terms to the offer
- What terms control when an acceptance changes terms in the offer
- Contract formation under U.C.C. §2-207(3) when the writings fail to form a contract

---

A. Two Situations Covered by U.C.C. §2-207

At common law, if a response to a written offer varies from the offer, such as by adding or changing terms, it is not an acceptance of the offer but a counter-offer. This is known as the "mirror image" rule, that the offer and acceptance have to be identical, as if looking at each other in the mirror. Thus, if Hank, via email, offers to mow Dean's lawn every Saturday for a year for $200 per month, and Dean responds that he accepts but adds that Hank warrants his work will be of good workmanship, Dean has not actually accepted. Instead, Dean has made a counter-offer, as his response added terms to the offer. Without an offer and acceptance, there is no contract, and yet it would not be uncommon for Hank to begin working, as if there were a contract. So, courts can be confronted with a situation where there is no contract but both parties act as if one existed. If that is the case, the courts will follow the intent of the parties that a contract exists and look for evidence of what the terms of that contract are by using the "last shot" doctrine. Essentially, whichever party made the last clear communication regarding terms of the contract—the "last shot"—will be deemed to have defined the contract that the other party accepted by beginning work. Therefore, should Hank begin work, he will be

35

deemed to have accepted Dean's last-shot counter-offer and the contract will be on Dean's terms.

Though the mirror image rule has softened at common law over the years, it still exists. The drafters of Article 2 believed that this rule made little sense in commercial contexts in which merchants frequently exchange purchase orders and invoices without looking carefully at each other's boilerplate language. Varying the hypothetical from above, assume that Hank's Hardware Company offers to buy 1000 hammers at $5 per hammer from Dean Supply Inc. via a purchase order that is faxed. The purchase order contains lines for the item, quantity, and price that are hand-written-in, and preprinted boilerplate language on the back governing warranties that will come with hammers. Dean Supply Inc. responds by sending an invoice, again with the item, quantity, and price charged hand-written-in, and with its own pre-printed boilerplate terms on the back, including a disclaimer of all warranties, express or implied. Hank's Hardware pays the invoice and Dean Supply Inc. sends the hammers. Under the common law, Dean Supply's terms would control, as the invoice, with its different warranty terms, would be a counter-offer that Hank's Hardware accepted by paying the invoice.

The drafters of Article 2 felt such a result was unwarranted because 1) the two parties really only care about the handwritten terms, i.e., item, quantity, and price, and 2) the enforceability of boilerplate terms should not turn on the fortuitousness of whose form was sent last. Thus, U.C.C. § 2-207 (known as the "Battle of the Forms" section) was created to address such a situation. Specifically, section 2-207(1) provides:

> A definite and seasonable expression of acceptance or a written confirmation which is sent within a reasonable time operates as an acceptance even though it states terms additional to or different from those offered or agreed upon, unless acceptance is expressly made conditional on assent to the additional or different terms.[*]

Unfortunately, the drafters attempted to do more in section 2-207 than just address situations where a written offer and acceptance do not match up; they also added the phrase "or a written confirmation." This addition is somewhat confusing given that a confirmation envisions that a contract has already been formed. Therefore, section 2-207 addresses two different situations: 1) instances

---

in which there is a written offer and a written acceptance that does not match up with the offer; and 2) instances in which a contract is formed orally, and one party sends a follow-up confirmation detailing the terms of the contract. To simplify your understanding of section 2-207, we have addressed the confirmation provision separately in Chapter 5. We spend the remainder of this Chapter addressing contracts upon the exchange of forms.

B. Contract Formation with a Written Offer and Acceptance Under U.C.C. § 2-207(1)

Section 2-207(1) alters the common law mirror image rule by recognizing that an acceptance with additional or different terms can still operate as an acceptance. We will refer to such contract formation, moving forward, as having a contract "on the forms." If there is a contract on the forms under section 2-207(1), then we move to section 2-207(2) to help resolve what the terms of the contract are, given the variations between the offer and acceptance. If there is not a contract on the forms, we move to section 2-207(3) to determine if there is nonetheless a contract by conduct. Section 2-207(1) therefore presents a fork in the 2-207 road, meaning you will either proceed to 2-207(2) or 2-207(3) but not both (there either is, or is not, a contract on the forms). Before delving further into those two subsections, we must first resolve when there is a contract on the forms under 2-207(1).

Section 2-207(1) permits contract formation despite the presence of additional or different terms with three major caveats: 1) the acceptance must be definite; 2) the acceptance must be seasonable; and 3) the acceptance can not make acceptance conditional upon the terms in the acceptance becoming a part of the contract. The concept of a seasonable acceptance is not terribly difficult to understand. It means that the acceptance must come in the time set forth in the offer, and if no such time is listed, then in a reasonable time period given the context in which it is made. Understanding the other two caveats requires a bit more explanation.

To understand what it means for an acceptance to be "definite," it is useful to recall why section 2-207 was drafted in the first place—to address boilerplate terms in an offer and acceptance. Section 2-207 was drafted prior to the advent of the electronic age, when the exchange of forms often involved preprinted forms with blanks where the important details of the bargain would be written in. Though not always the case, the hand-written terms were usually the core transactional terms—what would probably be deemed "definite" terms under 2-207(1)—and the preprinted terms were boilerplate.

Currently, it is not unusual for offers and acceptances to be completely typed, but the concept remains that an acceptance which changes the core transactional terms of the offer will not qualify as an acceptance. Thus, an acceptance that agrees to sell 1,000 bushels of oranges in response to a purchase order for 1,000 bushels of apples would not be an acceptance, as it is not definite (it is literally apples and oranges). In some instances, it will be easy to identify the definite terms, as the item being purchased, the quantity, and the price are often "definite" terms that must match up. However, other terms may be less clear. For instance, if an offer to sell goods has, amongst its terms, a provision that payment is to be "cash on delivery," and the acceptance has a term providing for 30 days credit, a subsequent dispute may arise as to whether there was a definite expression of acceptance. In such instances, contextual evidence of the importance of the terms to the transaction may be required to resolve the issue.

The last caveat, "unless acceptance is expressly made conditional on assent to the additional or different terms," is meant to prevent contract formation on the forms when an offeree tries to insist that the terms in the acceptance are controlling. This phrase should not be read too broadly, however, and most courts require clear language revealing that the offeree is not willing to go through with the transaction unless its terms are to be controlling. Some offerees have tried to argue that the presence of additional or different terms is a clear indication that they wished to only proceed on their terms, but such a reading would run counter to the very purpose of section 2-207. Though the precise language, "expressly made conditional," need not be used, there must still be a clear expression that the offeree does not wish to proceed unless its terms are to control.

C. What Terms Control When an Acceptance Adds Terms to the Offer

Hank's Hardware Company offers to buy 1000 hammers at $5 per hammer from Dean Supply Inc. via a purchase order. The order has boilerplate language requiring that all disputes be resolved via binding arbitration. Dean Supply Inc. sends its response, accepting the offer, but in its boilerplate language, it has added a disclaimer of all implied warranties and expressly retained the right to bring suit in the courts of its local jurisdiction. Assuming there is a contract on the forms, the next question becomes what to do with additional and different terms found in the acceptance. This inquiry is resolved by section 2-207(2), or at least in part. We say in part because, unfortunately, despite both additional and different terms being mentioned in section 2-207(1), section 2-207(2) only refers to additional terms. We will address how to deal with additional terms in this section and how to deal with different terms in the following section.

1. Additional terms when a non-merchant is involved

U.C.C. section 2-207(2) provides:

> The additional terms are to be construed as proposals for addition to the contract. Between merchants such terms become part of the contract unless:
>   (a) the offer expressly limits acceptance to the terms of the offer;
>   (b) they materially alter it; or
>   (c) notification of objection to them has already been given or is given within a reasonable time after notice of them is received.

U.C.C. § 2-207(2).* It is worth lingering a moment on the first line. Note that this line makes no caveats regarding merchants—that comes in the next line. By designating additional terms as "proposals for addition to the contract," it means that in any situation in which a non-merchant is involved, the proposed additional terms can be ignored and do not become a part of the contract unless the offeror expressly assents to them (this is true for different terms as well). As a consequence, when a non-merchant is involved, the contract will be on the offeror's terms and the offeree's additions are ignored.

2. Treatment of additional terms as between merchants

The next line of section 2-207(2) changes this result when the contract is between merchants. As between merchants, the additional terms will become a part of the contract subject to the three conditions listed. The first and third conditions are not as heavily litigated as the second. Under (a), if the offeror makes clear in the offer it will not accept additions or changes to the proposed bargain, then the additional terms will not make their way into the contract.[1]

---

* Uniform Commercial Code, copyright © by the American Law Institute and the National Conference of Commissioners on Uniform State Laws. Reproduced with the permission of the Permanent Editorial Board for the Uniform Commercial Code. All rights reserved.

1. Be wary not to confuse an offeror's right to limit acceptance to the terms in the offer with an attempt by an offeree to make acceptance expressly conditional on its own terms. The latter will prevent a contract in the forms; the former will not but will guarantee that no additional terms make their way into the contract.

Even if an offeror does not include such a clause, under subsection (c), the offeror is still afforded a "reasonable time" within which to object to the additional terms' presence after receiving notification of the terms. Typically, this will be sometime before performance has been completed, but as is often the case when a term like "reasonable" is used, contextual factors may influence the determination.

The most litigated of the three caveats is subsection (b), which provides that an additional term that materially alters the contract will not become a part of the contract. At the outset, a word of caution should be offered not to confuse a term that materially alters a contract with the concept of definiteness from section 2-207(1). Definiteness refers to the terms that form the heart of the transaction—the ones the parties are likely thinking of when they enter into the contract. A boilerplate term may not be a definite term in the sense that it is not a core transactional term, but could still be one that materially alters the expectations of the parties.

Though section 2-207 gives no further definition of what a "material alteration" is, the comments do provide some guidance. Comment 4 to section 2-207 states that a typical materially-altering clause is one that would "result in surprise or hardship if incorporated without express awareness by the other party." Comments 4 and 5 go on to list clauses that typically would and would not result in surprise or hardship. Clauses that are usually materially altering include:

> [A] clause negating such standard warranties as that of merchantability or fitness for a particular purpose in circumstances in which either warranty normally attaches; a clause requiring a guaranty of 90% or 100% deliveries in a case such as a contract by cannery, where the usage of the trade allows greater quantity leeways; a clause reserving to the seller the power to cancel upon the buyer's failure to meet any invoice when due; a clause requiring that complaints be made in a time materially shorter than customary or reasonable.

U.C.C. § 2-207, c. 4.* Typical clauses that would not materially alter a contract include:

> [A] clause setting forth and perhaps enlarging slightly upon the seller's exemption due to supervening causes beyond his control, similar

to those covered by the provision of this Article on merchant's excuse by failure of presupposed conditions or a clause fixing in advance any reasonable formula of proration under such circumstances; a clause fixing a reasonable time for complaints within customary limits, or in the case of a purchase for sub-sale, providing for inspection by the sub-purchaser; a clause providing for interest on overdue invoices or fixing the seller's standard credit terms where they are within the range of trade practice and do not limit any credit bargained for; a clause limiting the right of rejection for defects which fall within the customary trade tolerances for acceptance "with adjustment" or otherwise limiting remedy in a reasonable manner (see Sections 2-718 and 2-719).

U.C.C. § 2-207, c. 5. Though the comments give some guidance on these by way of example, it should be noted that these are just generalities. The guiding principle for whether a term materially alters the contract is to ask, "would this clause work surprise or hardship upon the party upon whom enforcement would be sought?" If the answer is "yes," then the clause is materially altering and does not become a part of the contract.

Turning back to our hypothetical between Hank's Hardware and Dean Supply is useful to demonstrate this principle in action. We will assume that both Hank's and Dean Supply are merchants. The additional term that is added by Dean Supply is a disclaimer of all implied warranties. Assuming Hank's offer did not limit acceptance of the offer to the terms in the offer, and that Hank's did not object within a reasonable time period, then the issue of whether the disclaimer will become a part of the bargain will come down to whether it materially alters the contract. A mechanical application of the comments, in particular comment 4, would seem to indicate that the clause does materially alter, but this ignores the subtlety of the analysis. The clause must still work a surprise or hardship upon Hank's. If it is typical to disclaim such implied warranties in the industry, then the disclaimer probably would not materially alter the contract. Therefore, one must be careful not to jump too quickly to any conclusion about the status of any given clause based on the comments.

D. What Terms Control When an Acceptance Changes Terms in the Offer

As noted above, though section 2-207(1) permits contract formation despite the presence of additional or different terms, it does not explicitly provide for what to do with the differing terms. This has caused a jurisdictional split in how to approach differing terms in the offer and acceptance between merchants. One approach is to simply treat differing terms the same as additional terms under 2-207(2). Another approach is to simply ignore the proposed differing term. A third approach applies what has been called the "knock-out rule" and is the majority approach.

1. Treat as additional approach

This approach deems the omission of the word "different" from section 2-207(2) as a drafting error. While this would be a pretty large error, there is some support for this approach found in the comments. Comment 3 notes that "[w]hether or not additional or *different* terms will become a part of the agreement depends upon the provisions of subsection (2)." Building upon this language in the comments, some courts simply read "different" into the opening line of section 2-207(2) so that it reads as, "The additional [or different] terms are to be construed as proposals for addition to [or to change] the contract." Under this approach, if both parties are merchants, then the analysis would proceed as described above in section C.2., i.e., the changes would be proposals to alter the contract that take effect unless one of the caveats in subsections (a)-(c) are met.

2. Ignore the proposed change approach

This approach can be viewed as being based in one of two arguments. First, similar to the reasoning above, the omission of "different" was a drafting error, so we must proceed through the three subsections of (a)-(c). However, given that the offeror has already presented the terms it wants in positive terms, it is viewed as having implicitly objected to any changes, and thus, under subsection (a) or (c), the proposed change fails.[2]

A second, perhaps more persuasive, rationale is that the omission is not a drafting error at all. By omitting "different" terms, the drafters intended there to be no path under section 2-207 for an offeree to change a term in the offer absent the offeror's express assent. Under either rationale offered, however, the result is the same—the contract is on the offeror's terms in the offer and the proposed differing terms in the acceptance are simply ignored and are of no effect.

---

2. An argument could also be made under (b) that changing a term in the offer will always work a surprise and hardship, and thus would materially alter the contract.

3. The "knock-out rule"

The final approach is the "knock-out rule," so called because the differing terms literally knock each other out, leaving a gap in the contract that the court will fill. Though this approach has no basis in the text of section 2-207, nor in the comments, it is a similar approach to that found in 2-207(3) (as we will explore below). Despite the lack of a statutory basis for this approach, it has been adopted in a majority of jurisdictions, perhaps due to the flexibility it offers the judge in crafting a term to fill the newly-created gap. Filling this gap can sometimes be accomplished through a statutory gap-filler, of which there are a number in Article 2.

Applying what we have just learned, let's turn back to our Hank's/Dean Supply contract (again assuming they are both merchants). Recall that Hank's offer set forth that all disputes would be through binding arbitration, while Dean Supply expressly retained the right to bring suit in the courts of its local jurisdiction. This is clearly a different term as it directly conflicts with Hank's arbitration provision.[3] Under the first approach, we would have to determine if changing the arbitration clause would impose surprise or hardship upon Hank's such that it would materially alter the contract. Under the second, the analysis is quite simple; Hank's terms control and Dean Supply's terms are ignored. Under the knock-out rule, neither party's terms survive. Hank's arbitration provision and Dean Supply's dispute provision knock each other out of the contract. If a court chose to gap-fill with the default rules, all disputes would go to court, as there is no default rule that requires arbitration. This result would depend on a court looking no further than the default rules, but that is not necessarily the only place to look to fill the gap. As we will learn in Chapter 7, before resorting to gap-fillers, courts should consider other contextual evidence such as course of performance, course of dealing, and trade usage. For now, it is enough to know that the parties' differing terms knock each other out and create a gap that must be filled by the court.

---

3. Not all such terms are as clear-cut. Arguments about whether an additional term is really different abound, especially when there is a presumptive set of rules lurking in the background. For instance, had Hank's offer been silent on the mode of dispute resolution, and Dean Supply been the one inserting an arbitration clause, Hank's might argue that it was silent in its offer because it wanted the normal set of rules, i.e., disputes being brought in a court with jurisdiction over the matter, to be controlling. In this sense, Dean Supply would not be adding but changing a term in the offer. Despite such arguments, generally courts will require a term in the acceptance to affect an express term in the offer before designating it a "differing" term.

One final nuance of the knock-out rule is worth noting before moving on. You may have noticed that the result of the knock-out rule is that Dean Supply was still able to avoid the arbitration clause. This suggests an opportunity for gaming the system when an offeree does not like the terms of the offer and knows that there is a default rule that is more favorable to the offeree. A crafty offeree can simply address the matter in the offer in a different way in the acceptance, knowing that a court applying the knock-out rule will ultimately gap-fill with the term they wanted in the first place. This strategy is not without its risks (such as a court finding a different default rule should apply), but it is a consequence of the knock-out rule that you should be alert to.

E. Contract Formation Under U.C.C. § 2-207(3) When the Writings Fail to Form a Contract

The previous two sections addressed what the terms of a contract are when there is a contract on the forms. But recall that not all acceptances lead to a contract on the forms. An acceptance that is not definite or seasonable does not create a contract. Even if an acceptance is definite and seasonable, if it is made expressly conditional upon its own terms, again there is no contract on the forms. If a contract fails on the forms, and the parties do nothing more, then there is no contract, and that is the end of the matter. But what happens if the parties move forward as if they had a contract? Perhaps neither party noticed a price disparity between the forms, or the offeror did not notice the expressly conditional language in the acceptance (remember that section 2-207 assumes neither party is reading each other's forms very carefully). In any event, the parties have moved forward and are acting as if a contract exists; if a dispute arises, how should the court determine the content of the parties' contract?

Section 2-207(3) addresses this situation, stating:

> Conduct by both parties which recognizes the existence of a contract is sufficient to establish a contract for sale although the writings of the parties do not otherwise establish a contract. In such case the terms of the particular contract consist of those terms on which the writings of the parties agree, together with any supplementary terms incorporated under any other provisions of this Act.

U.C.C. § 2-207(3).* This provision is generally in line with section 2-204 which, you may recall form Chapter 3, envisions a broad conception of contract formation. Section 2-207(3) provides that there is in fact a contract, but not on any one party's form. Instead, we must compare the two forms—wherever the forms agree, those terms become a part of the contract. But any terms which disagree, or which appear in one form, but not the other, are disregarded. In this regard, the rule from 2-207(3) is similar to the knock-out rule in that conflicting terms are discarded, but 2-207(3) is even broader in that it also discards terms that do not appear in both forms.

Again, turning to our Hank's/Dean Supply hypothetical, recall that there is both an additional disclaimer of warranties and a conflicting dispute resolution provision. Assume further that Dean Supply had inserted a clause in its boilerplate language stating "the acceptance is expressly conditional upon the terms found herein being controlling." Hank's did not see this provision, and the two move forward as if they have a contract, with Hank's paying $5,000 and Dean Supply providing the 1,000 hammers. Later, a dispute arises over the merchantability of the hammers.

Due to the "expressly conditional" clause, there was no contract on the forms, but the two parties' conduct definitely evidences a contract by performance. In such an instance, under 2-207(3), there is a contract but only on the terms upon which the parties agree. This means that Dean Supply's disclaimer of warranties will be discarded as it is not found in the offer, but both parties' dispute resolution provisions will be discarded. The end result will likely be that Hank's must bring suit in court (rather than via arbitration), but the upshot is that the implied warranty of merchantability will not be disclaimed.

Checkpoints

- Section 2-207 applies to two situations: contracts on the forms, and confirmations of prior oral agreements.

- If an acceptance is definite and seasonable, there will be a contract on the forms, unless the acceptance is expressly conditional on imposition of its own terms.

- Definite terms are non-boilerplate, core transactional terms.

- For contracts on the forms, additional terms in the acceptance are proposals that can be ignored by the offeror if **a non-merchant is involved**.

- For contracts on the forms, **as between merchants**, additional terms in the acceptance are proposals that become a part of the contract unless: the original offer expressly limits acceptance to the terms in the offer; the offeror objects to the terms in a reasonable amount of time; or the additional terms materially alter the contract.

- Material alteration turns on whether the new terms would impose **surprise or hardship** on the party upon whom enforcement is sought.

- For contracts on the forms, **as between merchants**, different terms in the acceptance are subject to one of three jurisdictional approaches: the treat as additional approach, the ignore the proposed change approach, and the "knock-out rule" approach.

- Under the majority "knock-out rule" approach, differing terms knock each other out and the court gap-fills.

- If there is no contract on the forms, but the parties nonetheless proceed as if they have a contract, then there is a contract, but only on the terms upon which the offer and acceptance agree — other terms fall away and the court may gap-fill where needed.

Chapter 5

Battle of the Forms — Confirmations

Roadmap

- How confirmations arise
- What terms control when a confirmation adds to or changes the terms of an oral agreement
- The rolling contract approach to contract formation
- The intersection of rolling contracts with U.C.C. § 2-207

A. How Confirmations Arise

As noted in the previous Chapter, U.C.C. § 2-207 addresses two situations: 1) instances in which there is a written offer and a written acceptance that does not match up with the offer; and 2) instances in which a contract is formed orally, and one party sends a follow-up confirmation detailing the terms of the contract. In this Chapter, we address the second situation involving confirmations.

Confirmations can arise in a number of situations. For instance, say John, a grain trader for DeMoss Grain, buys and sells wheat from farmers. The contracts are formed orally over the phone, but to memorialize the deal, and at the insistence of DeMoss's in-house lawyer, John sends a written confirmation to the farmers after each oral conversation. The confirmation contains the key details discussed over the phone, as well as a number of boilerplate terms meant to protect DeMoss's interests. The farmers don't have their own lawyers and don't particularly care about the boilerplate additions, so long as the confirmation correctly states the deal as agreed upon.

Another way confirmations arise is when goods are sold in-store or over the phone. Recall that typically the advertised price is a solicitation, and the consumer is the one who makes the offer when he or she checks out, and the seller accepts by taking payment. It is not unusual for goods to have additional

47

terms inside the box, sometimes referred to as "shrink-wrap" terms, as they are within the sealed packaging. As the contract has already been formed in-store (or possibly over the phone), these additional terms could also be deemed as confirmations, though not always, as we will explore below.

Section 2-207(1) addresses confirmations, but it is a strange place to address them, as most of 2-207(1) deals with when an acceptance qualifies as an acceptance, creating a contract on the forms. The very concept of a confirmation envisions a contract has already been formed. Thus, it is perhaps easier to view the reference to confirmations in 2-207(1) as nothing more than an acknowledgement that additional terms in a confirmation are to be addressed by 2-207(2). Similarly, as a contract has already been formed, section 2-207(3) should not apply to confirmations. The big take away here is that, when addressing an oral contract with a follow-up confirmation, only 2-207(2) is relevant. Attempts to address contract formation under 2-207(1) or (3) are misplaced in a confirmation setting.

B. What Terms Control When a Confirmation Adds to or Changes the Terms of an Oral Agreement

Recall that section 2-207(2) only addresses additional terms, causing a jurisdictional divergence on what to do with differing terms in an acceptance between merchants. However, as the contract is already formed in a confirmation situation, any attempt to change the terms of the contract would amount to a unilateral modification of the contract. Though U.C.C. § 2-209 does away with the need for consideration in modifying a contract, it still requires an agreement to modify. Thus, regardless of merchant status, an attempt to change a term in the confirmation requires the other party to expressly agree to the change; otherwise the proposed change can be ignored.[1]

If the confirmation simply adds terms to the agreement, then we follow the same path as we would with additional terms in a contract on the forms situation. We first ask if the contract is between merchants. If not, the additional terms are proposals for addition to the contract that can be ignored, unless expressly agreed upon by the other party. If the contract is between merchants,

---

1. However, as explained in Chapter 6, the statute of frauds will not permit the enforcement of a contract beyond a quantity in the writing. This creates an opportunity for a crafty party who wishes to change the quantity to a lower amount to do so through the provisions of section 2-201(1).

the additional terms will become a part of the contract unless one of the caveats in subsections 2-207(2) apply.

C. The Rolling Contract Approach to Contract Formation

In Chapter 3, we posed a fictional situation in which you go into an electronics store and see language-learning software advertised at $200. Based upon the general presumption that this is not an offer, but a solicitation, if you buy the software, you make the offer and the merchant accepts (probably by charging you). Based on the above, any additional terms found in the box of the software would be a confirmation, governed by section 2-207(2). However, in 1996, Judge Frank H. Easterbrook turned much of what we just learned on its head in the now famous (or infamous, depending on your viewpoint) case of *ProCD, Inc. v. Zeidenberg*, 86 F.3d 1447 (7th Cir. 1996).

1. *ProCD, Inc. v. Zeidenberg* and establishment of the rolling contract approach

The facts at issue in *ProCD* mirror, in many ways, the hypothetical used in Chapter 3. Matthew Zeidenberg entered into a local retail store and bought ProCD's product, "Select Phone," which was a CD-ROM disk containing over 95,000,000 telephone listings compiled by ProCD. Inside the package was a user guide containing a "Single User License Agreement" prohibiting the purchaser from copying the software other than for personal use. The license provided that "[b]y using the discs and the listings licensed to you, you agree to be bound by the terms of this License. If you do not agree to the terms of this License, promptly return all copies of the software . . . to the place where you obtained it." The box the software came in made reference to the license on the outside in small print but did not give any details. Zeidenberg purchased the software and soon realized he could copy the information and make it available to the public himself. To this end, he incorporated under the name Silken Mountain Web Services, Inc., ignoring the license agreement, and eventually made his database available over the internet.

ProCD brought suit to enjoin him claiming a violation of the license agreement. The district court considered whether the contract offer was accepted once Zeidenberg had received the goods and had an opportunity to inspect them, or whether the contract was formed in the store, and thus the terms of the license should be viewed under U.C.C. § 2-207. Reviewing section 2-206, the court concluded the contract was formed in the store, and that the additional terms of the license agreement were mere proposals that could be ignored by Zeidenberg under section 2-207(2), which would require Zeidenberg's express consent. Thus, the district court's approach was generally in line with our understanding of contract formation and confirmations as reviewed in Chapter 3 and above.

On appeal, Judge Easterbrook began his analysis by noting that Zeidenberg alleged, and the district court found, the offer occurred when the goods were placed on the shelf. Easterbrook did not take issue with this premise (though it is questionable), but instead took issue with the district court's treatment of the acceptance, which it held took place in the store. Easterbrook questioned this premise stating, "[W]hy would Wisconsin fetter the parties' choice in this way?" 86 F.3d at 1450–51. Easterbrook then described the advantages of permitting standard term agreements to be enforceable, despite the fact that they are often read for the first time after the buyer has the goods. Among these advantages was the saved time and expense of trying to describe all of the terms on the outside of a box. While there may be practical and economic advantages (particularly to the vendor/seller) in doing business in such a way, what of the district court's analysis under section 2-207? Easterbrook summarily dismissed its application stating, "Our case has only one form; U.C.C. § 2-207 is irrelevant." This conclusion of course ignores the fact that section 2-207 *does* apply to a single form in instances involving a confirmation.

Instead of analyzing under section 2-207 (or possibly section 2-206 which is not even mentioned), Easterbrook turned to U.C.C. § 2-204 as the guiding principle for such "terms later" contracts. Section 2-204 broadly provides that a contract may be formed "in any manner sufficient to show agreement," which Easterbrook used to justify his view that the vendor or seller is the master of its offer and can choose to invite acceptance by conduct, such as by using the product. This view of contract formation is limited by the caveat that the buyer must be given an opportunity to review and reject the offer, but otherwise, such contracts are enforceable. Thus, as Zeidenberg had been given notice of the license agreement, and continued to use the software, he was bound by the license agreement's terms.

The analytical approach championed by Judge Easterbrook has become known as the "rolling" or "layered" contract approach. The effect of this approach is to ignore the in-store transaction (or simply relegate it to some sort of preliminary agreement), and call the form which comes later the actual offer. By the offeree keeping the goods (or failing to return them), the offer is accepted. Note that this conception does avoid implication of section 2-207. Section 2-207 addresses two situations: 1) instances in which there is a written offer and a written acceptance that does not match up with the offer; and 2) instances in which a contract is formed orally, and one party sends a follow-up confirmation detailing the terms of the contract. Section 2-207 **does not** address situations in which there is a written offer and acceptance by conduct. Thus by calling the later form the offer, section 2-207 is avoided, not because it only involves one form, but because the one form is the offer.

Despite suffering from some analytical flaws (such as ignoring that section 2-207 does apply in instances when one form is involved), *ProCD* has been widely cited and adopted in a number of decisions on the issue of whether "rolling" or "layered" contracts are enforceable. Unfortunately, a number of these courts have failed to analyze why the common understanding of contract formation should be displaced by the "rolling" contract, and instead simply cite to *ProCD* and its progeny, adopting their approach.

2. Limitations on the rolling contract approach

The rolling contract theory does have limits as to how terms can be presented. A consistent theme throughout many rolling contract cases is the right of the buyer to return the goods should the buyer not agree to terms presented. This is really no more than the concept that an offeree is free to accept or reject an offer. The court in *DeFontes v. Dell, Inc.*, 984 A.2d 1061 (R.I. 2009) (a case involving Dell's ability to compel arbitration through its rolling contract standard terms), summarized some of the limitations on this approach:

> Yet in adopting the so-called "layered contracting" theory of formation, we reiterate that the burden falls squarely on the seller to show that the buyer has accepted the seller's terms after delivery. Thus, the crucial question in this case is whether defendants reasonably invited acceptance by making clear in the terms and conditions agreement that (1) by accepting defendants' product the consumer was accepting the terms and conditions contained within and (2) the consumer could reject the terms and conditions by returning the product.

Id. at 1071. Essentially, this limitation means that the offeror must conspicuously communicate to the offeree that the offeree has the right to reject the offer, and if they do choose to reject, how to do so. In addition to the above limitations, rolling contracts are still vulnerable to the other doctrines of contract voidability, such as unconscionability.

D. The Intersection of Rolling Contracts with U.C.C. § 2-207

The rolling contract approach to contract formation presents a bit of a quandary when dealing with situations in which a contract is consummated orally, and a form follows. The approach is frequently adopted when dealing with purchases of goods in-store or over the phone, in which the goods arrive with a document containing additional terms and conditions. In such a situation, a court may be forced to choose between the traditional approach, under which 2-207 would apply, and the rolling contract approach.

Consider the following hypothetical: Brock buys a laptop in-store from Venture Industries. At the time of the purchase, no mention is made of additional terms and conditions that will apply to the sale. When Brock gets home and opens the box the laptop is in, he discovers, for the first time, a form with additional terms and conditions, one of which requires all disputes to be resolved through binding arbitration. The laptop turns out to be defective, and Brock wishes to sue Venture Industries.

Under the approach outlined in parts A and B above, the terms and conditions page is a confirmation. As there are additional terms, these would be proposals for addition to the contract. If Brock is not a merchant, he can ignore these terms and they will not bind him, meaning he can proceed to sue in a court that has jurisdiction. Even if Brock is a merchant, the terms must still clear the caveats set forth in section 2-207(2)(a)-(c). However, under a rolling contract approach, the terms and conditions are the offer. So long as the form clearly explained that if he did not agree to the terms, he could return the product, then Brock would be bound, as his use would be an acceptance of the offer. Therefore, under this approach, Brock must settle his dispute through the arbitration process.

Consider also our grain trader, John, from above. Under section 2-207, John's additional terms are not necessarily a part of the oral contract with the farmers, though they may very well come in under section 2-207(2). Under a rolling contract approach, John's confirmation could be viewed as the offer, which the farmers accept through their performance.[2] Thus John could avoid section 2-207 altogether and the chance his terms won't apply. Indeed, one gets the sense that all a party needs to do to apply its terms is to ship, after an oral

---

2. This approach has not been limited to instances involving consumers. *See, e.g.,* *M.A. Mortenson Co. v. Timberline Software Corp.,* 998 P.2d 305 (Wash. 2000) (en banc) (involving the sale of computer software between two businesses).

agreement, favorable contract terms, with an opportunity to reject by the other party, and these terms will be honored—a result which harkens back to the "last-shot" doctrine that U.C.C. § 2-207 was meant to address. For this reason, not all courts are in agreement over the application of the rolling contract approach. Though this approach has sometimes been labeled the "majority" approach, this may be an overstatement, which ignores the nuances of when the approach has been applied.[3]

Checkpoints

- Section 2-207 applies to two situations: contracts on the forms, and confirmations of prior oral agreements.

- Different terms in the confirmation are ignored, unless expressly agreed to by the other party, as a party cannot unilaterally amend a previously formed contract.

- Additional terms in a confirmation are proposals for addition. If a nonmerchant is involved, the proposed additions are ignored unless expressly agreed upon.

- As between merchants, additional terms in a confirmation will become a part of the contract subject to the caveats listed in section 2-207(2)(a)-(c) (as discussed in the previous Chapter).

- Particularly in situations involving shrink-wrap terms, some courts have adopted a "rolling" (or "layered") contract approach.

- The rolling contract approach considers the later form to be the offer (rather than a confirmation) which can be accepted or rejected by the recipient.

- Under the rolling contract approach, the later form must still conspicuously give the recipient the right to reject the offer, and explain how to do so.

- The rolling contract approach may result in terms becoming a part of the contract that would not survive an analysis under section 2-207(2).

---

3. One of us has advocated that the distinguishing characteristic between when a rolling contract approach is appropriate, and when section 2-207 should apply, is the nature of the transaction involved. Contracts that by their very nature involve foreseeable ongoing obligations, such as technical services, are more likely to involve more complex terms and conditions, and it would probably be within both parties' contemplation that other terms and conditions apply to the transaction than what appear at the point of sale. In such situations, a rolling contract approach would seem appropriate and efficient. In more discreet sales, such as the sale of a sandwich, there are little or no further anticipated contacts between the parties regarding the transaction beyond the sale, and thus section 2-207 would be more appropriate. *See* Colin P. Marks, *Not What, but When Is an Offer: Rehabilitating the Rolling Contract*, 46 Conn. L. Rev. 73 (2013).

Chapter 6

Statute of Frauds

Roadmap

- An introduction to the Statute of Frauds
- The threshold requirements of 2-201(1)
- The "between merchants" exception
- Part performance exceptions
- Admission exception
- Interaction of § 2-201 with §§ 2-207 and 2-209

A. An Introduction to the Statute of Frauds

The Statute of Frauds is a bit of an anachronism from our common law past, but it remains alive and well under state laws. The Statute of Frauds is meant to prevent fraudulently asserted contract claims from making their way to trial by requiring that certain contracts be evidenced by a signed writing. The Statute of Frauds does not apply to all contractual disputes—two notable areas where it does apply are for transfers of an interest in land and contracts that cannot be performed within one year of the contract's making. One other area, which is of primary concern to this text, applies to contracts for goods for which the purchase price is $500 or more.

When the Statute of Frauds does apply, it permits the defendant to make a motion to dismiss based upon the lack of a signed writing evidencing the alleged contract. Typically, the Statute requires three things: 1) a writing; 2) that is signed by the party against whom enforcement is sought; and 3) content of the material terms of the contract. These general requirements warrant further discussion, as the first two have similar treatment under Article 2 (but the third is treated quite differently).

The first general requirement, a writing, does not require an actual written contract. Indeed, if there were a written contract, the Statute would not likely be invoked. The writing can come from any number of sources, such as

55

official meeting minutes, correspondence between the parties, diary entries, or even notes jotted down on a napkin. Furthermore, the writing may be in electronic form. The Uniform Electronic Transactions Act (UETA), drafted by the NCCUSL in 1999, and adopted by 47 states, the District of Columbia and the U.S. Virgin Islands, establish that electronic forms are equivalent to a physical writing or signature. Thus emails or other stored electronic records can establish the writing requirement. Furthermore, the writing requirement can be met through multiple writings (though there must be some way of knowing that the writings can fairly be read together).

The signature requirement does not require both parties' signature; only the party against whom enforcement is sought. As with a writing, the concept of a signature is similarly broad. Comment 1 to section 2-201 notes that the term "signed" "includes any authentication which identifies the party to be charged." Article 1 similarly provides that the term "includes using any symbol executed or adopted with present intention to adopt or accept a writing." Under this broad approach to signature, a simple "X" will qualify if it is adopted by the signer as his or her signature. Business letterheads also qualify as symbols so adopted, and even an email address in an email correspondence may qualify.

It is worth noting that though the writing and signature requirements can be met in a number of ways, this does not "win" the plaintiff's case — it merely helps overcome the Statute of Frauds and defeat the motion to dismiss. The plaintiff must still convince a fact-finder that a valid contract exists.

B. The Threshold Requirements of § 2-201(1)

Section 2-201(1) provides when Article 2's version of the Statute of Frauds applies and what it requires. It reads:

> Except as otherwise provided in this section a contract for the sale of goods for the price of $500 or more is not enforceable by way of action or defense unless there is some writing sufficient to indicate that a contract for sale has been made between the parties and signed by the party against whom enforcement is sought or by his authorized agent or broker. A writing is not insufficient because it omits or incorrectly states a term agreed upon but the contract is not enforceable under this paragraph beyond the quantity of goods shown in such writing.*

The threshold requirement for application is simple—the contract must involve the sale of goods, and total purchase price must be $500 or more. Note this is an aggregate price, and not a price per good. A contract for 100 widgets at $5 per widget would fall under the Statute even though the individual price for each is well below $500. This may seem to be a rather low amount, but remember that it was first proposed in the 1950s and has not been amended since.

If the Statute applies, then section 2-201 requires, similar to the common law, that there be a writing, signed by the party against whom enforcement is sought, but then differs as to what content is required. While the common law frequently requires that the writing contain the material terms, section 2-201(1) specifically does not. This is reinforced in the comments which state, "[t]he required writing need not contain all the material terms of the contract and such material terms as are stated need not be precisely stated. All that is required is that the writing afford a basis for believing that the offered oral evidence rests on a real transaction." The one exception to this laxity in approach is with regard to quantity. Though omitted price or delivery terms present no obstacle, the section is clear that no contract is enforceable "beyond the quantity of goods shown in such writing." Ultimately, section 2-201(1) can be summed-up as requiring three things from the writing: 1) it must evidence a contract for the sale of goods; 2) it must be "signed"; and 3) it must specify a quantity. *See* U.C.C. § 2-201, c. 1.

C. The "Between Merchants" Exception

Though a party may fail to meet the minimum requirements of section 2-201(1), sections 2-201(2) and (3) provide exceptions to enforcement of the Statute of Frauds. The first such exception is the "between merchants" exception of section 2-201(2), which provides:

> Between merchants if within a reasonable time a writing in confirmation of the contract and sufficient against the sender is received and the party receiving it has reason to know its contents, it satisfies the requirements of subsection (1) against such party unless written notice of objection to its contents is given within 10 days after it is received.*

Though dense, this exception is actually quite easy to apply. First, recall from Chapter 1, that some provisions of Article 2 take a broad approach to "merchant" status while others take a narrow view. This is one of the provisions that takes the broad view. Thus, for section 2-201(2), one qualifies as a merchant simply by being knowledgeable of general business practices, such as the import of receiving a mailed confirmation (but must be acting in their business capacity in the transaction at issue).

If the alleged transaction is between merchants, section 2-201(2) permits a confirmation to substitute for the requirement that the party receiving the confirmation have signed the writing based upon two inquiries. First, we determine whether the confirmation is effective against the sender under 2-201(1). If so, then we ask, did the recipient object to the confirmations contents, in writing, within 10 days of receiving the confirmation. If not, then the exception is met.

The following example may help illustrate how both section 2-201(1) and section 2-201(2) work. Venture Industries manufactures helper robots that perform custodial tasks. Hank's Hoagie Shop, a sandwich restaurant chain, contacts a representative at Venture Industries and places an order for 25 helper robots at a cost of $300 per robot on October 1. The next day, Venture Industries sends an invoice to Hank's in the mail, billing Hank's for 25 helper robots at $300 per robot for a total of $7,500. The invoice is not signed by any person but has the Venture Industries official letterhead and logo on it. The invoice is received by Hank's corporate office on October 5, but no further action is taken. In a subsequent suit by Venture Industries, Hank's will have the ability to move to dismiss the case under section 2-201(1), because though there is a writing and content, the writing is lacking a signature from the party against whom enforcement is sought, i.e., Hank's.

This is where subsection 2-201(2) becomes relevant. First, we should see that this alleged contract is between merchants under the broad view of that term. Venture Industries is definitely a merchant, even under the narrow view as it deals in helper robots, but Hanks' will also qualify as it is probably safe to assume it is knowledgeable of general business practices. We now move on to our first inquiry, and should see that the invoice *would* be effective against Venture Industries under section 2-201(1). The invoice is a writing, it contains the quantity of goods to be sold and evidences a contract was made, and we do have Venture's signature in the form of the letterhead (which would be a symbol adopted by the company). As the writing would be sufficient as against Venture Industries, we now need to ask if Hank's objected to the contents in writing. We are told it did nothing in response, and thus Venture Industries has satisfied the exception under section 2-201(2), and need not worry about the Statute of Frauds barring its claim.

D. The Part Performance Exceptions

At common law, there is a judicially recognized exception to the Statute of Frauds involving one party's part performance in reliance on the alleged contract. This exception tends to be limited to real estate transactions and requires that the claimant's performance be unequivocally referable to the alleged contract.[1] Though limited at common law, the part performance exception has made its way into section 2-201 under subsection (3) in two ways. The first involves the claimant having begun on performance of a contract involving specially manufactured goods, and the second involves partial payment or partial acceptance of the goods. We address each in turn.

1. Specially manufactured goods exception

Subsection 2-201(3)(a)[*] provides:

> A contract which does not satisfy the requirements of subsection (1) but which is valid in other respects is enforceable
> (a) if the goods are to be specially manufactured for the buyer and are not suitable for sale to others in the ordinary course of the seller's business and the seller, before notice of repudiation is received and under circumstances which reasonably indicate that the goods are for the buyer, has made either a substantial beginning of their manufacture or commitments for their procurement. . . .

This exception to 2-201(1) is reserved for sellers of specially manufactured goods and has four requirements. First, the specially manufactured goods cannot be suitable for sale to others in the *ordinary* course of the seller's business (note the inquiry is not whether they are capable of sale to others, as just about

---

1. This exception acts as a somewhat weak substitute for a writing, in that at least one party believed that a contract existed and started acting on that belief. Of course, that party could just be trying to game the system, which is why it's only a weak substitute, and viewed skeptically.

* Uniform Commercial Code, copyright © by the American Law Institute and the National Conference of Commissioners on Uniform State Laws. Reproduced with the permission of the Permanent Editorial Board for the Uniform Commercial Code. All rights reserved.

anything could be sold to others given a low enough price). Second, the seller must demonstrate it has begun performing the contract either by making a substantial beginning of the goods' manufacture, or by making commitments for their procurement. Commitments for their procurement could involve the ordering of building materials for the manufacture of the goods. Third, the beginning of performance or commitments for procurement must occur under circumstances which reasonably indicate that the goods are for the buyer. This is an important modifier to the second requirement, as it means that not every action or procurement will qualify. For instance, if the ordering of the building materials is a common good used by the seller in the manufacture of many other goods, the procurement may not reasonably indicate that the goods are for the buyer.[2] Finally, the beginnings or commitments must take place before the seller receives notice of repudiation from the buyer.

Interestingly, though section 2-201(1) insists that a writing is unenforceable beyond a stated quantity, and other exceptions to 2-201(1) incorporate this limitation in some form, there is no such limitation under 2-201(3)(a). Thus, if a seller of specially manufactured goods can meet the above requirements, it does not matter if the beginning of the work is only on a portion of the created goods, or if the commitments for procurement are for only a portion of the ordered goods. The entire contract can be enforced under section 2-201(3)(a), assuming a fact-finder can be convinced as to what that quantity is.

2. Payment/acceptance exception

In addition to the "specially manufactured" exception, there is a more general part performance exception available to both sellers and buyers under section 2-201(3)(c). It provides that "[a] contract which does not satisfy the requirements of subsection (1) but which is valid in other respects is enforceable . . . (c) with respect to goods for which payment has been made and accepted or which have been received and accepted."

Returning to our Venture Industries hypothetical from part C above, if neither party had sent a writing, but Venture Industries delivered the 25 helper robots, and Hank's accepted them, Venture would be able to avoid dismissal under section 2-201(1) due to subsection 2-201(3)(c). Similarly, if Hank's had paid the full $7,500, and Venture deposited the funds in its bank, section 2-201(1) would be no defense. The comments to section 2-201 explain,

---

2. This is similar to the concept at common law that for the part performance exception to apply, the conduct must be unequivocally referable to the alleged contract.

"[r]eceipt and acceptance either of goods or of the price constitutes an unambiguous overt admission by both parties that a contract actually exists. . . . This is true even though the actions of the parties are not in themselves inconsistent with a different transaction such as a consignment for resale or a mere loan of money."

There is a nuance, however, to the payment/acceptance exception that is not readily apparent from the text. Assume that in the Venture Industries hypothetical, Hank's paid a down payment of $3,000 (recall that the robots cost $300 each). Venture deposits the check, but Hank's subsequently refuses to pay any more on the contract. Should Venture be able to avoid the Statute of Frauds completely even though only a portion of the payment has been made? The answer is "no." In keeping with section 2-201(1)'s provision that no contract is enforceable beyond a quantity listed in the writing, Venture may only enforce the contract based on the proportional amount paid. The same would be true with regard to any goods delivered and accepted. The comments make clear that an apportionment is the favored approach. Comment 2 states:

> If the court can make a just apportionment, therefore, the agreed price of any goods actually delivered can be recovered without a writing or, if the price has been paid, the seller can be forced to deliver an apportionable part of the goods. The overt actions of the parties make admissible evidence of the other terms of the contract necessary to a just apportionment.[*]

Thus, if Hank's has only paid $3,000, the exception under 2-201(3)(c) will only permit Venture to enforce the contract up to 10 worker robots.

E. Admission Exception

The final exception to the Statute of Frauds, found in section 2-201(3)(b), is meant to address the possible abuse of the Statute as a device to avoid contracts that have actually been entered into. It provides that a contract that fails to meet section 2-201(1) is still enforceable "if the party against whom enforcement is sought admits in his pleading, testimony or otherwise in court that a contract for sale was made, but the contract is not enforceable under this

---

provision beyond the quantity of goods admitted."[3] This provision may seem straightforward, but the limits of its application are contested.

For instance, if a defendant admits in its pleadings that a contract was made, despite lacking a writing, this exception is clearly met, but what if the defendant denies the existence of a contract? Should the plaintiff be able to continue its discovery efforts in an attempt to obtain an admission? If the defendant signs a sworn affidavit denying the existence of a contract, should the plaintiff be permitted to still depose the defendant in the hopes of admitting to a contract (and thus committing perjury)? At what point are the defendant's denials sufficient to support a motion to dismiss based on section 2-201(1), or must they go all the way to swearing in open court that no contract exists before a motion will be granted?

The language of the provision states that the admission may come in court. Further, comment 7 to section 2-201 notes that the admission may be in open court stating "[i]f the making of a contract is admitted in court, either in a written pleading, by stipulation or by oral statement before the court, no additional writing is necessary for protection against fraud." Some courts have taken this as an invitation to permit cases to continue all the way to the cross-examination stage of trial. However, this largely defeats the purpose of having a writing requirement in the first place. Based upon this concern, some courts will limit how far the plaintiff may continue to conduct discovery after an initial denial of a contract in the pleadings. How far discovery may continue is far from uniform, but most courts will continue to allow some discovery before granting a motion to dismiss.

F. Interaction of § 2-201 with §§ 2-207 and 2-209

Section 2-201 may have implications with other sections of Article 2. In this portion, we highlight two in particular. The first involves confirmations sent under section 2-207. Recall that section 2-207 applies to written confirmations that follow an oral agreement. As noted above in part C, such a confirmation may be useful in meeting the exception under section 2-201(2), and as between merchants, additional terms must be analyzed under section 2-207(2) (explored in Chapter 5). You may also recall that, as a contract has already been made, attempts to modify the contract are generally unsuccessful as they

3. Note that as with §§ 2-201(2) & 2-201(3)(c), § 2-201(3)(b) limits enforceability to the quantity in keeping with § 2-201(1), in this case to the quantity admitted to.

are unilateral attempts at contract modification that would require the other party's assent. But what if the only term that has been modified in the confirmation is the quantity term and the confirmation is the only writing that evidences the contract? Under section 2-201(1), the contract is not enforceable beyond the quantity listed. Therefore, while it is true that one party cannot unilaterally modify a contract, due to the preclusive effect of section 2-201(1), if that modification affects a quantity, and the confirmation is the only written documentation of the quantity, a court should not allow the contract to be enforced beyond that listed quantity, absent another exception's application.

The other section that explicitly implicates section 2-201 is section 2-209 addressing modifications. Section 2-209(1) does away with the need for consideration to support a contract modification. However, section 2-209(3) notes that "[t]he requirements of the statute of frauds section of this Article (Section 2-201) must be satisfied if the contract as modified is within its provisions." Therefore, assume Art orally agrees to sell his painting of "Dogs Playing Poker" to Bert for $400. As the threshold amount is not met, section 2-201 does not apply and the contract is enforceable. Before the sale goes through, Art learns that his painting is actually worth $800. He asks Bert if he will agree to modify the contract price to $600 (still giving Bert a bargain) and Bert agrees. Under section 2-209, this modification is valid, as there is no need for Art to give any additional consideration, but as the new price is now over the $500 threshold, section 2-201(1) does apply, and Bert will be able to avoid enforcement of any alleged $600 oral contract.

Checkpoints

- Writings and signatures may be in electronic form.

- A signature may consist of any symbol intended to be adopted by a party, including letterheads of businesses and email addresses.

- Section 2-201(1) requires a writing indicating a contract, with a signature by the party against whom enforcement is sought, and a quantity.

- Section 2-201(1) has four exceptions: a "between merchants" exception, a "specially manufactured goods" exception, a payment/acceptance exception, and an admission exception.

- The "between merchants" exception allows a confirmation that would be enforceable against the sender, to be enforceable against the recipient if there is no written objection within 10 days.

- The "specially manufactured goods" exception only applies to sellers who have made a substantial beginning or commitments for procurement.

- The payment/acceptance exception allows enforcement of a contract but only in proportion to what has been paid or accepted.

- Under the admission exception, most courts permit some discovery before granting a motion to dismiss, to permit a plaintiff to solicit an admission.

- Section 2-201(1) may implicate other sections, in particular section 2-207 with regard to confirmations and section 2-209(3) when a modification brings a contract within section 2-201.

Chapter 7

Contract Interpretation and the Parol Evidence Rule

Roadmap

- Interpretive and constructive tools under the U.C.C.
- Judicial approaches to ambiguity and contract interpretation
- Introduction to the parol evidence rule under the U.C.C.
- Application of the parol evidence rule to partially integrated contracts
- Application of the parol evidence rule to fully integrated contracts
- Avoiding application of the parol evidence rule

A. Interpretive and Constructive Tools Under the U.C.C.

Contract interpretation is technically two different things: interpretation and construction. Contract interpretation is the process of discerning the meaning of the words in a contract, while contract construction is implying the existence of terms, though they may not be articulated in the contract. The tools used for contract interpretation and construction under the U.C.C. are very similar to the common law. Article 1 lays out specific sources to consult when interpreting and constructing terms, as well as a hierarchy.

The first thing to be consulted when interpreting a contract are the express terms of the contract. This is based upon the objective test, and an assumption that the clearest way to determine the intention of the parties is to look at the express terms used by the parties in the contract itself. U.C.C. § 1-303 provides that express terms should be read in light of, and consistent with, three other sources: course of performance, course of dealing, and trade usage. Article 1 defines each of these terms as follows:

(a) A "course of performance" is a sequence of conduct between the parties to a particular transaction that exists if:
(1) the agreement of the parties with respect to the transaction involves repeated occasions for performance by a party; and
(2) the other party, with knowledge of the nature of the performance and opportunity for objection to it, accepts the performance or acquiesces in it without objection.
(b) A "course of dealing" is a sequence of conduct concerning previous transactions between the parties to a particular transaction that is fairly to be regarded as establishing a common basis of understanding for interpreting their expressions and other conduct.
(c) A "usage of trade" is any practice or method of dealing having such regularity of observance in a place, vocation, or trade as to justify an expectation that it will be observed with respect to the transaction in question. The existence and scope of such a usage must be proved as facts. If it is established that such a usage is embodied in a trade code or similar record, the interpretation of the record is a question of law.

U.C.C. § 1-303.* These definitions can be a bit dense, but they are not that difficult to understand. "Course of performance" simply refers to how the parties have acted under the contract at issue. "Course of dealing" is how these same parties involved in the dispute have acted under previous contracts with each other. "Usage of trade" then refers to how other parties in the same industry act in such contracts. To be even more direct, at the end of the day, these three doctrines can be boiled down to various forms of "that's just how things are done 'round here."

The drafters of the code believed that parties do not make contracts in a vacuum. Therefore, all express language should be read in light of course of performance, course of dealing, and trade use, and "must be construed whenever reasonable as consistent with each other." A simple example of a common term that does not literally mean what it says, illustrates the need for such an approach; consider the term "2 × 4 board" in construction. Read literally, this would mean two inches by four inches as the board's depth and width, but in reality, the board is one and a half inches by three and a half inches. Thus "2 × 4" when read in light of the relevant usage of trade actually means "1½ × 3½" inches.

Of course, not all express terms can be harmonized with the course of performance, course of dealing or trade usage. When one or more of these sources conflict, section 1-303 provides the following hierarchy should be followed: "(1) express terms prevail over course of performance, course of dealing, and usage of trade; (2) course of performance prevails over course of dealing and usage of trade; and (3) course of dealing prevails over usage of trade." Note that this hierarchy applies even in the absence of express terms. This is because courts may fill the gaps left in the parties' agreement through construction by using course of performance, course of dealing and trade usage, subject to the hierarchy.

Therefore, if Sal and Bert enter into an installment contract which is silent as to mode of delivery, a court would look to the hierarchy to supply the missing term. If Sal has repeatedly delivered the goods to Bert's place of business under the contract, this will control even if it is standard in the industry for the buyer to pick the goods up at the seller's place of business. But regardless of the normal trade usage, Sal and Bert can reach the same result, more predictably, by expressly providing for such in the contract. Though express terms are at the top of the hierarchy, as you should see from the 2 × 4 example, there can be a fine line between when the express terms can be read in harmony with the other factors listed, such as usage of trade, and when they are in conflict. Also, it should be noted that these other concepts, such as trade usage, can expressly be displaced. So, if a contract specified wood to be cut exactly at 2 inches depth by 4 inches in width, and explicitly disavowed trade usage, then the wood should be cut to those specifications.

B. Judicial Approaches to Ambiguity and Contract Interpretation

When contract disputes arise, courts are often faced with two parties who disagree over the meaning of a key term. When the meaning of a term is in dispute, courts must first determine, as a matter of law, whether the term is ambiguous or unambiguous. If the court determines that a term is unambiguous, it simply assigns the unambiguous meaning to the term and that is the end of the matter. However, if a court determines that the term is ambiguous, then the fact-finder must determine what the parties meant by the term, and in doing so, is permitted to hear evidence outside of the contract, for the limited purpose of clarifying the ambiguity. This would include not just the relevant course of performance, course of dealing and usage of trade, but could also include other extrinsic evidence that relates to the contract but that does not appear on the face of the contract, such as statements between the parties or the circumstances surrounding the agreement.

Given the importance of deciding whether a term is ambiguous or not, the next natural question is to ask what evidence the judge gets to consider when making the ambiguity determination. At common law, one approach, known as the plain meaning rule, did not permit the judge to look outside of the contract in making such a determination (except, perhaps, to dictionary definitions). The U.C.C. expressly rejects such an approach, however, at least in so far as course of performance, course of dealing and usage of trade are concerned. *See* §2-202, comment 1.c. Turning back to our "2×4" board, if a dispute arose over the meaning of "2×4," the court would be permitted to look at the relevant trade usage of the term in deciding on whether it is ambiguous. After hearing the relevant trade usage, the court might very well decide the term unambiguously refers to a board that is 1½×3½ inches.

When a party seeks to introduce evidence that there exists an agreement that is not found in the contract, courts are faced with a similar challenge. At common law, under the parol evidence rule, if a contract is fully integrated, it cannot be modified by evidence of earlier or contemporaneous agreements. A contract is said to be fully integrated if it is meant to be the full and final expression of the parties' agreement. If a contract is not fully integrated, it is said to be partially integrated, meaning it is complete as to the terms it addresses, but is capable of being supplemented, and extrinsic evidence may be introduced so long as it does not contradict the writing.

As with the ambiguity analysis, the court determines as a matter of law whether a contract is fully or partially integrated. Also, the question of whether the court can consider extrinsic evidence in making this determination depends on the jurisdiction. Some courts adopt a "four corners" approach, similar to the plain meaning approach, which restricts the court to looking only at the contract when deciding whether, on its face, it appears to be fully integrated. Under such an approach, the presence of a merger clause— a clause stating that the contract represents the parties' complete and final agreement—may be particularly influential. Other courts adopt a softer contextual approach, which allows the court to consider extrinsic evidence when making its determination as to whether the contract is fully or partially integrated.

C. Introduction to the Parol Evidence Rule Under the U.C.C.

The parol evidence rule can be found in U.C.C. section 2-202, however, some explanation is required to understand how the rule integrates concepts such as fully and partially integrated. Section 2-202 provides:

> Terms with respect to which the confirmatory memoranda of the parties agree or which are otherwise set forth in a writing intended by the parties as a final expression of their agreement with respect to such terms as are included therein may not be contradicted by evidence of any prior agreement or of a contemporaneous oral agreement but may be explained or supplemented
>
> (a) by course of performance, course of dealing, or usage of trade (Section 1-303); and
>
> (b) by evidence of consistent additional terms unless the court finds the writing to have been intended also as a complete and exclusive statement of the terms of the agreement.*

The rule is similar to the common law parol evidence rule in that it only bars the introduction of prior or contemporaneous agreements, not subsequent, but the analogies to fully and partially integrated agreements take a little more discernment. In the first part of the section, where the provision refers to terms in a writing that are "intended by the parties as a final expression of their agreement with respect to such terms," it is speaking of contracts that are partially integrated. Reference to fully integrated agreements is found in sub (b), where it speaks of writings that are "intended also as a complete and exclusive statement of the terms of the agreement." Similar to the common law, Article 2 restricts the introduction of extrinsic evidence in fully integrated contracts, but as we explore below, is explicitly more permissive of certain types of evidence.

1. Application of the parol evidence rule to partially integrated contracts

Section 2-202 generally addresses what evidence may be introduced if a contract is partially integrated. Specifically, it references the introduction of

---

* Uniform Commercial Code, copyright © by the American Law Institute and the National Conference of Commissioners on Uniform State Laws. Reproduced with the permission of the Permanent Editorial Board for the Uniform Commercial Code. All rights reserved.

course of performance, course of dealing and usage of trade, as well as other "evidence of consistent additional terms." This last reference covers prior and contemporaneous oral agreements not found in the writing. The explanation and supplementation of a partially integrated writing, while allowed by 2-202, is subject to two caveats.

The first is that the supplemental evidence cannot contradict a term found in the writing. This is explicitly set forth in section 2-202, and is reinforced in subsection (b) which only permits "consistent additional terms." Thus, if a partially integrated writing provides that the price of goods is $1,000, evidence of a prior oral agreement that the price is actually $700 should generally be excluded, as it would contradict the explicit price listed in the contract.[1] The same is true for course of performance, course of dealing, and usage of trade. For instance, if a contract provides that the buyer will pick up goods from the seller's place of business, the buyer should not be permitted to introduce course of dealing evidence that typically the seller delivers the goods to the buyer, as this would be in direct contradiction of the express terms in the writing.

The second caveat is that additional terms, under subsection (b), should not be admitted if the terms would mislead a jury. This caveat is found in comment 3 to section 2-202 which states: "If the additional terms are such that, if agreed upon, *they would certainly have been included in the document in the view of the court,* then evidence of their alleged making must be kept from the trier of fact." (emphasis added). This caveat is meant to prevent one party from introducing evidence of significant new obligations or conditions that never made their way into the writing, but could apply to less significant terms as well. Its clearest application would be in a heavily negotiated contract that took months to conclude, and went through multiple drafts. In such a situation, a court should be reluctant to allow evidence of a negotiated term that ultimately was rejected in the final writing. Other times, however, a term is so important or bizarre, that there is no way the parties would not have thought of including it among the obligations in the writing. For instance, evidence of a prior oral agreement that the sale of an ordinary used car would be plated in gold before delivery would certainly seem to be the sort of thing the parties would include in the final writing, and should be excluded.

---

1. We say generally, as there is always the possibility that a skilled advocate could convince a court that the $700 price evidence is merely explaining, rather contradicting, the $1000 price term.

2. Application of the parol evidence rule to fully integrated contracts

Section 2-202 makes no mention of fully integrated contracts until subsection (b). There, it provides that introduction of evidence of consistent additional terms is not permitted if a contract is "intended also as a complete and exclusive statement of the terms of the agreement." Note, however, that this restriction on fully integrated agreements is not present in subsection (a) with regard to course of performance, course of dealing, and usage of trade. This is due to the drafters' belief that all contracts are drafted within the context of the relationship of the parties.

Comment 2 to section 2-202 makes note of the relevance of these concepts when interpreting a contract.

> Paragraph (a) makes admissible evidence of course of dealing, usage of trade and course of performance to explain or supplement the terms of any writing stating the agreement of the parties in order that the true understanding of the parties as to the agreement may be reached. Such writings are to be read on the assumption that the course of prior dealings between the parties and the usages of trade were taken for granted when the document was phrased. Unless carefully negated they have become an element of the meaning of the words used. Similarly, the course of actual performance by the parties is considered the best indication of what they intended the writing to mean.[*]

Therefore, even if a contract is fully integrated, a party may nonetheless introduce evidence of course of performance, course of dealing, or usage of trade so long as it is being used to explain or supplement the writing. As with partially integrated agreements, such evidence can never be used to contradict a term in the writing.

D. Avoiding Application of the Parol Evidence Rule

As the parol evidence rule has the power to prevent valuable information from making its way to the jury, it is important to understand that it does not

---

[*] Uniform Commercial Code, copyright © by the American Law Institute and the National Conference of Commissioners on Uniform State Laws. Reproduced with the permission of the Permanent Editorial Board for the Uniform Commercial Code. All rights reserved.

apply to all situations involving contract interpretation and construction. In this section, we will discuss three situations in which the parol evidence rule will not apply. The first two come from section 2-202, and the last one derives from the validity of the contract in the first instance.

First, the parol evidence rule only applies to *prior or contemporaneous* statements, not subsequent statements. If evidence is offered of a promise made after the contract has been formed, it should not be barred under the parol evidence rule. Such subsequent statement may be subject to limitations on contract modification found in section 2-209; particularly, 2-209(2) which provides that, "[a] signed agreement which excludes modification or rescission except by a signed writing cannot be otherwise modified or rescinded. . . ." Therefore, if a car salesman sells a used car "as is," but two weeks after the sale agrees to warrant tires, evidence of such an agreement would not be barred by the parol evidence rule, but might be subject to any clause in the contract limiting modifications to only those signed and in writing.

Second, the parol evidence rule only applies to terms "set forth in a writing intended by the parties as a final expression of their agreement with respect to such terms." Not all writings are intended to be a final expression of the parties' agreement. For instance, if two parties send multiple drafts back and forth but never agree on a "final contract," but move forward anyway, it can't be said that the drafts are a "final expression" of their agreement. In such a situation, oral testimony and prior drafts should all be admissible to determine the parties' intentions with regard to the contract.

Finally, voidability defenses, such as fraud and unconscionability, generally avoid application of the rule. This is because such defenses call into question the validity of the contract. However, fraud defenses can be complicated by the presence of a merger clause, particularly one that claims neither party relied on any prior statements that do not appear in the contract itself. Courts have struggled with what effect to give such merger clauses when an allegation of fraud is involved. Some hold that one party cannot contract around its own fraud, and give such clauses no effect. Other courts hold that the presence of the clause negates any justifiable reliance by the party claiming fraud.[2]

---

2. Even in such courts, for at least for some, a distinction is made as to whether the clause that disclaims reliance is detailed and specific, or general, with the latter being insufficient.

Checkpoints

- Contracts are to be interpreted within the context in which they are made.

- When interpreting contracts, the following hierarchy is to be followed: express terms, followed by course of performance, course of dealing, and finally usage of trade.

- Course of performance is how the parties have acted under the contract in dispute.

- Course of dealing is how the same two parties have acted in similar previous contracts with each other.

- Usage of trade is how other parties in the industry act in similar circumstances.

- Courts determine, as a matter of law, whether contract terms are ambiguous, and whether contracts are fully or partially integrated.

- The U.C.C. generally rejects a "plain meaning" approach to ambiguity.

- Under the U.C.C., if a contract is partially integrated, then extrinsic evidence may be introduced so long as it does not contradict the writing.

- Under the U.C.C., if a contract is fully integrated, then extrinsic evidence may not be introduced, except for course of performance, course of dealing, and usage of trade, so long as it is not used to contradict the writing.

- The parol evidence rule does not apply to subsequent agreements, nor to writings **not** intended as a final expression of the parties' agreement.

- The parol evidence rule generally does not apply when a voidability defense is at issue.

- The presence of a merger clause may call into question the availability of a fraud defense in some jurisdictions.

Chapter 8

Express Warranties

Roadmap

- How express warranties arise
- Affirmations of fact, promises, and descriptions
- Sample or model
- The basis of the bargain
- The role of puffery

A. How Express Warranties Arise

Article 2 provides for the enforcement of express warranties made by sellers of goods under section 2-313.*

(1) Express warranties by the seller are created as follows:

(a) Any affirmation of fact or promise made by the seller to the buyer which relates to the goods and becomes part of the basis of the bargain creates an express warranty that the goods shall conform to the affirmation or promise.

(b) Any description of the goods which is made part of the basis of the bargain creates an express warranty that the goods shall conform to the description.

(c) Any sample or model which is made part of the basis of the bargain creates an express warranty that the whole of the goods shall conform to the sample or model.

(2) It is not necessary to the creation of an express warranty that the seller use formal words such as "warrant" or "guarantee" or that he have

---

* Uniform Commercial Code, copyright © by the American Law Institute and the National Conference of Commissioners on Uniform State Laws. Reproduced with the permission of the Permanent Editorial Board for the Uniform Commercial Code. All rights reserved.

a specific intention to make a warranty, but an affirmation merely of the value of the goods or a statement purporting to be merely the seller's opinion or commendation of the goods does not create a warranty.

This section recognizes three broad ways in which an express warranty may arise. The first two relate to words used by the seller, either oral or written, so we will address those two together below. The third way, by sample or model, is addressed next. Note that in all three methods, it must become the "basis of the bargain" before liability attaches. We will address that provision in part B.

1. Affirmations of fact, promises, and descriptions

Subsection (a) provides that "[a]ny affirmation of fact or promise made by the seller to the buyer which relates to the goods and becomes part of the basis of the bargain creates an express warranty." The most straight-forward example of a warranty under this section would be statements or writings made that actually use the word "warranty" or "guarantee"; however, use of such words is not required to create a warranty under this section, nor does the seller need to intend to make a warranty. This is made explicit in subsection (2)'s caveat, "[i]t is not necessary to the creation of an express warranty that the seller use formal words such as 'warrant' or 'guarantee' or that he have a specific intention to make a warranty."

Subsection (a) covers not only promises, but also "affirmation[s] of fact." Thus, if a buyer asks a car dealer, "This model jeep has four-wheel drive, right?" and the dealer responds "Yes," the dealer is just as liable in warranty as had the dealer proactively told the buyer it had four-wheel drive. This is consistent with the Code's approach that anything that forms the basis of the bargain has the potential to be an actionable warranty.

> In actual practice affirmations of fact made by the seller about the goods during a bargain are regarded as part of the description of those goods; hence no particular reliance on such statements need be shown in order to weave them into the fabric of the agreement. Rather, any fact which is to take such affirmations, once made, out of the agreement requires clear affirmative proof. The issue normally is one of fact.

U.C.C. §2-313, cmt. 3.* However, while a promise or affirmation can become the basis of a warranty, an opinion often will not.

---

* Uniform Commercial Code, copyright © by the American Law Institute and the National Conference of Commissioners on Uniform State Laws. Reproduced with the

Subsection (2) recognizes the opinion defense, as well as a valuation defense, stating "an affirmation merely of the value of the goods or a statement purporting to be merely the seller's opinion or commendation of the goods does not create a warranty." The value exception is easy to justify. Imagine a buyer and seller haggling over the price of a good. The seller invariably asserts that the good is worth an amount higher than the buyer is initially willing to pay, but is convinced by the seller that the good is worth the asking price. If the buyer later learns that the same good could be purchased for less elsewhere, the seller should not be subject to a warranty action simply for asking a high price (though other assertions could form the basis of a warranty action).

The opinion defense can be a difficult road to navigate, as many affirmations could be recast as mere opinions, rather than warranties. Consider the following two statements made by the manager of an art gallery to a prospective purchaser regarding a painting: a) "This is an original."; b) "This artwork is superb." Both statements could be cast as an affirmation of fact, but could also be viewed as mere opinions. In such situations, it is useful to ask two questions: 1) is the statement at issue objectively verifiable; and 2) did the maker of the statement use equivocal language? Statements that are capable of being objectively verified are more likely to be viewed as affirmations than opinions. Similarly, the more specific a statement, the more likely it will be an affirmation. Based on these two questions, our first statement would seem to qualify as an affirmation. Whether the painting is an original is verifiable and is specific. The second statement, however, would seem to lean toward opinion. The word "superb" is not easy to verify objectively, and is not very specific. Superb in what way? Its colors? Technique? Size? Thus, we would tend to favor viewing the first statement as an affirmation and the second as an opinion. However, context matters, and the parties' relative sophistications may also play a role. If the prospective purchaser is an experienced art collector who understands the gallery manager is simply opining on the first statement, it may not qualify as a warranty, though this may turn more upon it not being the basis of the bargain (discussed below), than on the words that are used.

The second category of express warranties under section 2-313 is descriptions. While descriptions of the goods can be quite detailed, such as by size, color, materials, etc., they are also made simply by describing the goods being sold. For instance, if a car dealership describes the item for sale as an "automobile," it cannot then try to substitute a bicycle upon the consummation of the sale. The comments describe the purpose of this type of warranty as follows:

> In view of the principle that the whole purpose of the law of warranty is to determine what it is that the seller has in essence agreed to sell, the policy is adopted of those cases which refuse except in unusual circumstances to recognize a material deletion of the seller's obligation. Thus, a contract is normally a contract for a sale of something describable and described. A clause generally disclaiming "all warranties, express or implied" cannot reduce the seller's obligation with respect to such description and therefore cannot be given literal effect under Section 2-316.
>
> This is not intended to mean that the parties, if they consciously desire, cannot make their own bargain as they wish. But in determining what they have agreed upon good faith is a factor and consideration should be given to the fact that the probability is small that a real price is intended to be exchanged for a pseudo-obligation.

U.C.C. § 2-313, cmt. 4.* The basic principle at the heart of descriptions would appear to be simply that the seller must sell the good promised. The substitution of a bicycle for an automobile would quite clearly run afoul of this principle, but other cases are less clear. For instance, suppose the seller agreed to sell an automobile on its lot for $5,000 to the buyer. Later, to the buyer's dismay, he learns the automobile has no engine. Given that one usually equates the term "automobile" with something that is capable of independent locomotion, could it be fairly said that what was sold was an automobile at all? Further, what if the seller disclaimed all warranties express or implied? The Code appears to reject an approach that, even in light of the disclaimers of all warranties, would permit the seller to succeed on such a defense. However, too broad an application of this principle would seem to overlap with the concept of the implied warranty of merchantability, explored in the next Chapter. In other words, the question becomes how far does the description warranty extend beyond the class of goods described? Courts have reached varying results.

---

2. Sample or model

Subsection (1)(c) addresses two different, but similar, ways a warranty may be made — samples and models. Though these do not involve verbal or written representations, a sample or model can just as easily convey representations about qualities of the final product that is to be sold. A sample is drawn from the bulk or inventory of goods that are the subject matter of the sale. A model, on the other hand, is not drawn from the bulk of goods, but is nonetheless meant to act as a representation of the good to be sold. Perhaps an easier way to distinguish the two is that a sample is literally a representation of the good to be sold, while a model is an illustrative representation of the good to be sold.

The simple fact that a sample or model is offered or available for inspection does not automatically lead to a warranty by description. For instance, if a seller of coal offers up a lump of coal for inspection, but expressly caveats that the actual coal to be sold will be of inferior quality, the coal offered would not be a sample, and its use as a model would be subject to the caveat. Similarly, if the same seller had piles of coal on its lot, and the buyer, while on site, inspected the coal, it would not necessarily follow that the coal so inspected was intended to be a sample or model by the seller, unless words or circumstances indicated otherwise. As with contractual language, the surrounding circumstances, including customs in the trade, should be considered in determining if a warranty has been made. "A description need not be by words . . . [o]f course, all descriptions by merchants must be read against the applicable trade usages with the general rules as to merchantability resolving any doubts." U.C.C. § 2-313, cmt. 5.

B. The Basis of the Bargain

Article 2 does not require actual reliance before a warranty becomes enforceable; rather, the promise, affirmation of fact, description, sample or model must form "part of the basis of the bargain." Though Article 2 rejects "reliance" as the basis for a warranty action, the Code gives little guidance as to what "basis of the bargain" means. A few generalities can be drawn from the Code and developed caselaw. First, a warranty does not need to make its way into the final contract language to be binding — statements, samples and models that become a basis of the bargain during contract negotiations may create actionable warranties. As comment 7 to section 2-313 notes, "[t]he precise time when words of description or affirmation are made or samples are shown is not material. The sole question is whether the language or samples or models are fairly to be regarded as part of the contract." Of course, whether the language, or samples, or models became a part of the contract may be subject to a parol evidence defense, as discussed in Chapter 7, but you should see that warranties can arise from the contract negotiations.

Second, the express warranty does not need to be the sole or even primary reason for entering into the transaction. Further, in adopting a "basis of the bargain" standard, the drafters were rejecting the old standard by which reliance was required. Thus, any statement that might influence the purchasing decision should be sufficient for a plaintiff's prima facie case.

Third, though reliance isn't necessary, that doesn't mean it is irrelevant. The wording of section 2-313 may present nothing more than a rebuttable presumption in favor of the plaintiff. If a plaintiff can show that a promise was made that would likely influence the purchasing decision, the defendant can then present evidence that the alleged promise was not the basis of the bargain, such as by showing that the plaintiff did not rely on the statement. For instance, if Jeremy responds to an advertisement for the sale of a Camaro automobile with a sun roof, and upon inspection of the car sees that there is no sunroof, but purchases the car anyway, it will be difficult for Jeremy to argue that the sunroof was a basis of the bargain. Though the description would qualify as a warranty, the defendant seller need only point to Jeremy's inspection of the car to show that the sunroof was not a basis of the bargain.

One recurring issue involving basis of the bargain is what to do with express warranties that are not discussed or that arrive after the consummation of the contract. For instance, most car purchases involve a number of warranties that, though available prior to purchase, are not discussed or read during the negotiation and sale of the car. It is only once a problem arises that the buyer digs out the paperwork to see what warranties were made. Similarly, many sales of goods come with warranties that are not seen until after the product is brought home and opened (recall our discussion of shrink-wrap agreements in Chapter 5). In both situations, a seller could argue that there is no way that the warranty, unknown by the buyer, could have become the basis of the bargain. In addressing such situations, courts have arrived at a number of ways, sometimes strained, to find for the aggrieved buyer.

Some courts simply impute a generalized knowledge of the existence of warranties during the negotiation process, if the sale is of a good frequently accompanied by express warranties, such as the sale of a new car. The buyer, the theory goes, generally knows that the purchase comes with a warranty of some kind, and that is enough to satisfy the basis of the bargain requirement, and shift the burden to the defendant. Alternatively, courts cast warranties that appear later as contract modifications, under section 2-209, which require no consideration to support them (though this approach appears to ignore the requirement that the modification be by agreement). This modification approach appears to be explicitly endorsed by the comments to section 2-313: "If language is used after the closing of the deal (as when the buyer when taking delivery asks and receives an additional assurance), the warranty becomes a modification, and need not be supported by consideration if it is otherwise reasonable and in order (Section 2-209)." U.C.C. § 2-313, cmt. 7.

When the affirmation or promise is made soon after a sale has been completed, some courts find for the buyer on the theory that, had the buyer known the true state of affairs, it could have returned the goods, particularly if the good was sold by a seller with a return policy. For instance, assume Jeremy buys shoes at his local shoe store. After the purchase, and unrelated to the sale, he mentions that he is taking his family hiking. The seller tells Jeremy that the shoes are excellent hiking shoes. In reliance on this statement, Jeremy uses the shoes for hiking, but they fall apart, as they are not suitable for hiking. The condition of the shoes will prevent Jeremy from taking advantage of the return policy, and express warranty may be the only avenue to recovery in contract.

Add to the above anther possible way that post-sale affirmations may be enforceable as express warranties. Recall in Chapter 5 that some courts adopt a rolling contract approach to post-sale forms. Under this approach, the shrink-wrap terms are the actual offer, which the buyer accepts by keeping and using the good. Under this approach, it would seem that the buyer would have a very clear path to showing that the warranties were a basis of the bargain, without the need for some of the legal gymnastics that courts, trying to find for the buyer, have engaged in.

C. The Role of Puffery

Related to the basis of the bargain discussion is the concept of puffery. Puffery is closely related to the opinion defense, in that certain statements simply aren't actionable as they may be exaggerated statements of opinion, or "seller's talk." Broadly speaking, puffery exists in two general forms: (1) exaggerated statements of bluster or boast upon which no reasonable consumer would rely;

and (2) vague or highly subjective claims of product superiority, including bald assertions of superiority. Both forms, however, appear to negate express warranties based on the basis of the bargain requirement.

In the first category, general statements such as "best in town," "A-1," and "high quality" are simply statement of bluster that every reasonable consumer should know are not to be trusted. For instance, if Buddy goes into Zooey's Diner and buys a cup of coffee because he sees a sign that reads "World's Best Cup of Coffee," he will not be successful on a breach of express warranty claim when the coffee turns out to be just a crappy cup of coffee. While the court could throw the case out based on the statement being an opinion, it could also reject the claim because no reasonable person would rely on such a puffed-up statement.

Similarly, vague statements of superiority provide no basis for relief. If a seller advertises that his electronics store "buries the competition's prices," what exactly does this mean? What precisely is being made the basis of any subsequent bargain? Suits based on such vague language are routinely dismissed under the puffery defense, but frequently what is really meant is that the statements could not be the basis of the parties' bargain.

While at first blush, this may seem to encourage sellers to engage in what is, at its heart, somewhat deceptive behavior, courts seem willing to permit the continued use of puffery without liability. This may be, in part, due to a fear that making too many statements actionable would lead to chilling advertising, and put sellers on guard to only make the blandest of statements that convey no real information ("eat our brand of potato chips—They're EDIBLE!"), but given that puffing statements don't convey much useful information, this seems unpersuasive. It is likely that courts expect consumers to act reasonably in their transactions, and not to check their common sense at the door when making purchasing decisions.

Checkpoints

- Express warranties can be created by promises, affirmations of fact, descriptions, samples, or models.

- The word "warranty" or "guarantee" need not be used for a statement to be actionable as an express warranty.

- Affirmations of value and opinions are **not** actionable as express warranties.

- All express warranties must be viewed within the context that they are made.

- Express warranties may be based on pre-sale negotiations and statements that do not end up in the final sale contract.

- Aggrieved buyers need not show reliance on the statement, only that the statement became some part of the basis of the bargain.

- Post-sale warranties, though subject to a basis of the bargain defense, may be enforceable under a number of theories.

- Puffery, or seller's talk, is not actionable, as such statements could not become the basis of the bargain for any reasonable buyer.

- Puffery includes both exaggerated boasts which would be unreasonable to believe and vague or highly subjective claims of product superiority.

Chapter 9

Implied Warranties

Roadmap

- Introduction to implied warranties
- The implied warranty of merchantability
- When does the implied warranty of merchantability arise?
- What does it mean to be merchantable?
- The implied warranty of fitness for particular purpose

A. Introduction to Implied Warranties

Comment 1 to section 2-312 distinguishes express warranties from implied warranties:

> "Express" warranties rest on "dickered" aspects of the individual bargain, and go so clearly to the essence of that bargain that words of disclaimer in a form are repugnant to the basic dickered terms. "Implied" warranties rest so clearly on a common factual situation or set of conditions that no particular language or action is necessary to evidence them and they will arise in such a situation unless unmistakably negated.[*]

In so noting, the drafters of Article 2 signaled a move away from the rule of *caveat emptor* in favor of a default rule in which many sales would come with a set of default warranties. The two implied warranties we will discuss in this Chapter are the warranty of merchantability and the warranty of fitness for a

---

particular purpose. There is, however, a third implied warranty—the implied warranty of title—which we will discuss in Chapter 11. As to all of these warranties, the drafters felt that the better rule was that such warranties exist "unless unmistakably negated." One of the most important and obvious reasons for this is that we want commercial transactions to have lower due diligence requirements. The requirement isn't zero, but implied warranties mean the buyer doesn't have to inspect for the basics. This is also why, as we shall see, the narrow definition of merchant is used for merchantability—because the buyer shouldn't have to spend time and money on due diligence when the seller is the "expert." With that said, as we will learn in the next Chapter, the warranties of merchantability and fitness are not incredibly difficult to disclaim. For now, we will simply focus on mastering when these two warranties apply and what they entail.

B. The Implied Warranty of Merchantability

The implied warranty of merchantability, found in section 2-314, acts as a sort of implied quality guarantee and is closely related to the area of products liability. Section 2-314 provides:

(1) Unless excluded or modified (Section 2-316), a warranty that the goods shall be merchantable is implied in a contract for their sale if the seller is a merchant with respect to goods of that kind. Under this section the serving for value of food or drink to be consumed either on the premises or elsewhere is a sale.

(2) Goods to be merchantable must be at least such as
(a) pass without objection in the trade under the contract description; and
(b) in the case of fungible goods, are of fair average quality within the description; and
(c) are fit for the ordinary purposes for which such goods are used; and
(d) run, within the variations permitted by the agreement, of even kind, quality and quantity within each unit and among all units involved; and
(e) are adequately contained, packaged, and labeled as the agreement may require; and
(f) conform to the promises or affirmations of fact made on the container or label if any.

(3) Unless excluded or modified (Section 2-316) other implied warranties may arise from course of dealing or usage of trade.*

The first subsection provides for when the merchantability warranty will arise. Subsections (2) and (3) then address what it means for a good to be merchantable. We address each in turn below.

1. When does the implied warranty of merchantability arise?

Subsection (1) establishes two prerequisites to when the warranty of merchantability will arise. First, there must be a contract for the sale of goods. Second, the seller must be a "merchant with respect to goods of that kind."

The first requirement is not likely to come into question often. Many cases will involve clear sales, though it is worth highlighting that this provision includes sales for used goods (in which case, such status will affect how merchantability is judged). Further, there is no need for the buyer to have taken possession for there to be a contract, nor for the buyer to have yet paid. Thus, a patron of a restaurant will likely be covered by the warranty of merchantability even though he or she has not yet paid (assuming the ordering of the food is the offer and the serving of the food is the acceptance). There can be close situations, however. For instance, should a shopper at a grocery store be covered when, prior to check out, a glass jar in his cart explodes and cuts him? On the one hand, the timing seems fortuitous to the seller, as the jar could have just as easily exploded post-sale. On the other hand, the Code provision is clear as to the necessity of a contract for the sale, and other avenues of holding the seller liable, such as through tort, seem better suited. The latter approach should therefore be favored.

The second requirement touches upon an area we covered in Chapter 1, Part C. Recall that some provisions of Article 2 refer to a merchant in the broad sense that he or she is knowledgeable of general business practices. Other provisions refer to a merchant in the narrower sense that the person actually deals in goods of the kind at issue. Section 2-314 refers to the narrower definition of merchant. Thus, an isolated sale, even by someone who in another context might qualify as a merchant, will not be subject to the merchantability warranty. For instance, a commercial fisherman would undoubtedly be a merchant, for 2-314 purposes, with regard to the sale of fish. However, as comment 3 notes: "A person making an isolated sale of goods is not a 'merchant' within the meaning of the full scope of this section and, thus, no warranty of merchantability would apply." Therefore, the same fisherman likely would **not** be a merchant with regard to the sale of his boat.

2. What does it mean to be merchantable?

Subsection (2) provides a laundry list of minimum standards, but as the comments make clear, the list is not meant to be exhaustive. "Subsection (2) does not purport to exhaust the meaning of 'merchantable' nor to negate any of its attributes not specifically mentioned in the text of the statute, but arising by usage of trade or through case law. The language used is . . . [intended] to leave open other possible attributes of merchantability." This reference to developing standards with reference to surrounding standards is also explicitly found in subsection (3), which allows for merchantability to be further defined by course of dealing and trade usage. Note also that subsections (a) through (f) are connected by an "and." This means that, to be merchantable, the good must satisfy all of these subsections.

Subsections (2)(a) and (b) further establish merchantability with reference to the general trade, and these two subsections should be read together. Note that the standard is not a defect-free warranty, but rather, one of fair, average quality such as would pass without objection in the trade. Some products are known to have standards of deviation in the trade, but are still acceptable. For instance, chocolate often contains insect parts and sometimes rat hairs. In fact, the FDA has established standards for the level of permissible insect parts and rat hairs which require no action on its part as these levels are deemed safe.[1] If you were to discover a rat hair in your chocolate bar, so long as the bar passed muster in the trade, it would still be merchantable, albeit gross. Of course, this hypothetical is also unlikely to result in any harm. Some alleged defects, such as small fish bones in fish or the presence of nuts in a dessert, can result in real harm, but again, so long as they pass muster in the trade,

---

1. The FDA has standards for many foods, not just chocolate. *See Defect Levels Handbook: The Food Defect Action Levels, Levels of natural or unavoidable defects in foods that present no health hazards for humans,* available at https://www.fda.gov/Food/Guidance Regulation/GuidanceDocumentsRegulatoryInformation/SanitationTransportation/ucm 056174.htm.

subsections (a) and (b) will be of no use (though subsection (e) might come into play, as we will discuss).

Subsection (2)(c) is perhaps the most often litigated of the list. Claims that goods are not fit for their ordinary purposes often coincide with claims of design defects, but again, the reference point is what passes muster in the trade. For instance, one could allege that a vacuum with a long cord is not satisfactory for the ordinary use of vacuuming because the user is subject to tripping over the cord. The plaintiff's argument would be that a retractable cord—or perhaps no cord at all—is required for a vacuum to be fit for its ordinary purpose. To prove it, the plaintiff would need to call an expert witness who could testify as to the good's ordinary use, and whether a corded vacuum can be satisfactorily used. Since the reference point is what actually works in the trade, defendant would respond with evidence that vacuums with non-retractable cords are normal in the trade, and the claim would fail. Of course, a defective design claim could still be brought under tort law, but that's a separate question.

Subsection (e) is another avenue that a plaintiff can pursue, especially if the contract involves goods that require special packaging. The provision that goods be adequately contained and packaged could be at play in our exploding glass jar hypothetical, but also covers situations in which goods have been damaged during shipping (though this would implicate the risk of loss provisions as well). For defects that are normal in the trade, such as fish bones in fish or nuts in a dessert, this provision may also require adequate notice of these inherent dangers. As above, reference will be made to the standard in the trade, and many cases brought under subsection (e) could be made under subsections (a) through (c).

The final subsection (f) may seem a bit confusing at first, as it addresses express, rather than implied, warranties. To require that goods "conform to the promises or affirmations of fact made on the container or label if any" would seem to be speaking directly about enforcing express warranties. However, recall that for express warranties to be actionable, they must become a basis of the bargain. As section 2-314 has no such requirement, subsection (f) permits plaintiffs to make claims of merchantability when it is difficult to prove the basis of the bargain element of express warranties.

C. Implied Warranty of Fitness for a Particular Purpose

Section 2-315 provides the other major implied warranty—that of fitness for a particular purpose. Unlike the warranty of merchantability, the fitness warranty can apply to both merchant and non-merchant sellers alike. That section provides:

> Where the seller at the time of contracting has reason to know any particular purpose for which the goods are required and that the buyer is relying on the seller's skill or judgment to select or furnish suitable goods, there is unless excluded or modified under the next section an implied warranty that the goods shall be fit for such purpose.[*]

This can be broken down into three essential elements: 1) the seller must have reason to know of the buyer's particular purpose; 2) the seller must have reason to know the buyer is relying on the seller's skill or judgment to furnish or select appropriate goods; and 3) the buyer must, in fact, rely upon the seller's skill or judgment.

As to the first two elements, in many cases, the buyer will explicitly tell the seller what his or her particular purpose is for buying a good. For instance, if a man walks into a shoe store and announces he needs a new pair of running shoes, the purpose has been clearly communicated.[2] However, the comments clarify that such an explicit announcement is not always necessary.

> Whether or not this warranty arises in any individual case is basically a question of fact to be determined by the circumstances of the contracting. Under this section the buyer need not bring home to the seller actual knowledge of the particular purpose for which the goods are intended or of his reliance on the seller's skill and judgment, if the circumstances are such that the seller has reason to realize the purpose intended or that the reliance exists. The buyer, of course, must actually be relying on the seller.[**]

So, if the same man were to attend a runner's expo, where several shoe merchants were peddling their wares, and the man mentioned at one stand that

---

[*] Uniform Commercial Code, copyright © by the American Law Institute and the National Conference of Commissioners on Uniform State Laws. Reproduced with the permission of the Permanent Editorial Board for the Uniform Commercial Code. All rights reserved.

2. If the seller responds by explicitly stating that the shoes he is showing the customer are specially for running, then express warranties may exist as well.

[**] Uniform Commercial Code, copyright © by the American Law Institute and the National Conference of Commissioners on Uniform State Laws. Reproduced with the permission of the Permanent Editorial Board for the Uniform Commercial Code. All rights reserved.

he is an avid runner, the seller could be imputed with the requisite knowledge that the man is there to look at running shoes, even though it was never explicitly mentioned.[3]

Some brief mention should be made here as to the distinction between an ordinary purpose, which would impact the merchantability warranty, and a particular purpose. The comments are again useful, and continue our shoe-buying theme:

> A "particular purpose" differs from the ordinary purpose for which the goods are used in that it envisages a specific use by the buyer which is peculiar to the nature of his business whereas the ordinary purposes for which goods are used are those envisaged in the concept of merchantability and go to uses which are customarily made of the goods in question. For example, shoes are generally used for the purpose of walking upon ordinary ground, but a seller may know that a particular pair was selected to be used for climbing mountains.

So, if our shoe buyer walks into a store and buys shoes that fall apart when subjected to simply walking, this would not involve a particular purpose, though a claim for merchantability may now exist. However, if the buyer said he needed a new pair of shoes for a formal dinner party, and was recommended running shoes, then the fitness warranty would apply rather than merchantability—as running shoes are fit for their ordinary purpose, but not for fancy formal dinners.

The last element requires the buyer's reliance. In instances in which the buyer is less informed about the products at issue, reliance will be clear. So when will reliance be an issue? Comment 5 provides some guidance, noting:

> If the buyer himself is insisting on a particular brand he is not relying on the seller's skill and judgment and so no warranty results. But the mere fact that the article purchased has a particular patent or trade name is not sufficient to indicate nonreliance if the article has been recommended by the seller as adequate for the buyer's purposes.[*]

---

3. Of course, the seller could make the argument that, the more expert the runner is, the less likely it is that he is relying on some shoe salesman's expertise (since he has his own experience to draw upon).

* Uniform Commercial Code, copyright © by the American Law Institute and the National Conference of Commissioners on Uniform State Laws. Reproduced with the permission of the Permanent Editorial Board for the Uniform Commercial Code. All rights reserved.

Thus, if our runner enters a store and states that he wants Nike brand running shoes, the selection of Nike is most likely on our shoe buyer. However, that is not to say that the actual model chosen could not still be the subject of a fitness claim. Along with the purchaser who demands a particular brand, some buyers have knowledge equal, or even superior, to the seller. In such cases, the seller may again dispute whether the purchaser relied on the seller's, rather than his own, knowledge.

Checkpoints

- Article 2 contains default implied warranties of merchantability and fitness for a particular purpose.

- The warranty of merchantability only applies to contracts for the sale of goods in which the seller is a merchant with regard to goods of the type at issue.

- Whether a good is merchantable depends heavily on what passes without objection in the trade.

- Merchantable goods must also be fit for their ordinary purpose — an inquiry that will often require expert testimony.

- To be merchantable, goods must also be adequately packaged and labelled.

- Merchantability also requires that goods live up to any express promises made on the container or label, regardless of whether such statements were the basis of the bargain.

- The fitness warranty applies to merchants and non-merchants alike.

- The fitness warranty has three elements: 1) the seller must have reason to know of the buyer's particular purpose; 2) have reason to know the buyer is relying on the seller's skill or judgment; and 3) the buyer must, in fact, rely upon the seller's judgment.

Chapter 10

Disclaiming and Limiting Warranties

Roadmap

- The use of contract to disclaim or limit warranty
- Disclaiming express warranties
- Disclaiming implied warranties
- Disclaiming implied warranties under § 2-316(2)
- Disclaiming implied warranties: the easy way
- Disclaiming implied warranties by inspection
- Disclaiming implied warranties under § 2-316(3)(c)
- Limiting remedies

A. The Use of Contract to Disclaim or Limit Warranty

In many instances, particularly with regard to express warranties, sellers are fine standing behind the products they sell. However, this does not mean they want to be open to every consequence of an express or implied warranty. Sellers may be wary that the buyer uses the product in a way that the seller did not intend when making an express warranty, or that an agent has made an unauthorized representation that has now become a basis of the bargain. Sellers can turn to contract law to help limit the scope of warranties, the remedies sought, or even the very existence of a warranty.

Article 2 specifically authorizes the use of contractual language to address these concerns. Section 2-316(1) permits the use of contractual language to explain, but not contradict, express warranties. Subsections 2-316(2) and (3) further permit the complete elimination of the implied warranties of merchantability and fitness. Finally, section 2-316(4) permits sellers to contractually limit the remedies available to an aggrieved buyer, subject to the limitations found in section 2-719. We address each in turn below.

B. Disclaiming Express Warranties

Section 2-316(1) provides:

> Words or conduct relevant to the creation of an express warranty and words or conduct tending to negate or limit warranty shall be construed wherever reasonable as consistent with each other; but subject to the provisions of this Article on parol or extrinsic evidence (Section 2-202) negation or limitation is inoperative to the extent that such construction is unreasonable.*

At first blush, this provision would seem to do little for the seller, as it specifically forbids a seller from trying to back out of an express warranty through a contractual disclaimer. The comments echo this, noting, "This section is designed principally to deal with those frequent clauses in sales contracts which seek to exclude 'all warranties, express or implied.' It seeks to protect a buyer from unexpected and unbargained language of disclaimer by denying effect to such language when inconsistent with language of express warranty. . . ." U.C.C. § 2-316, cmt. 1. However, this is not to say the seller cannot limit the application of an express warranty — just that any such limitation must not be inconsistent with the express warranty and the reasonable expectations of the buyer. Therefore, warranty language stating that the warranty is subject to "proper maintenance and cleaning," or subject to the use for which the product is intended should stand and be effective, so long as they are not unreasonable.

This section contains another avenue for the seller to use contractual language to limit express warranties when it notes the section is subject to the parol evidence rule. Recall from Chapter 7 that some sellers use the preclusive nature of the parol evidence rule to their advantage by including "merger clauses" which proclaim that there have been no agreements made other than what is in the contract and that the buyer has not relied on anything other than the written contract. Further, to prevent agents from making statements that become a part of the contract, sellers will frequently insert "no authority"

---

clauses, which state that the seller's agents have no authority to make any representations other than what is found in the written contract. The drafters of
Article 2 acknowledged the use of such clauses in the comments, stating, "The
seller is protected under this Article against false allegations of oral warranties by its provisions on parol and extrinsic evidence and against unauthorized representations by the customary 'lack of authority' clauses."

C. Disclaiming Implied Warranties

Given that an implied warranty of merchantability is implied in every merchant's sale of goods, and that breach of this warranty can lead to consequential damages that are perhaps disproportionate to the value of the sold good
itself, it is understandable why many merchant sellers would seek to disavow
such warranties and liability. The U.C.C. explicitly permits such disclaimers,
but with some limitations. Section 2-316(2) provides a very specific method
for disclaiming the implied warranties of merchantability and fitness. This
demanding standard is a contrast to the very next subsection, (3)(a), which
provides a much easier way to disclaim all such warranties. We discuss each,
as well as two other alternatives, below.

1. Disclaiming implied warranties under § 2-316(2)

A merchant may disclaim both the implied warranty of merchantability
and the warranty of fitness for a particular purpose under section 2-316. Subsection (2) specifically provides:

> Subject to subsection (3), to exclude or modify the implied warranty of
> merchantability or any part of it the language must mention merchant-
> ability and in case of a writing must be conspicuous, and to exclude or
> modify any implied warranty of fitness the exclusion must be by a
> writing and conspicuous. Language to exclude all implied warranties
> of fitness is sufficient if it states, for example, that "There are no war-
> ranties which extend beyond the description on the face hereof."

This provision permits an oral disclaimer so long as the word merchantability is used, as well as a written disclaimer of merchantability, but only if it
mentions merchantability and only if it is conspicuous. Disclaimers on warranties of fitness must be in writing and must also be conspicuous, but the
Code does not specifically require mention of a particular word or phrase, such
as "warranty" or "fitness." Though the Code blesses the phrase, "There are
no warranties which extend beyond the description on the face hereof," this

would be insufficient to disclaim the warranty of merchantability. Therefore, it is not unusual for a typical disclaimer to specifically mention both implied warranties by name.

Subsection (2) requires that both written disclaimers be "conspicuous." This term is specifically defined in section 1-201(1) as follows:

(10) "Conspicuous", with reference to a term, means so written, displayed, or presented that a reasonable person against which it is to operate ought to have noticed it. Whether a term is "conspicuous" or not is a decision for the court.

Conspicuous terms include the following:

(A) a heading in capitals equal to or greater in size than the surrounding text, or in contrasting type, font, or color to the surrounding text of the same or lesser size; and

(B) language in the body of a record or display in larger type than the surrounding text, or in contrasting type, font, or color to the surrounding text of the same size, or set off from surrounding text of the same size by symbols or other marks that call attention to the language.*

Though this section makes mention of specific ways that a term can be made conspicuous, such as by using all capital letters in the heading, comment 10 to section 1-210 makes clear that other methods may be sufficient, and that "the test is whether attention can reasonably be expected to be called to it." Despite the language in section 1-210(10), some courts have held that it is not enough to simply capitalize the heading or to capitalize particular words such as "merchantability" and "fitness for a particular purpose," as that does not draw attention to the fact that the warranties are disclaimed. In response, some sellers find it prudent to print the entire disclaimer in bold-face capitals. For instance, below is the disclaimer used by Amazon.com on their website:

DISCLAIMER OF WARRANTIES AND LIMITATION OF LIABILITY
THE AMAZON SERVICES AND ALL INFORMATION, CONTENT, MATERIALS, PRODUCTS (INCLUDING SOFTWARE) AND OTHER SERVICES INCLUDED ON OR OTHERWISE MADE

---

* Uniform Commercial Code, copyright © by the American Law Institute and the National Conference of Commissioners on Uniform State Laws. Reproduced with the permission of the Permanent Editorial Board for the Uniform Commercial Code. All rights reserved.

AVAILABLE TO YOU THROUGH THE AMAZON SERVICES ARE
PROVIDED BY AMAZON ON AN "AS IS" AND "AS AVAILABLE"
BASIS, UNLESS OTHERWISE SPECIFIED IN WRITING. AMA-
ZON MAKES NO REPRESENTATIONS OR WARRANTIES OF
ANY KIND, EXPRESS OR IMPLIED, AS TO THE OPERATION OF
THE AMAZON SERVICES, OR THE INFORMATION, CONTENT,
MATERIALS, PRODUCTS (INCLUDING SOFTWARE) OR OTHER
SERVICES INCLUDED ON OR OTHERWISE MADE AVAILABLE
TO YOU THROUGH THE AMAZON SERVICES, UNLESS OTHER-
WISE SPECIFIED IN WRITING. YOU EXPRESSLY AGREE THAT
YOUR USE OF THE AMAZON SERVICES IS AT YOUR SOLE RISK.

TO THE FULL EXTENT PERMISSIBLE BY LAW, AMAZON DIS-
CLAIMS ALL WARRANTIES, EXPRESS OR IMPLIED, INCLUD-
ING, BUT NOT LIMITED TO, IMPLIED WARRANTIES OF
MERCHANTABILITY AND FITNESS FOR A PARTICULAR PUR-
POSE. AMAZON DOES NOT WARRANT THAT THE AMAZON
SERVICES, INFORMATION, CONTENT, MATERIALS, PROD-
UCTS (INCLUDING SOFTWARE) OR OTHER SERVICES
INCLUDED ON OR OTHERWISE MADE AVAILABLE TO YOU
THROUGH THE AMAZON SERVICES, AMAZON'S SERVERS OR
ELECTRONIC COMMUNICATIONS SENT FROM AMAZON ARE
FREE OF VIRUSES OR OTHER HARMFUL COMPONENTS. TO
THE FULL EXTENT PERMISSIBLE BY LAW, AMAZON WILL NOT
BE LIABLE FOR ANY DAMAGES OF ANY KIND ARISING FROM
THE USE OF ANY AMAZON SERVICE, OR FROM ANY INFOR-
MATION, CONTENT, MATERIALS, PRODUCTS (INCLUDING
SOFTWARE) OR OTHER SERVICES INCLUDED ON OR OTHER-
WISE MADE AVAILABLE TO YOU THROUGH ANY AMAZON
SERVICE, INCLUDING, BUT NOT LIMITED TO DIRECT, INDI-
RECT, INCIDENTAL, PUNITIVE, AND CONSEQUENTIAL DAM-
AGES, UNLESS OTHERWISE SPECIFIED IN WRITING.

See Amazon Conditions of Use *available at* https://www.amazon.com/gp/help
/customer/display.html/ref=footer_cou?ie=UTF8&nodeId=508088

2. Disclaiming implied warranties: the easy way

Despite the specific language required under section 2-316(2), subsection (3)
provides a number of alternatives, which will also be effective in disclaiming
implied warranties. The one perhaps most easy to meet is subsection (3)(a),

which provides: "Notwithstanding subsection (2)[,] unless the circumstances indicate otherwise, all implied warranties are excluded by expressions like 'as is', 'with all faults', or other language which in common understanding calls the buyer's attention to the exclusion of warranties and makes plain that there is no implied warranty." This would appear to give some leeway to the merchant seller to fashion a general disclaimer, but courts have not always looked kindly on what might otherwise appear to be equivalent language. For instance, simply excluding "all warranties, express or implied" has been held insufficient to effectively disclaim the implied warranties of merchantability and fitness. Furthermore, though there is no express requirement that an "as-is" type of clause be conspicuous, many courts have required such. To be safe, many sellers pair "as is" language with the safe harbor language found under section 2-316(2).

3. Disclaiming implied warranties by inspection

Section 2-316(3)(b) provides:

> [W]hen the buyer before entering into the contract has examined the goods or the sample or model as fully as he desired or has refused to examine the goods there is no implied warranty with regard to defects which an examination ought in the circumstances to have revealed to him. . . .

This provision can be broken down into two elements. First, there must be a pre-contractual examination, or pre-contractual refusal to examine the goods. Second, such inspection should have revealed the complained of defect to the buyer. While this method of disclaiming implied warranties may seem so broad as to prevent warranties in any number of situations where the goods are available for inspection, the comments and case law have made clear that it is not so broad.

The exception is meant to reach situations "in which the circumstances surrounding the transaction are in themselves sufficient to call the buyer's attention to the fact that no implied warranties are made or that a certain implied warranty is being excluded." U.C.C. § 2-316, cmt. 6. Consistent with this purpose, simply making the goods available for inspection is not enough to invoke subsection (b).

> There must in addition be a demand by the seller that the buyer examine the goods fully. The seller by the demand puts the buyer on notice that he is assuming the risk of defects which the examination ought to reveal. The language "refused to examine" in this paragraph is intended to make clear the necessity for such demand.

U.C.C. § 2-316, cmt. 8.* The import of this subsection is essentially that by making the demand, the seller is highlighting that there may be something wrong with the goods. So if Sam is selling his car to Burt, and Burt asks if there are any defects, and Sam replies, "I don't know, you really should take it for a test drive before buying," if Burt refuses, he will not be able to later claim the car is unmerchantable for a defect that he should have discovered had he so taken it for a test drive. Sam's caution has placed Burt on notice in much the same way an explicit "as is" clause would.

The second element can also come into play to limit the seller's ability to disclaim warranties. Only defects that ought to be discovered by an examination are covered. Latent defects, or defects that would require more than a mere examination, are not the type of defect that can be disclaimed by subsection (b). On the other hand, "[a] failure to notice defects which are obvious cannot excuse the buyer." *Id.* In considering whether a defect ought to have been discovered, the buyer's particular skill and knowledge are relevant to the analysis. Therefore, a professional buyer or merchant of the same goods will be held to a higher standard than a lay person, but again only as to defects that a fellow professional buyer or merchant ought to have discovered.

4. Disclaiming implied warranties under § 2-316(3)(c)

The final method of disclaiming implied warranties is found in section 2-316(3)(c), but is really nothing more than the recognition of two concepts we have already covered: contract interpretation and what it means to be merchantable. Subsection (c) provides that "an implied warranty can also be excluded or modified by course of dealing or course of performance or usage of trade." Recall from Chapter 7 that all contracts are to be interpreted within the context that they are made, and that express terms are to be read, whenever possible, as consistent with the course of performance, course of dealing, and usage in the trade. Subsection (c) simply clarifies that such concepts may also act to exclude implied warranties. Also, recall from Chapter 9 that the merchantability warranty turns heavily on what is acceptable in a given trade.

Of course, if the complained of defect is acceptable within a given trade, this would seem to be a moot provision as the good is merchantable. Trade usage, however, may also influence disclaimers. For instance, assume a seller of microprocessors attempts to disclaim the warranty of merchantability, but fails to use conspicuous wording, thus making the disclaimer ineffective under section 2-316(2). If it is common in the trade to disclaim merchantability, the seller may be able to convince a court that the disclaimer became a part of the parties' contract, despite the failure to strictly comply with subsection (2). This would be based, not so much on the actual disclaimer used, but on the interpretive rule that contracts are read in light of the course of performance, course of dealing and usage in the trade.

D. Limiting Remedies

Another method to avoid liability in warranty is to simply limit the buyer's remedies. Section 2-316(4) specifically authorizes this, stating: "Remedies for breach of warranty can be limited in accordance with the provisions of this Article on liquidation or limitation of damages and on contractual modification of remedy (Sections 2-718 and 2-719)." Before delving into remedy limitation, it is worth noting that an effective warranty disclaimer should largely do away with the need to limit remedies, because if a good is sold "as is," then there is no warranty that could be breached. Comment 2 to section 2-316 is in accord, stating:

> This Article treats the limitation or avoidance of consequential damages as a matter of limiting remedies for breach, separate from the matter of creation of liability under a warranty. If no warranty exists, there is of course no problem of limiting remedies for breach of warranty. Under subsection (4) the question of limitation of remedy is governed by the sections referred to rather than by this section.

Despite these comments, some courts, perhaps moved by the plight of a sympathetic plaintiff, have still allowed cases to move forward despite adequate warranty disclaimer language. For this reason, many sellers find it prudent to not just disclaim warranties, but also to add contractual limitations on a buyer's remedies.

A buyer's remedies may be limited under section 2-719(1), which provides that:

> (1) Subject to the provisions of subsections (2) and (3) of this section and of the preceding section on liquidation and limitation of damages,
>
>   (a) the agreement may provide for remedies in addition to or in substitution for those provided in this Article and may limit or alter the measure of damages recoverable under this Article, as by limiting

the buyer's remedies to return of the goods and repayment of the price
or to repair and replacement of non-conforming goods or parts; and
    (b) resort to a remedy as provided is optional unless the remedy is
expressly agreed to be exclusive, in which case it is the sole remedy.*

Subsection (b)'s statement that the limited remedy is optional unless it is
expressly agreed to be exclusive has caused some courts to find for buyers when
sloppy language has been used that did not make clear that a remedy was
"exclusive." However, careful drafting should be sufficient to circumvent this
outcome. Also, some courts have held that remedy limitations must be conspicuous, though no such requirement is found in the text.

While subsection (1) permits limitation, it is subject to two statutory limitations. The first is that the exclusive or limited remedy cannot "fail of its
essential purpose." *See* U.C.C. §2-719(2) ("Where circumstances cause an
exclusive or limited remedy to fail of its essential purpose, remedy may be had
as provided in this Act."). Comment 1 clarifies that "it is of the very essence
of a sales contract that at least minimum adequate remedies be available," and
that where other circumstances cause an otherwise fair clause "to deprive either
party of the substantial value of the bargain, it must give way to the general
remedy provisions of [Article 2]." The most typical scenario in which a remedy
limitation clause fails its essential purpose is where the seller fails to effectively
repair or replace a defective good in accordance with the limited remedy within
a reasonable time period (or sometimes at all), or where the buyer is unable to
tender the goods for repair due to their complete destruction.

Where an exclusive repair or replace clause does fail its essential purpose,
there is a split of authority whether this entitles an aggrieved buyer to also pursue consequential damages as well as direct damages. Some courts have held
that the limitation on consequential damages is dependent on the exclusive
remedy and, therefore, if the exclusive remedy fails, all other remedies, including consequential damages, should be available to the buyer. Other courts,
however, have held that exclusions of consequential damages should be viewed
as independent of the exclusive remedy, and thus should continue to be barred.
It seems that, again, careful drafting could resolve this issue, such as by a seller
adding language that "in no case shall the buyer be entitled to consequential
damages and such limitation is independent of exclusive repair or replace
remedy."

---

* Uniform Commercial Code, copyright © by the American Law Institute and the
National Conference of Commissioners on Uniform State Laws. Reproduced with the
permission of the Permanent Editorial Board for the Uniform Commercial Code. All
rights reserved.

Subsection (3) contains a second limitation; that restrictions on consequential damages, which are unconscionable, "may be limited or excluded." We address the doctrine of unconscionability found in section 2-302, in Chapter 15. For now, it is worth noting that section 2-302 already grants courts such powers for any clause or contract that it deems unconscionable, and thus this provision would seem to add little to the Code. However, subsection (3) goes on to provide limitations on consequential damages "for injury to the person in the case of consumer goods [which] is prima facie unconscionable[,] but limitations of damages where the loss is commercial is not [prima facie unconscionable]." Thus, subsection (3) does two things: first, it explicitly authorizes contractual exclusions on consequential damages, subject to the usual burden of the plaintiff to show that such clause is unconscionable; and second, it shifts the burden to the seller only in a narrow class of cases that involve consumer goods and a limitation on injuries to person.

Checkpoints

- Express warranties may be reasonably modified, but not negated, through other contractual language.

- Express warranties are still subject to the parol evidence rule and merger clauses.

- Implied warranties of merchantability and fitness may be excluded through the use of safe harbor language found in section 2-316(2), but must be conspicuous.

- Implied warranties of merchantability and fitness can also be disclaimed through "as is" clauses or clauses of similar import.

- Implied warranties may be negated by an examination, if the examination ought to have revealed the defect, taking into consideration the buyer's expertise.

- A refusal to examine may also be the basis of a disclaimer, but the seller must essentially demand that the buyer conduct such an examination.

- Disclaimers may also be found through course of performance, course of dealing and trade usage.

- Apart from disclaiming warranties, sellers may also limit the buyer's remedies so long as the limitation does not "fail of its essential purpose."

- Sellers may limit a buyer's remedies to repair or replace.

- Sellers may also exclude consequential damages, but such limitations for personal injuries involving consumer goods are prima facie unconscionable.

Chapter 11

Warranty of Title

Roadmap

- How title is transferred
- Void versus voidable title
- Entrustment
- The implied warranty of title
- Disclaiming the implied warranty of title
- The warranty against infringement

A. How Title Is Transferred

Every sale comes with an implied warranty of good title. Before delving into this warranty, however, it is useful to review how transfer of title works and how it can go awry. In many instances, this warranty is not problematic, as the seller has good title itself. However, what if the seller had encumbered the goods with a security interest? Or perhaps the seller was only a part owner of the good? What has then been transferred?

Article 2 answers this in sections 2-401 and 2-403. Section 2-401 sets forth that title passes once the goods have been identified to the contract, subject to any conditions agreed upon by the parties and the provisions of Article 9 which addresses secured transactions. Section 2-403 provides, "(1) A purchaser of goods acquires all title which his transferor had or had power to transfer except that a purchaser of a limited interest acquires rights only to the extent of the interest purchased." Together, these provisions provide that the buyer can only buy the goods to the extent that the seller's interest allows. If the seller has title to the goods encumbered by a security interest, then the buyer is also buying the goods subject to a security interest. If the seller is only part owner of the goods, then all the seller can transfer is the seller's interest. This all seems simple enough, but what if the seller obtained the goods through fraud such that the original owner could have sued to get the goods back? Or what if the seller had bought the goods with a bad check? What title passes then? The answer depends on whether the seller had voidable, as opposed to void, title.

1. Void versus voidable title

When a seller has voidable title, it is nonetheless able to pass good title onto a good faith purchaser for value. The seller will have voidable title in situations that may give rise to a voidability defense or entitle the original owner to sue for recovery of the goods in question. Section 2-403(1) addresses a number of specific situations that have arisen through the years under which good title can be passed despite the seller having only voidable title.

> ... A person with voidable title has power to transfer a good title to a good faith purchaser for value. When goods have been delivered under a transaction of purchase the purchaser has such power even though
>> (a) the transferor was deceived as to the identity of the purchaser, or
>> (b) the delivery was in exchange for a check which is later dishonored, or
>> (c) it was agreed that the transaction was to be a "cash sale", or
>> (d) the delivery was procured through fraud punishable as larcenous under the criminal law.

U.C.C. § 2-403(1).* Subsection (a) addresses where the original owner was deceived by an impersonator into handing over the goods. Subsection (b) addresses bounced checks. Subsection (c) addresses situations where the original buyer and seller agree that title will not pass until the seller is paid, despite the goods changing hands. Finally, subsection (d) addresses criminal fraud, such as by forging a check. The common theme in these scenarios is that the original seller voluntarily relinquishes the goods, but has the right to revoke consent under certain circumstances. Thus, the original buyer has a voidable title (because the original seller can revoke in the future) but not a void title (where the original buyer had not voluntarily transferred the goods). With a voidable title, the original buyer can pass good title onto a subsequent buyer.

Good title does not automatically pass to any buyer, however, as the buyer must act in good faith and purchase for value. The value requirement essentially

---

means that the beneficiaries of gifts do not get to enjoy good title, presumably because they have given nothing up for the goods, and so it would not be burdensome for them to relinquish the goods if the original owner revokes consent and voids the original transaction. The good faith requirement can be trickier. Good faith is defined in section 1-201(b)(2) as "honesty in fact and the observance of reasonable commercial standards of fair dealing." This involves both a subjective and objective requirement. Thus, if a subsequent buyer knows the seller obtained the goods by fraud, section 2-403(1) will not help the buyer; but neither will ignoring clear warning signs that would be normal in the trade. For instance, a used car dealer should understand the importance of getting the certificate of title on cars it buys. If it buys a car without the certificate, it may not be a good faith purchaser under this section.

One other aspect of section 2-403(1) should be pointed out: once a buyer qualifies as a good faith purchaser for value, title is no longer clouded with the "voidable" label. The title is now good and can be passed along freely, even to those who would not necessarily have qualified as a good faith purchaser themselves. For instance, assume that Frank is selling his rare baseball collection to Sid for $5,000 which Sid pays by check. Val knows Frank and finds out that Sid's check bounced, much to the chagrin of Frank. Val would not qualify as a good faith purchaser if she purchased from Sid, as she knows about the bad check. However, assume that Sid sold the baseball collection to Jennifer, a good faith purchaser, for $5,000 cash. Jennifer would now have good title and Val would be free to buy the baseball collection from her, even though she knows of how Frank got ripped off. In this way, section 2-403(1) acts as a sort of title sanitizer—once a transaction has been cleansed of its voidable title, it is freely transferable to anyone.

So far, we have addressed voidable title and the effect it has on downstream transactions, but how does one get void title? The most obvious instance of one obtaining void title is through theft. If Sid had stolen Frank's baseball collection from his house, Sid would have void title. The consequence of void title is that even good faith purchasers only get void title. Thus, if Jennifer bought the collection for $5,000, and Frank was later able to show that the collection actually belonged to him but was stolen by Sid, Frank would be able to get the baseball collection back from Jennifer. Jennifer's only recourse would be to go after Sid for breach of warranty of title, which we address below.

At this point, you may be wondering why these two situations are treated differently. In one situation, Sid defrauded Frank and got the baseball collection. In the other he stole it, but in each situation, Sid is the wrongdoer who has paid nothing for the cards, and Frank is innocent, so why is Frank deprived the right in the first situation of getting his cards from Jennifer, but not in the second? The drafters apparently felt that Frank is less culpable in the outright theft situation, whereas in the bad check situation, he at least was in a position to try and protect himself. Further, this must be balanced with our innocent third party, Jennifer. At the end of the day, we don't want title issues too easily interfering with commercial transactions, but in cases of outright theft, the equities finally favor the victim, Frank.

2. Entrustment

Section 2-403(1) is not the only section in which the drafters favored the innocent purchaser. The Code provides similar protection to purchasers who buy from merchants to whom goods have been voluntarily left or "entrusted." Subsections (2) and (3) provide:

> (2) Any entrusting of possession of goods to a merchant who deals in goods of that kind gives him power to transfer all rights of the entruster to a buyer in ordinary course of business.
> (3) "Entrusting" includes any delivery and any acquiescence in retention of possession regardless of any condition expressed between the parties to the delivery or acquiescence and regardless of whether the procurement of the entrusting or the possessor's disposition of the goods have been such as to be larcenous under the criminal law.[*]

First note that these provisions only apply to instances in which the goods have been entrusted "to a merchant who deals in goods of that kind." Therefore, this is one of the instances in which the narrow definition of merchant, referenced in Chapter 1, is applied. Second, note that the purchaser must be a "buyer in the ordinary course of business." This is a defined term under Article 1, but it is important to note that it is a misleading one. The term does not mean that the buyer has to buy such goods in the ordinary course of business, but that they buy from one who sells in the ordinary course of business. In other words, it just means someone who buys from a merchant, though there is more to the definition. Section 1-201 defines buyer in ordinary course of business as "a person that buys goods in good faith, without knowledge that the sale violates the rights of another person in the goods, and in the ordinary course from a person, other than a pawnbroker, in the business of

---

[*] Uniform Commercial Code, copyright © by the American Law Institute and the National Conference of Commissioners on Uniform State Laws. Reproduced with the permission of the Permanent Editorial Board for the Uniform Commercial Code. All rights reserved.

selling goods of that kind." From this definition we see that it is not enough that the buyer purchases from a merchant, but must do so without knowledge that the sale violates the rights of a third party. This is not quite the same as the good faith standard we discussed in relation to section 2-403(1), though similar policy issues are at play. The knowledge requirement for buyer in the ordinary course is an actual knowledge standard, and therefore constructive knowledge will not disqualify a buyer.

It is not enough that the purchase be from a merchant by a buyer in the ordinary course—the goods must also have been entrusted as that is defined in subsection (3). Owners may entrust their goods for any number of reasons. A car owner might leave a car at the auto shop for repair. An owner of a rare piece of art might agree to allow a gallery to display one the pieces in her collection for a limited time. The key, as demonstrated by the use of the word "acquiescence," is that the possession was made voluntarily. Once it is so entrusted, a buyer in the ordinary course can buy the goods with good title, and the entruster's only recourse will be against the merchant who sold the goods. At this point, it may have occurred to you that the art gallery could sell a priceless work of art entrusted to its care, or an auto mechanic could sell a luxury vehicle entrusted to it for repairs, so what is stopping them? First off, such actions could run afoul of criminal statutes. Second, as noted, such a merchant would still be civilly liable to the entruster. Finally, and perhaps most importantly, it is just bad business. Mechanics that have a reputation for selling their patrons' cars won't last long, and art galleries will have a hard time getting anyone to trust them to display their priceless pieces if they are known to sell them when in their care.

B. The Implied Warranty of Title

With a clear understanding of some of the ways title issues can arise, we can now address the implied warranty of title. Section 2-312 provides:

(1) Subject to subsection (2) there is in a contract for sale a warranty by the seller that
  (a) the title conveyed shall be good, and its transfer rightful; and
  (b) the goods shall be delivered free from any security interest or other lien or encumbrance of which the buyer at the time of contracting has no knowledge.*

---

* Uniform Commercial Code, copyright © by the American Law Institute and the National Conference of Commissioners on Uniform State Laws. Reproduced with the

As noted above, when good are sold, they are sold subject to the seller's title. Unless the provisions of section 2-403 save the buyer, this means that title may be clouded, such as being subject to a security interest. While secured transactions are a topic for a different text, it is sufficient to say that this means that the goods can be taken from the buyer if the debt that gave rise to the security interest is not paid. Similarly, if the goods are conveyed with void, as opposed to voidable, title, the goods could be reclaimed and taken from the buyer.

Section 2-312 gives the aggrieved buyer the right to go after the seller for damages incurred due to the violation of the warranty. Note that this is not a provision limited to merchant sellers but applies to all sellers. At a minimum, the damages will usually be the purchase price, but there may be additional expenses, such as in defending against an action to repossess the goods. This does not mean that the seller becomes liable for every action brought by a third party against the buyer. The comments note that the purpose of the provision is so that the buyer can expect good title, and "will not be exposed to a lawsuit in order to protect it." The purpose, therefore, is to not expose the buyer to a substantial cloud on the title of the goods; however, frivolous lawsuits would not pose such a threat, and should not implicate the warranty.

C. Disclaiming the Implied Warranty of Title

Though every sale comes with a warranty that the title is good and rightful, comment 6 to section 2-312 notes, "The warranty of subsection (1) is not designated as an 'implied' warranty, and hence is not subject to Section 2-316(3). Disclaimer of the warranty of title is governed instead by subsection (2), which requires either specific language or the described circumstances." Thus, unlike the implied warranty of merchantability or of fitness, the warranty of title has its own specific way that it is disclaimed, and "as is" language by itself will not be sufficient.

Under section 2-312(2), "A warranty under subsection (1) will be excluded or modified only by specific language or by circumstances which give the buyer reason to know that the person selling does not claim title in himself or that he is purporting to sell only such right or title as he or a third person may have." This raises two questions: 1) what language will be sufficient to disclaim the warranty; and 2) what circumstances will give the buyer "reason to know" that there may be a cloud on the title?

As to what language will suffice, neither the Code itself nor the comments give much guidance. The reference to "specific" language means that a general "as is" clause will not suffice, and courts have generally been unforgiving of equivocal or ambiguous language. However, a simple, specific statement such as, "The seller does not warrant the title of these goods" would seem sufficient. The Code does not require that the warranty disclaimer be conspicuous, but it would seem prudent to do so, given the import of the disclaimer.

As for what other circumstances may give rise to the buyer having reason to know that the warranty of title is disclaimed, the comments provide guidance. Comment 5 states:

> that sales by sheriffs, executors, certain foreclosing lienors and persons similarly situated may be so out of the ordinary commercial course that their peculiar character is immediately apparent to the buyer and therefore no personal obligation is imposed upon the seller who is purporting to sell only an unknown or limited right.*

The idea behind such sales is that they are forced sales in which what is being sold is an unknown or limited right, in a setting where one would not expect the normal rules of commerce to necessarily apply. However, Article 9 foreclosure sales[1] do not give rise to such a disclaimer, and section 9-610 of that Article provides that such a disposition includes the warranties imposed under section 2-312 unless properly excluded.

D. The Warranty Against Infringement

Section 2-312 contains one other warranty — the warranty against infringement. Section 2-312(3) provides:

> Unless otherwise agreed a seller who is a merchant regularly dealing in goods of the kind warrants that the goods shall be delivered free

---

* Uniform Commercial Code, copyright © by the American Law Institute and the National Conference of Commissioners on Uniform State Laws. Reproduced with the permission of the Permanent Editorial Board for the Uniform Commercial Code. All rights reserved.

1. Article 9 permits foreclosing secured creditors to self-help repossession and to sell the goods themselves, without the assistance of a sheriff.

of the rightful claim of any third person by way of infringement or the like but a buyer who furnishes specifications to the seller must hold the seller harmless against any such claim which arises out of compliance with the specifications.

This provision, which only applies to merchant sellers (again using the narrow definition), addresses claims of patent, trademark, copyright infringement and the like against the buyer. It only requires that the goods be delivered free from such claims, so if a buyer's subsequent unanticipated use happens to infringe a patent, there would be no claim. Note also that, if it is the buyer that provides the specifications, then it must hold the seller harmless. Thus, an innocent seller of specialty goods requested by the buyer to certain specifications will not be subject to suit by the buyer when a patent infringement claim is brought because the goods, as specified by the buyer, infringe the patent.

Comment 4 to section 2-312 clarifies that, "This section rejects the cases which recognize the principle that infringements violate the warranty of title but deny the buyer a remedy unless he has been expressly prevented from using the goods." This would seem to indicate that the buyer can maintain a claim against the seller for litigation costs incurred in successfully defending against a claim. However, does the fact that the buyer won mean that the seller didn't violate the warranty of infringement? This would seem an odd result. Perhaps the better approach would be to uphold claims of a section 2-312(3) violation when a colorable claim has been made against the buyer, but not for frivolous suits. The provision is rarely litigated, however, and so there is little guidance in the case law.

Checkpoints

- Sellers generally can convey no more title than they themselves have, subject to voidability and entrustment exceptions.

- If the seller has voidable title, the seller may convey good title to a good faith purchaser for value.

- If a merchant seller has been entrusted with goods, the seller may convey good title upon a buyer in the ordinary course of business.

- Every sale of goods comes with a warranty that title is good, rightful, and free of all liens.

- The warranty of title may be disclaimed by either specific language or by the circumstances.

- To disclaim by specific language, the language must be clear and unequivocal, and should probably be conspicuous.

- The circumstances that will give rise to a disclaimer of title are ones outside the normal commercial practices, in which it is known that the seller is selling an unknown or limited right, such as a sheriff's sale.

- Every sale by a merchant also comes with a warranty against infringement, which covers subsequent claims against the buyer such as for patent, trademark, or copyright infringement.

Chapter 12

Breach and Cure

Roadmap

- Perfect tender rule
- Reject the whole
- Accept non-conforming goods
- Accept commercial units and reject the rest
- Duty to mitigate
- Opportunity to cure
- Installment Contracts

A. Perfect Tender Rule

Enforcing contracts under the U.C.C. requires a clear standard for contract breach, so that the buyer knows when the seller has done enough to qualify as having delivered the goods as promised. If the contract has complicated provisions for payment, the seller might also need to know whether the buyer has kept its promises, but the more complex questions of contract enforcement under the U.C.C. will typically involve the seller's performance, and whether the goods delivered are as promised. The standard for sales of goods under the U.C.C. is perfect tender, and it requires the seller to provide exactly what the contract describes. Any deviation from the contract terms, no matter how small, will be enough for the buyer to refuse to pay. U.C.C. § 2-601 makes that clear:

> Subject to the provisions of this Article on breach in installment contracts . . . and unless otherwise agreed under the sections on contractual limitations of remedy . . . , if the goods or the tender of delivery fail in any respect to conform to the contract, the buyer may

(a) Reject the whole; or

(b) Accept the whole; or

(c) Accept any commercial unit or units and reject the rest.*

We will discuss the exception for installment contracts in part D, below. For now, notice that it is not just the quality of the goods delivered that must comply perfectly with the contract terms, but also the manner of delivery. If the contract has a specific deadline for tender of goods, showing up even a few minutes late will be a breach. If the contract is specific regarding the company to be used in delivering the goods, using a different service — even if equivalent — will be a breach. To reiterate, any deviation from the express terms will be a breach, and will entitle the buyer to refuse to perform.

It is important to understand the benefits and drawbacks of choosing a strict standard for performance, like the perfect tender rule. The primary advantage is that it respects the autonomy of individuals, because it holds them to exactly what they promised and assures them that they will be entitled to nothing less than what they bargained for. This is particularly important for those who place an unusually high value on some contract term. If required to seek only damages for breach, these individuals with unusual preferences — known as idiosyncratic bargainers — will almost certainly be undercompensated because a jury will not appreciate the high value they place on the term in question. Perfect tender protects these individuals, as long as they bargain for exactly what they want. As a secondary benefit, perfect tender also encourages parties to be precise about what they really value during the bargaining process, since all express terms will be strictly enforced.

Perfect tender is not without its disadvantages, the greatest of which is turning minor variations from the contract into potentially contract-killing disputes. For example, if ShoeCo contracts to sell a shipment of shoes to RetailMart, to arrive on Friday by 4:30 p.m., then a shipment arriving after 4:30 p.m. is non-conforming and may be rejected. Imagine that there is particularly heavy traffic on Friday, and the delivery truck gets stuck in traffic, arriving at 4:35 p.m. Under a more relaxed standard, the shoes would satisfy the contract, and RetailMart would have to pay, although perhaps with a slight discount to compensate for any costs resulting from the minor delay. Under a perfect tender standard, however, RetailMart can refuse to accept the entire shipment, and ShoeCo would have to take back perfectly good shoes and pay shipping both directions. Importantly, in terms of the standard of performance, the U.C.C. does not ask why RetailMart is refusing the shoes;[1] they were not delivered as promised, so RetailMart can say no, and ShoeCo loses the sale and pays the extra cost of transport.

Courts refer to this problem as "forfeiture," referring to the fact that all of ShoeCo's efforts up to that point are forfeit—wasted—because RetailMart has exercised its right to enforce all contract terms strictly, even the delivery time. The danger is not just that ShoeCo will be a little poorer afterwards. Instead, the threat of forfeiture can be used by RetailMart to extract new concessions from ShoeCo. If ShoeCo agrees, rather than face the losses and additional costs of breach, the overall terms of the contract have been effectively changed under circumstances that can seem somewhat coercive, especially if the concessions are larger than the actual harm suffered from the five-minute delay. The U.C.C. was designed to facilitate voluntary commercial transactions, and the possibility of this coercive and extortionate behavior by a non-breaching buyer contradicts that basic principle.

The U.C.C. is able to make perfect tender work because three separate factors serve to lessen the dangers of forfeiture. First of all, we have the rule regarding usage of trade, defined in section 1-103 and applied to contracts in section 2-202, which is that generally accepted customs in a particular industry or geographic location will be considered as terms of the contract even if they aren't expressly stated. This is the technical version of when people say, "that's just how things are done around here." These customs aren't included in the contract, but everyone in that industry—or that geographic location—just understands that the terms are part of every contract. Returning to our example, perhaps, a location with heavy traffic might have a custom of accepting shipments as on-time even if they are up to 10 minutes late. In that case, the shipment of shoes would still be considered on-time, since the local custom transforms "4:30 p.m." into "4:30 to 4:40 p.m." Other interpretive rules may also come into play, such as whether previous contracts between ShoeCo and RetailMart have allowed slightly-late shipments (course of dealing, defined in section 1-303(b) and applied in section 2-202) or whether past deliveries have been accepted, even though late (course of performance, defined in section 1-303(a)). In effect, there is a two-step process: first, identify what perfect tender requires, given the text of the contract and these interpretive rules; and second, identify whether the goods meet that standard.

---

1. Every U.C.C. contract is also governed by the standard of good faith, and some courts have held that a pretextual rejection (rejecting out of spite but claiming rejection based on non-conformity) is a violation of that standard of good faith.

In addition to these interpretive rules, the U.C.C. adopts a right to cure. We will discuss this in section C, below, but the short answer is that when the buyer identifies what is wrong with the goods, the seller has a right to at least try and make it right. This won't help ShoeCo, obviously, since you can't fix being late, but if the shoes were the wrong color, ShoeCo might have the right to try to deliver conforming shoes to RetailMart and avoid not getting paid.

Finally, the nature of the market for goods helps to soften the blow of a severe rule like perfect tender. In most of the markets covered by Article 2 of the U.C.C., there are numerous buyers and sellers, so every buyer has a large number of potential suppliers and every seller can market its products to a large number of potential buyers. This largely eliminates the forfeiture problem, because a buyer who tries to leverage a minor breach into a big payout will find that the seller has willingly sold the goods to someone else. This concept may be more easily understood if we compare it to a contract under the common law. BuildCo has contracted with Jim, a homeowner, to construct a new garage with an 84-inch-high door. As BuildCo finishes the garage, it realizes that the door is only 83 inches tall. Under a perfect tender rule, Jim could refuse to pay, even though he has a garage that is fully functional. And BuildCo can't just take the garage and go, so Jim can offer to pay only at a significantly discounted rate. By contrast, even under the perfect tender rule, if RetailMart threatens to refuse delivery of shoes unless ShoeCo agrees to a large discount, ShoeCo can sell the shoes to RetailMart's biggest competitor, WarehouseMart.

Now that we have some idea of why a perfect tender rule was chosen for the U.C.C., we should spend some time illustrating how it functions, in practice. When a shipment of non-conforming goods arrives, the buyer must first identify the non-conformity and then make a choice of how to proceed. As described above, the options are to reject the entire shipment, accept the shipment, even though the goods are non-conforming, or accept some and reject the rest, so long as the amount accepted counts as a "commercial unit."

1. Reject the whole

The perfect tender rule requires—as its name implies—perfection, and if the goods do not conform to the contract in every way, the buyer is not required to accept them. Put another way, the goods described by the contract have never arrived so, in essence, the buyer is the recipient of a random shipment of goods from the seller. The seller, who shipped the goods, has not shipped the goods described by the contract, but some other random pile of goods.

Now, the buyer has no goods that meet its needs and the seller has a pile of goods that have somehow escaped and are now at the buyer's premises.

The buyer gets to choose this outcome, since another option is to accept the goods, but if the buyer wishes to reject, there are some rules that it has to follow. The primary section dealing with rejection is section 2-602, which states:

> (1) Rejection of goods must be within a reasonable time after their delivery or tender. It is ineffective unless the buyer seasonably notifies the seller.
>
> (2) Subject to the provisions of the two following sections on rejected goods (Sections 2-603 and 2-604),
>
> (a) after rejection any exercise of ownership by the buyer with respect to any commercial unit is wrongful as against the seller; and
>
> (b) if the buyer has before rejection taken physical possession of goods in which he does not have a security interest under the provisions of this Article (subsection (3) of Section 2-711), he is under a duty after rejection to hold them with reasonable care at the seller's disposition for a time sufficient to permit the seller to remove them; but
>
> (c) the buyer has no further obligations with regard to goods rightfully rejected.
>
> (3) The seller's rights with respect to goods wrongfully rejected are governed by the provisions of this Article on Seller's remedies in general (Section 2-703).

U.C.C. § 2-602.* Subsection 1 requires that buyer must reject within a reasonable time and notify seller "seasonably," and section 2-605 requires buyer to let seller know exactly *how* the goods fall short of the contract description. For a definition of "seasonable," we go to section 1-205, which describes seasonable notice as notice within a reasonable time. Of course, that means that exactly how fast the buyer needs to notify the seller will be case specific and contextual. The type of goods, how easy it is to identify the non-conformity, what forms of communication are available, and so on will be factors that will determine what counts as "seasonable" notice. A buyer will want to be careful,

however, because failure to reject — including providing seasonable notice —
counts as acceptance, as described below.

The buyer will also want to be careful with that random pile of goods that
might be sitting on its loading dock. Recall that, because it has rejected the
goods, they still belong to the seller. The buyer will have to treat the goods as
any other non-owner would. Since it is in possession of goods that do not
belong to it, section 2-602(2) requires it to take reasonable care of the goods in
order to give seller a chance to take them away. If the goods are damaged while
in buyer's care, seller might be able to sue buyer for damages. Likewise, if buyer
starts acting like the owner — perhaps refusing to let seller remove the goods —
seller will be able to treat buyer like a stranger that has stolen the goods.

Section 2-603 goes even further, describing circumstances under which
buyer is required to sell the goods as an agent of the seller:

> (1) Subject to any security interest in the buyer (subsection (3) of Sec-
> tion 2-711), when the seller has no agent or place of business at the
> market of rejection a merchant buyer is under a duty after rejection
> of goods in his possession or control to follow any reasonable instruc-
> tions to make reasonable efforts to sell them for the seller's account
> if they are perishable or threaten to decline in value speedily. Instruc-
> tions are not reasonable if on demand indemnity for expenses is not
> forthcoming.
> (2) When the buyer sells goods under subsection (1), he is entitled to
> reimbursement from the seller or out of the proceeds for reasonable
> expenses of caring for and selling them, and if the expenses include no
> selling commission then to such commission as is usual in the trade
> or if there is none to a reasonable sum not exceeding ten per cent on
> the gross proceeds.
> (3) In complying with this section the buyer is held only to good faith
> and good faith conduct hereunder is neither acceptance nor conver-
> sion nor the basis of an action for damages.

U.C.C. § 2-603.* Subsection 1 establishes the basic criteria for buyer's obligation to act as agent for seller in selling the non-conforming goods. First, the
buyer must be a merchant, under the broad definition discussed in Chapter 1.
Second, the seller must be without an agent or place of business at the location

---

* Uniform Commercial Code, copyright © by the American Law Institute and the
National Conference of Commissioners on Uniform State Laws. Reproduced with the
permission of the Permanent Editorial Board for the Uniform Commercial Code. All
rights reserved.

where the goods were rejected. Third, there must be reasonable instructions from the seller regarding sale of the goods, and those instructions will be reasonable only if they include indemnification for expenses in pursuing a sale. Fourth, the goods themselves must be perishable — such as most foodstuffs — or subject to rapidly declining value. With such a long list, the likelihood of a buyer bearing this responsibility is low. However slim the probability, section 2-603 is worth remembering because it creates the potential for a buyer who rightfully rejects non-conforming goods still being held liable for the entire value of the goods.

2. Accept non-conforming goods

Rewind now back for a moment to when the buyer decides what to do with the non-conforming goods that have just arrived. Perfect tender gives the buyer the right, but not the obligation, to reject them. In other words, it is up to buyer to decide whether the non-conformity is large enough to make it worth the effort of finding new goods. If not, the buyer is within its rights to accept them, flaws and all.

To understand why a buyer might do that, imagine the following example. A shipment of athletic shoelaces has just arrived at ShoeCo, but they are the wrong shade of blue (too light, for example). ShoeCo needs to ship 500 blue athletic shoes tomorrow and there is just enough time to lace the shoes before they get shipped out. Without time to find substitute laces at this late hour, ShoeCo must choose between defaulting on its contract obligations or accepting shoelaces that are blue, just not quite the right shade of blue. In either case, ShoeCo will likely be able to recover damages from the seller, as we will discuss in Chapter 20, but section 2-607(2) makes clear that accepting the goods means that ShoeCo waives the right to reject, but retains all other remedies available to it, including suing for damages. So, whether ShoeCo accepts the shoelaces will likely be a function of whether its customers will be more irritated that the shoes will have laces that aren't *quite* blue enough or that the shoes won't arrive, at all. It is entirely possible that ShoeCo will make the business decision to accept the goods and sue to recover the difference between the value of the shoelaces as promised and as delivered.

When it comes to acceptance, the U.C.C. provides three methods, described in section 2-606:

(1) Acceptance of goods occurs when the buyer
   (a) after a reasonable opportunity to inspect the goods signifies to the seller that the goods are conforming or that he will take or retain them in spite of their non-conformity; or

(b) fails to make an effective rejection (subsection (1) of Section 2-602), but such acceptance does not occur until the buyer has had a reasonable opportunity to inspect them; or

(c) does any act inconsistent with the seller's ownership; but if such act is wrongful as against the seller it is an acceptance only if ratified by him.

(2) Acceptance of a part of any commercial unit is acceptance of that entire unit.

U.C.C. § 2-606.* The easiest and most obvious way is for the buyer to say or otherwise indicate that the goods are acceptable, so ShoeCo can simply sign whatever shipping documents are presented, or perhaps call or text the seller to indicate that the goods are accepted. The second method was alluded to earlier, that a buyer who fails to make a seasonable rejection has accepted the goods. So, ShoeCo cannot wait too long to reject if that is what it intends to do; if it does, it may discover that it is now the proud owner of some blue shoelaces that it doesn't want. Finally, if the buyer starts acting like an owner would, such as using the shoelaces to prepare the athletic shoes for shipment, then ShoeCo has accepted the laces. Recall that a buyer who rejects, but later starts acting like an owner, can be treated as having converted the goods. If acts of ownership occur prior to any rejection, the buyer will be treated as the owner and will have to pay for the goods.

3. Accept commercial units and reject the rest

In our example, ShoeCo needs some laces right now, and feels significant pressure to not reject the shipment, even though it is non-conforming. If the seller has shipped 500 pairs of shoelaces and ShoeCo needs laces for 500 athletic shoes, then it might make sense to accept the entire shipment. However, what if the shipment is for 10,000 pairs of shoelaces? In that case, ShoeCo would like to be able to return all but what will satisfy its immediate needs. Fortunately, the U.C.C. provides just such an option, with one caveat: that ShoeCo must only keep "commercial units." According to section 2-105, that means keeping a number of goods that would normally be grouped together for sale.

If taking one unit away makes it harder to sell the group, then the group is a commercial unit. For most consumer goods, the examples are obvious. A carton with 11 eggs will not be sold, so 12 eggs would be a commercial unit. A carton with 23 cans of soda will not be sold, so 24 cans of soda are a commercial unit. With large goods, such as a truck, or a piece of construction equipment, one unit will likely be a commercial unit, since trucks and construction equipment don't come in a six-pack. For other goods, things can get a little more complicated, such as a set of living room furniture that contains a sofa, a love seat, and two recliners; as long as they are normally sold as a complete set, then the buyer would have to take or reject the entire set. To be clear, since a commercial unit is the amount that is "normally" grouped for sale, that amount can differ based on the goods, the industry, and perhaps the geographic location, to name a few relevant factors.

In the case of our not-blue-enough shoelaces, ShoeCo will have to consider what a normal commercial unit is for shoelaces. If it is 100 pairs, then ShoeCo can keep five commercial units and reject the rest. If, instead, shoelaces are sold in groups of 1,000 pairs, ShoeCo will have to keep one complete commercial unit, even though it only needs 500, or half of a commercial unit.

B. Duty to Mitigate

If the buyer chooses to accept the non-conforming goods, the only thing left to do is figure out how much the non-conformity is "worth," in damages. If the buyer rejects the goods, however, two mechanisms kick into action. The first is that the seller has the right to correct—or "cure"—the non-conformity, and we'll come back to that in section D. The second—and this will be applicable whether the seller attempts to cure or not—is that the buyer has a duty to make reasonable efforts to minimize, or mitigate, the losses suffered because the goods are non-conforming. If it doesn't, then it cannot collect any damages that it might have avoided.

Why impose this duty on the non-breaching party? After all, it has done nothing wrong, so why should it be required to do anything? There have been many philosophical justifications offered, but there are two simple justifications that will serve our purposes. First, it is reasonable to assume that most people in that situation would want to just move on with their lives, finding the best way to move forward, and someone who refuses to do so is likely to be motivated by spite. Since we don't want to encourage that sort of behavior within contracts, we set the duty in accordance with what we assume the vast majority of people will do, anyway. Second, the purpose of the U.C.C. is to facilitate commercial transactions. One transaction has fallen through, but we should encourage the non-breaching party to find a substitute transaction and move forward, making more deals.

In the context of a contract for goods, a buyer's mitigation will mean buying from someone else without unreasonable delay. The buyer might suffer some loss because of the delay or the costs of searching for a new supplier, but those losses will often be much less than if the buyer did nothing and lost out on lots of profits. A buyer might also have to pay contract damages if the seller's breach caused the buyer to breach, as well. The buyer might be able to recover damages from seller, but it could cause additional breaches downstream, affecting many more merchants and consumers. Requiring the non-breaching party to mitigate its loss will hopefully stop that chain of events, keeping the stream of commerce flowing. Notice, however, that the non-breaching party is only required to take *reasonable* measures to mitigate losses.

Returning to our previous example, if ShoeCo chooses not to accept the non-conforming shoelaces, it will not be able to ship out the 500 athletic shoes to RetailMart, as scheduled. RetailMart will lose the profit it would have gained from selling the shoes, ShoeCo will have to pay those damages, and ShoeCo's supplier will have to pay ShoeCo because its breach set off the chain of events. More about that later in Chapter 20, but for now, imagine that ShoeCo has other shipments of the same shoe that must go out in three days, five days, and ten days, respectively. ShoeCo may not be able to avoid the loss from today's shipment, but it must attempt to find another supplier of blue shoelaces for the upcoming shipments. Assume that it finds a substitute that can provide the right shoelaces in 8 days for $1 a pair, 4 days for $1.50, and 2 days for $4, and that the original price was $1 a pair.

It should be obvious that ShoeCo can largely avoid all damages by contracting to buy the shoelaces 8 days out. The duty to mitigate will require ShoeCo to make that deal. For the shipment 4 days out, ShoeCo will earn less profits— $0.50 worth for each shoe—if it takes the deal and pays more for substitute laces. Similarly, for the shipment 2 days out, ShoeCo will earn $3 less in profits for each shoe. For each shipment, ShoeCo's original supplier will be on the hook for those lost profits, and society will be better off because consumers will actually get shoes. If ShoeCo declines to make those purchases and ends up with damages of $5 per pair (a combination of lost profits and consequential damages), it will discover that it isn't able to recover the full amount. Because it could have made the first shipment—and avoided the $5 per pair damages—by paying the substitute supplier $4 per pair ($3 more than the original price of $1), it can only recover $3 per pair. The reason is that paying

$3 per pair extra would have avoided $5 per pair in damages, so $2 per pair in damages was caused by ShoeCo's refusal to mitigate. For the second shipment five days out, ShoeCo would have paid only $0.50 more, so $4.50 in damages was caused by ShoeCo's failure to mitigate. For the shipment ten days out, ShoeCo could have paid the same amount and wouldn't have suffered any damages. ShoeCo will therefore be able to recover only $0.50 per pair in damages from the second shipment and nothing for the third shipment. Notice that, because attempts at mitigation must be reasonable, ShoeCo is not entirely free in its mitigation efforts. It could not, for example, buy all the shoelaces it needs at the higher two-day price. That price is reasonable in order to meet its order that is three days out, but if it has the ability to wait four days to meet its five-day deadline, then it must pay the four-day price. Likewise, if it can wait eight days to meet its ten-day deadline, then it must pay the eight day price.

The duty to mitigate also extends to the seller, in the event that the buyer refuses to pay for the goods. As we will discuss in Chapter 19, a seller who is not paid has the right to sell to another buyer, and recover the difference between what would have been received under the contract and what is actually received from the new buyer. Basically, the seller is allowed to recover the profits lost because of the breach. In a simple case like that, the duty to mitigate kicks in to keep the seller from waiting too long to find a new buyer. A more complicated case arises if the buyer tries to cancel the deal while seller is still making the goods. In that case, the duty to mitigate normally requires the seller to stop production, sell the goods for whatever value it can receive, or perhaps sell for scrap.

Spending any amount of time searching the U.C.C. for the duty to mitigate will be a largely fruitless endeavor. Unlike the common law, which states the duty to mitigate expressly, the U.C.C. only implies it. For example, when one party refuses to perform under the contract, the non-breaching party is only allowed to wait a "commercially reasonable time" for the breaching party to change its mind. This implies that, after that commercially reasonable time, the breaching party must begin to act. Exactly what must the non-breaching party do? Chapter 19 will discuss the options available to seller, and Chapter 20 will discuss the options available to buyer. In both cases, however, a buyer or seller who wishes to recover damages must normally engage in mitigation efforts, finding someone else to perform in the place of the breaching party. Recall, also, from Chapter 1's discussion of the relationship between the U.C.C. and the common law, that the common law's provisions step in to fill any gaps in the U.C.C. Therefore, to the extent necessary, we can rely on the common law duty to mitigate.

C. Opportunity to Cure

The U.C.C.'s perfect tender rule could easily keep sellers up at nights, worried about whether the goods that have been shipped to buyers are going to meet the precise descriptions of the contract. If you are the CEO of Laces, Inc., for example, the laces you sent to ShoeCo *should be* the right shade of blue, but you've been having trouble with your dye machine, and you can't be too certain. Fortunately for you, section 2-508 provides you an opportunity to fix any mistakes that ShoeCo identifies:

> (1) Where any tender or delivery by the seller is rejected because non-conforming and the time for performance has not yet expired, the seller may seasonably notify the buyer of his intention to cure and may then within the contract time make a conforming delivery.
>
> (2) Where the buyer rejects a non-conforming tender which the seller had reasonable grounds to believe would be acceptable with or without money allowance the seller may if he seasonably notifies the buyer have a further reasonable time to substitute a conforming tender.

U.C.C. § 2-508.* That right is absolute before the time for performance is expired, in that the buyer *must* give the seller notice of any non-conformity and allow seller the chance to get replacement (and conforming) goods there before the time for performance expires. Of course, when the buyer provides notice of non-conformity, the seller must provide notice of intent to cure.

A more interesting and complicated scenario arises when the time of performance has expired. In that case, section 2-508 says that the seller has "a further reasonable time" to provide conforming goods, *if and only if* the seller "had reasonable grounds to believe" that the non-conforming goods would be accepted, "with or without money allowance." There are some technical terms that deserve further explanation. To keep everything in context, remember that these are goods that do not meet the description in the contract. For that reason, it is reasonable to assume that the goods are not as valuable to the buyer, so "money allowance" is a reference to a discount that the seller might give the buyer as compensation for the non-conformity. If the seller

---

* Uniform Commercial Code, copyright © by the American Law Institute and the National Conference of Commissioners on Uniform State Laws. Reproduced with the permission of the Permanent Editorial Board for the Uniform Commercial Code. All rights reserved.

knows that the goods are non-conforming, it might ship them anyway, believing that the buyer won't be bothered by the non-conformity or, if it is bothered, will accept a small discount. In a circumstance like that, the only remaining question is whether the seller had "reasonable grounds" for its belief. If so, the seller has additional time to provide conforming goods.

What if, however, the seller had no idea that the goods were non-conforming? By a strict reading, section 2-508 doesn't seem to cover that scenario. Only those sellers who know there is a non-conformity can possibly have a reasonable belief that it will be accepted, nevertheless. Courts have not limited section 2-508 to that strict reading. Instead, they have held that a seller who is unaware of the non-conformity might have a reasonable belief that the goods would be *accepted* if there was a reasonable belief that the goods were *acceptable*. While this is an interpretive stretch, it does have an intuitive appeal, since goods that meet the perfect tender standard *must* be accepted by the buyer.

Returning to our example, if Laces, Inc. knows that the laces are not blue enough but knows that ShoeCo regularly pairs shoes and laces of different colors, it might have a reasonable belief that the laces will be fine, although it might have to charge only $0.95 per pair. If so, then Laces, Inc. might have an additional day or two to ship shoelaces of the right hue to ShoeCo. Now, consider the alternative scenario, where Laces, Inc. believes that the shoelaces are the right color. If that belief is reasonable — in that they aren't just incompetent or negligent in checking their shipments — then Laces, Inc. may have a reasonable belief that the shipment would be accepted by ShoeCo and would get the same day or two to deliver a conforming shipment.

D. Installment Contracts

The U.C.C. has constructed a regime where the perfect tender rule does not often result in forfeiture and limits spiteful and opportunistic behavior by buyers. It does this through interpretive rules, the duty to mitigate, and an opportunity to cure. The possibility of forfeiture will always be there, however, and the reduced likelihood is small enough that society is better off even with that possibility. There is one area, however, where the U.C.C. abandons the perfect tender rule entirely, and that is the case of installment contracts.

Section 2-612 defines an installment contract as "one which requires or authorizes the delivery of goods in separate lots to be separately accepted," even if the contract attempts to distinguish each shipment as a separate contract. As an initial matter, notice that the key is not just that the goods arrive in different shipments, but that each shipment undergoes a separate accept/reject decision. What that means is that, even if all shipments arrive on the same day, the contract allows the buyer to accept or reject each shipment independently.

Taken as a whole, the language of section 2-612(1) indicates that courts will look to the function of the contract, rather than the specific language of the contract, in order to determine whether it is an installment contract. Why does it matter? Because a shipment that arrives as part of an installment contract cannot be rejected under the perfect tender standard. Instead, a buyer can reject an installment only if the non-conformity "substantially impairs the value of that installment and cannot be cured," or if the non-conformity is in the documents required by the contract. In other words, minor flaws cannot be the basis for rejection. And, even if the flaws are substantial, the buyer cannot reject the shipment if the seller provides adequate assurances of cure. If the parties have drafted a contract that functions like an installment contract, with independent shipments, then other language attempting to disclaim that status will be disregarded.

The different treatment of installment contracts also extends to when the contract, as a whole, has been breached. Only when one or more shipments are so flawed that they "substantially impair[] the value of the whole contract" will the buyer be able to terminate the whole contract and sue for damages on the whole contract. U.C.C. § 2-612(3). It may be difficult to imagine where the dividing line would be between minor defects and those that substantially impair the value of the contract. As one example, consider the non-conforming shoelaces that ShoeCo has received. If they are a slightly different shade of blue, that likely is minor and not grounds for cancelling the contract. If, however, the shoelaces are toxic, so that using them would destroy ShoeCo's ability to operate in the athletic shoe market ever again, the non-conformity is almost certainly large enough that it substantially impairs the value of the entire contract and ShoeCo can cancel the contract and seek out a new supplier.

Even if the contract is not breached, of course, the buyer can still sue for damages for deviations from the contract description, but the contract continues. Only when the value of the whole contract is breached does the buyer's right to terminate the contract kick in. If that point is reached, the buyer need no longer accept offers to cure but must observe a few procedural requirements if it wants to cancel the contract. First, the buyer must notify the seller that the contract is cancelled. Second, any lawsuit to recover damages from the breach should include past *and* future damages; any claim only for past damages will be interpreted as a desire to continue the contract into the future. Finally, the buyer should be careful not to act in a way that indicates an expectation that the seller will continue to perform, because the courts will also interpret that as the buyer's desiring to continue the contract.

Given the harsh nature of the perfect tender rule that the U.C.C. adopts as a broadly applicable rule, this exception for installment contracts may seem a little odd. If a contract is a one-time deal, we apply the strict requirement of perfect tender. If the contract is expected to extend over a number of independent shipments, we apply a much more lenient standard, making it harder for the buyer to get exactly what it wants. What is the rationale for the different standard? There are two main explanations. One is that the parties to an installment contract have something invested in the long-term relationship between the parties in addition to what they have invested in the transaction, itself, so they would prefer a less-harsh rule, in order to maintain the value of that relationship. The second explanation is that the long-term nature of the relationship makes the parties more vulnerable to the type of extortionary behavior that was discussed at the beginning of this chapter. If the seller knows that the buyer is relying on the installments—as buyer must, or it would have just bought what it needed as needed—then seller has leverage. Similarly, buyer must know that seller has planned its production schedule to include future installments and is relying on buyer to pay for them, so buyer may have leverage. In either circumstance, a more lenient rule can alleviate the temptation to engage in extortionary behavior.

Checkpoints

- Article 2 adopts the perfect tender standard for a seller's contract performance.

- The perfect tender rule requires performance in exact compliance with contract terms.

- The perfect tender rule also opens the door to extortionary pressures, which can lead to forfeiture.

- Article 2 mitigates the risk of forfeiture through interpretive rules, the duty to mitigate, the opportunity to cure, and the nature of markets for goods.

- If non-conforming goods are received, the buyer can reject the whole shipment, accept the whole shipment (and sue for damages), or accept one or more commercial units and reject the rest.

- If the buyer wishes to reject non-conforming goods, it must notify the seller of the specific nature of the non-conformity.

- The duty to mitigate requires the non-breaching party to take reasonable actions to lessen the harm caused by the breach.

- If a seller sends non-conforming goods, but can get a shipment of conforming goods to the buyer before the time of performance, the buyer must allow it.

- If a seller had reasonable grounds to believe non-conforming goods would be accepted, the seller may send conforming goods within a reasonable time after the time of performance.

- Article 2 adopts an exception to the perfect tender rule for installment contracts.

- An installment can be rejected only if the non-conformity substantially impairs the value of the shipment.

- An installment contract can only be terminated if one or more faulty shipments substantially impair the value of the whole contract.

Chapter 13

Anticipatory Repudiation and Adequate Assurances

Roadmap

- Repudiation of a contract
- Walking the mitigation/breach tightrope
- Demanding adequate assurances

A. Repudiation of a Contract

On occasion, one of the parties to a contract — say, the seller — will want out before they have had to perform. Maybe the seller has discovered that they can't produce the goods for the contract price, so they'll lose money on the deal. Or, perhaps, they have found another buyer that will pay more than their counterparty. Either way, the contract relationship is certain to deteriorate and, eventually, the seller could choose to end, or repudiate, the contract. Of course, the buyer then no longer has any obligation to pay for any goods not yet delivered. Repudiation is also breach, so the buyer will be able to sue for damages.

Article 2 does not describe how repudiation occurs but, under the common law, repudiation can be express or implied. Express repudiation is, as might be obvious, simply stating a refusal to perform under the contract. Express repudiation must be unambiguous, however. Implied repudiation occurs when one party acts in a way that makes it plainly impossible for them to perform. For example, Pat contracts to sell Terry a famous painting by Vincent Van Gough, entitled "Starry Night," on July 4. On June 30, Terry discovers that Pat has already sold the painting to Bill. Pat has not spoken to Terry to let Terry know that the contract is off, so there has not been an express repudiation, but since Starry Night is unique, it cannot be sold twice. Pat has made it impossible to perform and, as a result, has impliedly repudiated the contract. However, not all instances where the seller loses possession of the goods will lead to a repudiation. If Starry Night was seized by the sheriff to sell to pay off a lien, and Pat still had time to buy it back at the sale, a repudiation may not have occurred simply by the seizure by the sheriff.

Section 2-610 lists the options available to the party who has just found out that the other party has repudiated the contract. First, the non-breaching party is allowed to wait a commercially reasonable time, just in case the breaching party changes its mind. Before we proceed, it might be good to consider why someone might want to take this option (waiting) after receiving notice of repudiation. For some, it may be that they have a longstanding relationship with the other party, and they want to give every chance for the other party to do the right thing and perform. For others, it may be that finding a substitute is going to be costly and they are hoping that the other party will change its mind and avoid the extra costs. At any rate, notice that any waiting the non-breaching party does can only last a "commercially reasonable time," after which it must start its attempts at mitigation. As always, it will be impossible to know exactly how long a commercially reasonable time is, because it will depend on the industry, the goods, the geographical location, and so on.

If the non-breaching party chooses not to wait a commercially reasonable time — it is an option, not a requirement, after all — or after waiting a commercially reasonable time, the non-breaching party is allowed to pursue any of its options. In other words, repudiation triggers a brief buffer of time that the non-breaching party *can* take to wait for the other party to change its mind. During that buffer time, section 2-611 gives the breaching party a chance to change its mind and retract its repudiation. This right of retraction lasts until the repudiating party's next performance or until the non-breaching party accepts the repudiation or materially changes its position. Any attempt to retract, however, "must include any assurance justifiably demanded" by the non-breaching party. U.C.C. § 2-611(2).

If the breaching party is able to retract its repudiation, the non-breaching party will be excused if the delay caused by the repudiation affects the contract dates. The non-breaching party might even be entitled to compensation for any damages caused by the delay, even though the contract is back on once the repudiation is retracted. If the breaching party never retracts the repudiation, the buffer period will eventually end and the contract will end with a breach. All remedies are then on the table and the non-breaching party is excused from performance, though not from the duty to mitigate.

B. Walking the Mitigation/Breach Tightrope

The duty to mitigate complicates matters significantly for the non-breaching party in the case of repudiation prior to the date of performance (anticipatory repudiation). The reason is that the duty to mitigate kicks in when the other party has repudiated, but repudiation is not always clear. Even worse, actions in mitigation look a lot like breach. In fact, if the other party has not actually repudiated, then actions in attempted mitigation are the very definition of breach.

Assume that PatCo has agreed to sell TerryCorp 10,000 postcards with the image of Van Gough's Starry Night, and TerryCorp agrees to make PatCo its exclusive supplier. PatCo starts having trouble at its printing facility and is worried that it won't be able to meet the contract deadline. PatCo doesn't say anything, but word gets around to TerryCorp that there are production concerns. Eventually, the printing facility is shut down for some emergency maintenance. When TerryCorp hears about the shutdown, it assumes that the contract has been breached, and finds an alternative supplier, BobbyCo. If PatCo has actually breached the contract and is unable to perform, then TerryCorp's actions are not only a good idea, but required if it wants to avoid losing out on damages because it failed to mitigate, as we talked about in Chapter 12. However, if PatCo has not breached the contract — perhaps it is able to get its facility up and running in a couple of days, or perhaps it buys the postcards from BobbyCo, and ships 10,000 conforming postcards by the contract date — then TerryCorp is the one who has breached by buying from anyone other than PatCo. Instead of protecting its right to collect damages, TerryCorp will actually find itself paying damages.

This same uncertainty faces any party that has learned of possible repudiation by the other party. This uncertainty can be worsened if one of the parties is intentionally vague in its words and actions. It can be hard enough to know whether — and when — to start mitigation efforts when the other party is trying to comply with the contract, but is falling behind. The level of uncertainty is likely to be even worse if one party is trying to make the other party breach. For example, imagine that PatCo is not really having problems at its printing facility, but has identified another buyer who will pay 20% more than TerryCorp for the same postcards. If PatCo begins to act as if it is having difficulties, that will make TerryCorp nervous about possible repudiation. PatCo might even shut down production for a couple of days, hoping that TerryCorp will be worried enough that it will seek out an alternative supplier. If TerryCorp does so, then the breach has come from TerryCorp and PatCo is excused from its performance and can sell the postcards to its new buyer for 20% more.[1]

Whether as a result of legitimate difficulties or shenanigans by the other party, repudiation is often difficult to precisely identify. The common law attempts to clarify by setting a high bar for repudiation, allowing the non-breaching party to wait longer before the duty to mitigate kicks in. Section 2-610 places an additional limitation on when repudiation "counts"—when failure of performance will "substantially impair the value of the contract." In other words, repudiation as to a minor part of the contract will not trigger the provisions of Article 2, including the duty to mitigate. These common-law and U.C.C. provisions will provide some protection to the non-breaching party who is trying to determine whether repudiation has occurred, as will the right to demand assurances.

C. Demanding Adequate Assurance

Section 2-609 describes an "obligation on each party that the other's expectation of receiving due performance will not be impaired." In other words, when the parties sign a contract, they both have a right to expect that the other party will not do or say things that will make them question whether or not they will receive the promised performance. Of course, rights are not always respected and obligations are not always fulfilled, so there will be times when uncertainty creeps in, and one or both parties will begin to question the other. This could be inadvertent or intentional but, regardless, section 2-609 provides that "[w]hen reasonable grounds for insecurity arise with respect to . . . performance . . . the other party may in writing demand adequate assurance of due performance." When uncertainties arise, the uncertain party is entitled to request that the other party reassert its intention to perform. In the context of the previous section, the benefit of this statement of intent should be obvious—it is the opposite of repudiation, so the uncertain party need not worry about the need to mitigate.

A few points regarding demanding adequate assurances are worth highlighting. First of all, the demand must be in writing. Of course, there is nothing wrong with asking for assurances verbally, but it will not count as a demand under section 2-609 and there may be no duty to respond. Second, while

---

1. This behavior by PatCo would likely be a breach of the duty of good faith but, as with all such claims, TerryCorp would have a very difficult time proving it, especially if PatCo knows what it is doing.

section 2-609 phrases the right to demand assurances as an option — the uncertain party is allowed to demand assurances — some courts have ruled that demanding assurances is a duty, and failure to do so will be held against the non-breaching party if the courts have to determine who breached and when. Just as important, demanding assurances is a way of avoiding, or at least postponing, the mitigation/breach tightrope, so it is difficult to imagine a scenario when demanding assurances would not be an advisable first step before deciding for, or against, the commencement of mitigation efforts.

Third, the right to demand assurances kicks in when there are reasonable grounds for insecurity, which means that the right is contextual. Similarly, Article 2 is largely silent on what, exactly, constitutes "adequate" assurances, although section 2-611 does state that a repudiating party can be required to provide assurances. Also, section 2-609 states that commercial standards will be used to determine what meets both standards in a dispute between merchants. Given the stricter requirements on merchants throughout Article 2, it is likely that a consumer will be given more leeway, and a merchant less when it comes to a determination of reasonableness. This determination matters because the party causing the uncertainty might dispute even the right to demand assurances, claiming that there are not reasonable grounds for insecurity — essentially, that the other party is paranoid — or that the assurances demanded are too demanding.

Once the uncertain party has demanded assurances, two things happen. The first is that the demanding party may be entitled to suspend performance if doing so is "commercially reasonable." The second is that, if the other party receives the demand, and either does not respond, responds after a commercially reasonable time (there's that standard, again) not to exceed 30 days, or responds without providing "adequate" assurances, the uncertain party can treat the refusal to respond as a repudiation and begin efforts at mitigation and any remedies available to it. The party providing assurances will always claim that those assurances are adequate, so any attempt to treat assurances as inadequate and proceed as though the contract has been repudiated is likely to lead to litigation.

To see how this would work, we turn to our previous example. TerryCorp has been hearing the rumors about PatCo's production difficulties, so there is already some uncertainty about PatCo's ability to perform. TerryCo has its own contracts to meet, so it is concerned about the situation. When TerryCorp hears about the emergency shutdown, what were mere concerns become very real probabilities of default. TerryCorp has its lawyer draft a professional letter asking for an update on the shutdown, and asking for an official timetable for the production facility's reopening, as well as an official confirmation that PatCo will perform and provide the postcards. Two weeks later, PatCo sends a letter in response, promising to deliver the postcards, as promised, but providing no timetable for reopening the facility.

PatCo has responded, but in a way that might mean that the response doesn't count as adequate assurances. First of all, it took PatCo two weeks to respond. In a fast-moving market, or in a short-term contract, that might not be within a commercially reasonable time. For example, if the response comes only one week before performance is due, the response may not have come soon enough, giving TerryCorp the right to consider the contract as repudiated. Second, PatCo didn't give a timeline for reopening the production facility, which is the source of TerryCorp's uncertainty. Even though PatCo has stated that it will still perform, it hasn't given any evidence that it has the production capacity to actually perform. As a result, the assurances that PatCo has given are probably not "adequate," and TerryCorp can consider the contract repudiated. So, TerryCorp can immediately seek out substitute performance and sue for damages.

One word of caution should be offered here with regard to adequate assurances. Though the uncertain party may demand adequate assurances, it cannot attempt to unilaterally modify the contract through its assurances. For instance, assume that TerryCorp demands that PatCo post a bond in the amount of $10,000 as part of its assurances, so that, if PatCo breaches, TerryCorp can draw upon the bond to cover some of its damages. This would be an extra-contractual demand that would likely go beyond a mere assurance, and wander into the land of coercive behavior. In some instances, the line can be a close one. Generally, a simple explanation in writing of how the other party intends to address the concerns is not too onerous and will be upheld.

Checkpoints

- A party can repudiate a contract either expressly or impliedly.

- Express repudiation must be unambiguous.

- Implied repudiation occurs when actions make it plainly impossible to perform.

- The non-breaching party can wait a commercially reasonable time after repudiation, but must then start mitigation efforts.

- The breaching party can retract the repudiation at any time before the next deadline for performance or until the non-breaching party accepts the repudiation.

- If the non-breaching party is uncertain regarding repudiation, or the capacity of the other party to perform, it can demand reasonable assurances.

- If assurances don't come, aren't adequate, or aren't given in a commercially reasonable time, the uncertain party can consider the contract repudiated.

Chapter 14

Impracticability

Roadmap

- Excuse by impracticability
- Unexpected contingency
- Unallocated risk
- Performance is impracticable
- When identified goods are harmed
- Effect on the parties' responsibilities

A. Excuse by Impracticability

The doctrine of impracticability — or commercial impracticability to be more precise — comes into play when something unexpected happens and the landscape of the contract changes dramatically. If the change is severe enough, the parties might be excused from performance. The essence of excuse is that, under the right circumstances, the contract just goes away. In other words, the court declares that both parties get to go their separate ways and no further action is required by either side. Of course, if we let courts excuse performance on a regular basis, no one would be able to fully trust that the other side would do what they promised. As a result, excuse is only allowed in very specific circumstances.

Section 2-615 excuses performance when there is a "Failure of Presupposed Conditions."

(a) Delay in delivery or non-delivery in whole or in part by a seller who complies with paragraphs (b) and (c) is not a breach of his duty under a contract for sale if performance as agreed has been made impracticable by the occurrence of a contingency the non-occurrence of which was a basic assumption on which the contract was made or by compliance in good faith with any applicable foreign or domestic governmental regulation or order whether or not it later proves to be invalid.

U.C.C. § 2-615.* If something occurs and the parties had planned on it not happening and, as a result, didn't decide who would bear the risk, the seller's failing to deliver might not be a breach of the contract, but only if delivery is "impracticable." A seller's performance might also be excused if performance is impracticable because the seller was complying "in good faith with any applicable foreign or domestic governmental regulation or order."

1. Unexpected contingency

The most important thing to remember about the doctrine of excuse is that it does not exist to save parties from bad contracts. It is not enough, therefore, that something changes and now the contract is one that will cause the buyer or seller to lose money. The only way excuse is available is if the unexpected event was not anticipated by either of the parties. In fact, it goes even further than this. Section 2–615 says that excuse by impracticability is only available when the non-occurrence of the contingency was a basic assumption of the bargain. This type of legal phrasing drives most normal people crazy, so let's break this down.

When two parties are contemplating a bargain, they each must consider whether the bargain will be a good deal or not, including the things that could go wrong with the deal to make it less profitable. In a complicated world, there are almost an infinite number of things that could go wrong—contingencies— but only a finite amount of time to say yes or no to the deal. After all, even time costs money, so the more time spent worrying about contingencies, the costlier the deal becomes and the less likely it will be worth doing, at all. What that means is that parties to the contract only have time to worry about the most important contingencies, those that are more likely to occur, or those that have more severe consequences if they do. Many contingencies just aren't worth worrying about, because both parties are convinced that those particular bad outcomes just won't happen. In order to invoke excuse by impracticability, then, a party needs to be able to point to a contingency that both parties assumed would not occur. This is not just the list of everything that the parties left out of the contract, however, because the courts can rely on

---

implications from the contract language and context of the contract to reach their conclusion.

Consider an example: GrainCo has hired ShipCo to transport wheat from Kansas to California. The contract requires delivery by October 31 and sets the price at $5 per ton. The contract also provides that ShipCo will have an additional week to deliver the wheat if early snows close the Colorado mountain passes. As ShipCo begins loading the grain in Wichita, Kansas, it receives word that there has been an avalanche in Colorado and the rail lines are no longer serviceable. However, the avalanche was not caused by snow, but by an earthquake. Both parties assumed that snow-caused avalanches were possible, and the contract provides for how to deal with them. If snow had closed the pass, excuse by impracticability would not be available, because the parties thought of snow closures. But, because the contract is silent as to what happens if an earthquake is responsible for closing the passes, the court has to decide whether the parties planned on no other type of closure occurring. The court could conclude that the parties assumed that earthquakes wouldn't happen, so that impracticability is an available defense, or the court could conclude that the parties understood that closure of the passes was possible and place the burden on ShipCo to find another way to get the grain to California on time.

2. Unallocated risk

If a contingency occurs and the parties assumed it wouldn't, then impracticability might be available as an excuse, but the court will still want to check and see whether the risk was allocated somewhere in the contract. Section 2-615 says that the seller can be excused from performance for impracticability, "[e]xcept so far as a seller may have assumed a greater obligation." If the parties have allocated the risk expressly in the contract, this part of the analysis will be easy. In our previous example, for instance, if the passes are closed due to snow, ShipCo is given one extra week to perform. In that case, risk has been allocated between the parties. GrainCo bears some risk, because it must deal with the fact that the wheat may not arrive for an additional week. ShipCo also bears some risk, because it must find a way to get the wheat to California within that additional week.

More difficult is a situation where the contract is silent as to the allocation of risk. The court could conclude in that situation that the parties did not allocate the risk, and impracticability is on the table. Alternatively, the court could determine that the parties intended to allocate risk according to some broader principle of contract law, such as the least-cost-avoider doctrine. Under least cost avoider, courts presume that the parties to the contract wanted risk to be borne by the party that has the ability to mitigate the risk at the lowest cost. Doing so makes sure that risk is minimized and the total profits from the deal are maximized.

For example, ShipCo hears about the earthquake and the closed tracks and diverts the shipment south towards New Mexico. On the way, something ignites and sets one of the train cars on fire. Most of the grain is salvaged, but some is lost, and ShipCo might not be able to deliver the grain as promised—it might be in breach. The contract is silent regarding fires, so the court could excuse performance. More likely, however, is that the court will determine that the party in possession of the grain—ShipCo—agreed to bear the risk of a fire when it agreed to transport the grain. Why? Because it would be far more costly for GrainCo to protect its grain from fires than it would for ShipCo, who owns the train cars. ShipCo employees were in the best position to inspect the train cars and mitigate any fire risk before loading, and they are likely accompanying the grain to its destination. Because ShipCo could more easily and more cheaply keep the fire from happening in the first place, or put it out more quickly once it started, it is the least cost avoider of the problem, and the court may refuse to excuse it from performance.

3. Performance is impracticable

The final requirement that must be met before a contract can be excused is that performance is commercially impracticable. Commercial impracticability is one of those terms that only lawyers know and use but, as a simple baseline, you can think of it as meaning "outrageously expensive," because if the costs of performance aren't at least a little shocking, then it is highly unlikely that the contract is commercially impracticable. The standard under the common law was that excuse was available only when performance was literally impossible. That standard has been relaxed—although if performance is impossible, it will also be impracticable—but it would be a mistake to overstate how much the standard has been relaxed.

A contract is not impracticable merely because it would cause one party to lose money, even a lot of money. Instead, it must be so expensive that no one could be expected to perform and incur the expense. It may help to consider the difference between subjective impracticability and objective impracticability. When something is objectively impracticable, performance simply can't be accomplished without extreme expense. By contrast, when something is only subjectively impracticable, the individual responsible for performance believes that it can't be done without extreme expense, but it would fail a test for objective impracticability. For example, a farmer that has contracted to deliver 500 bushels of wheat only to have the crop destroyed by wildfire will find it personally impracticable to deliver the grain, but delivering 500 bushels of grain is not objectively impracticable — there are many other sources of grain that haven't been burned. The farmer will therefore be required to provide the grain, buying it from another farmer in order to comply with contractual obligations.[1] The exception to that would be if the farmer had promised grain from his own property.[2] In such a case — where the goods were identified to the contract (see below) — the contract would be objectively impracticable, and he would be excused from performance.

None of this answers the question: just how expensive does it have to be before it is impracticable? Some courts have set the standard at "unjust," in that it must be unjust to require performance. The U.C.C. does not force commercial actors to engage in behavior that is technically possible, but would waste a lot of resources. Some contracts, however, are just expensive, so an expensive performance might still be required if doing so is not completely outside normal parameters. Likewise, the test is not the impact on the parties, and a business might not be excused even though it faces bankruptcy if it performs, if that outcome is likely only because it had been irresponsible up to that point.

4. When identified goods are harmed

Section 2-613 describes a specific situation where impracticability is met:

> Where the contract requires for its performance goods identified when the contract is made, and the goods suffer casualty without fault of either party before the risk of loss passes to the buyer, or in a proper case under a "no arrival, no sale" term (Section 2-324) then
>
> (a) if the loss is total the contract is avoided; and
>
> (b) if the loss is partial or the goods have so deteriorated as no longer to conform to the contract the buyer may nevertheless demand inspection and at his option either treat the contract as avoided or

---

1. Just in case you are worried about the farmer, most farmers have insurance for just this sort of contingency. In fact, this distinction should impress upon you the importance of insurance, generally.

2. Comment 5 to section 2-615 notes, "Where a particular source of supply is exclusive under the agreement and fails through casualty, the present section applies rather than the provision on destruction or deterioration of specific goods [2-613]. The same holds true where a particular source of supply is shown by the circumstances to have been contemplated or assumed by the parties at the time of contracting."

accept the goods with due allowance from the contract price for the deterioration or the deficiency in quantity but without further right against the seller.

U.C.C. § 2-613.* The two requirements for this section to apply are that the goods are identified when the contract is made and that the harm to the goods not be the fault of either party. Identification of goods is, in essence, picking specific goods that the seller must deliver, as opposed to accepting whichever goods from seller's pile of similar goods seller chooses to send along.[3] So, if the parties had identified which goods were to be delivered and those goods were damaged, the seller is not allowed or expected to ship replacement goods. Instead, section 2-613 kicks in to determine the responsibilities of the parties. If the goods have been completely destroyed, then the contract cannot be completed, at no fault of either party. If the goods have only been damaged, the seller must still deliver, but buyer has limited options: either accept what has been delivered and pay a price discounted to reflect the goods' deteriorated value, or else consider the contract avoided.

B. Effect on the Parties' Responsibilities

If a court decides that performance is commercially impracticable, it will excuse performance. In that case, it is important to remember that the contract, itself, has been excused, so that both parties walk away. If by that time, one of the parties has already partially performed, it could possibly seek to

---

* Uniform Commercial Code, copyright © by the American Law Institute and the National Conference of Commissioners on Uniform State Laws. Reproduced with the permission of the Permanent Editorial Board for the Uniform Commercial Code. All rights reserved.

3. Generally, identification can occur however the parties jointly decide but, in the absence of express agreement, identification occurs

   (a) when the contract is made if it is for the sale of goods already existing and identified;

   (b) if the contract is for the sale of future goods other than those described in paragraph (c), when goods are shipped, marked or otherwise designated by the seller as goods to which the contract refers;

   (c) when the crops are planted or otherwise become growing crops or the young are conceived if the contract is for the sale of unborn young to be born within twelve months or the next normal harvest season after contracting whichever is longer.

U.C.C. § 2-501(1). The latter two provisions are inapplicable to this Chapter, but worth remembering, because other provisions in future Chapters will require an understanding of identification of goods.

recover the value of the benefit that it had bestowed, through a theory of unjust enrichment. For example, if ShipCo gets the grain to New Mexico only to discover that the train tracks there have also been destroyed by the earthquake, a court may find that ShipCo is excused from performance. That means that it no longer has any obligation to get the grain to California or anywhere else, but it also means that GrainCo has no legal obligation to pay ShipCo. ShipCo can leave the grain in New Mexico and find other grain shipments to haul, but what about the expenses that ShipCo has incurred getting the grain to New Mexico? Under a theory of quantum meruit—Latin for "as much as deserved"—the court can require GrainCo to pay ShipCo for whatever GrainCo has gained having the grain in New Mexico, rather than Kansas. If shipping by truck from New Mexico to California is $1 million cheaper than if the grain were in Kansas, GrainCo can be ordered to pay ShipCo $1 million. Importantly, however, notice that the amount is based on the *benefit* to GrainCo, not the *cost* to ShipCo. And notice that ShipCo is not *legally* entitled to this amount, but is asking the court to award the amount in equity, based on principles of fairness rather than strict legal principles.

In some instances, only a portion of the goods may become impracticable to deliver. For instance, suppose ABC Corp. is under contract to supply computers to both Company Y and Company Z. Company Y is to get 40 computers and Z is to get 10. A section 2-615 event occurs destroying much of ABC Corp.'s inventory so that only 10 remain. What are ABC Corp.'s options? It could choose to do one of three things: 1) it could satisfy Co. Z fully and leave Y in the lurch; 2) it could divert all its computers to Co. Y as it is a bigger customer; or 3) it could split delivery, but how? Section 2-615(b) favors the third approach.

> (b) Where the causes mentioned in paragraph (a) affect only a part of the seller's capacity to perform, he must allocate production and deliveries among his customers but may at his option include regular customers not then under contract as well as his own requirements for further manufacture. He may so allocate in any manner which is fair and reasonable.*

So what is a fair and reasonable split? A pro rata approach is usually acceptable. So here we have a commitment of 50 computers total and only 10 left, meaning 4/5 (or 8 computers) go to Co. Y and 1/5 (2) go to Co. Z.

Checkpoints

- Under the right circumstances, an unexpected occurrence can excuse performance.

- Excuse is available only if the occurrence is something that the parties assumed would not happen.

- Excuse is available only if neither party accepted the risk of the occurrence happening.

- Assumption of risk can be found implicitly, as through the least-cost-avoider doctrine.

- Excuse is available only if performance would be commercially impracticable, or so expensive as to make it unjust to require performance.

- If goods identified to the contract are harmed, the contract will be partially or completely avoided due to the impracticability of delivering the identified goods.

- If performance is excused for one party, the entire contract is excused and both parties can walk away.

- If either party has partially performed, it might recover the value of the benefit bestowed, based on equitable claims for unjust enrichment.

- If impracticability only affects part of the seller's ability to perform, the seller must allocate the goods to its customers in a fair and reasonable manner, usually on a pro rata basis.

Chapter 15

Unconscionability

Roadmap

- Unconscionability
- Procedural unconscionability
- Absence of meaningful choice
- Unequal bargaining power
- Contracts of adhesion
- Substantive unconscionability
- Unconscionability is rarely successful

A. Unconscionability

To understand what unconscionability is, and why we have it as a principle of contract law, we need to start with a reminder of the goals of contract law. We enforce contracts because we want to respect free individuals' intent to bind themselves to each other. We do this because we respect their autonomy as individuals, and because voluntary transactions make both sides better off. After all, a rational person will agree to a transaction only when she believes that what she stands to gain is worth more than what she has to give up. There will be times when parties to a transaction estimate the costs and benefits badly but, by and large, people do a pretty good job, particularly in contracts for the sale of goods. When we enforce contracts, people enter into more contracts, because they have confidence that they will receive what they were promised. In this way, contract law is about facilitating voluntary transactions so people can make their lives better. In the case of Article 2 of the U.C.C., facilitating the sale of goods makes a lot of people better off, because those goods are often resold to many more people.

What happens, though, when contracts aren't voluntary? We are hesitant to enforce those contracts because they likely won't make people's lives better. Instead, enforcing those contracts might actually be supporting exploitation.

If a party to a contract was literally forced to sign a contract, we call that coercion or duress, and we won't enforce that involuntary contract. If a contract was signed only because one party actively lied to the other—or, at the very least, hid important things about the transaction—we call that fraud or misrepresentation, and we won't enforce that contract because it wasn't really voluntary, either. We don't enforce contracts signed by those who don't have the mental capacity to consent, including those with severe mental disorders, those who are severely drunk, and those under the age of eighteen. This last one is more than a little paternalistic and demeaning to teenagers, but society had to draw a line and they chose the legal age of majority. It is fair to disagree, but you still need to know the law.

Section 2-302 of the U.C.C. also allows a judge to refuse to enforce a contract that it finds unconscionable, but what is unconscionability and how does it fit in with the rest of these doctrines? The U.C.C. does not define unconscionability, but relies on the common law definition, which distills largely to a question of severe unfairness. Most courts require that contracts be both procedurally unconscionable (which addresses contract formation) and substantively unconscionable (addressing the terms themselves) before granting relief. We address each of these below, but basically, the doctrine of unconscionability gives us a tool for dealing with contracts that don't look right, even though the parties all seem to have given real and meaningful consent. One way it is described is that unconscionable contracts yield an unfair surprise to one of the parties when enforced. That unfair surprise might arise from the process or the substance of the contract.

B. Procedural Unconscionability

A contract might be so fundamentally unfair that we won't enforce it if the party complaining about the contract didn't really have a fair chance to make a good bargain while the contract was being made. This is not duress or coercion, where the party was literally forced to sign, but the process was manipulative enough that it still doesn't feel right to enforce it. It is also not fraud, in that the party wasn't induced to sign by outright lies, but important terms were left unexplained and hidden. In other words, while the contract may have been entered into voluntarily, any choice was not meaningful. This is more likely to be the case when one of the parties has significantly more bargaining power, and can therefore manipulate the contracting process. The resulting contract may be unenforceable if it was created in a way that left one party without any real choice in the matter.

1. Absence of meaningful choice

If consent to the contract is induced through force or threats of force, that is duress and the contract will not be enforced. Unlike duress, procedural unconscionability still has the appearance of voluntary choice, but meaningful choice is said to be missing because the process did not allow the complaining party to really understand the terms. Perhaps the terms were buried in mountains of legalese, or maybe the terms themselves were written in such a complex way that the complaining party could not reasonably be expected to understand their meaning, given the knowledge, education, etc., of that party.

For example, imagine that Bert is hoping to buy a new car, and he has heard that electric cars are more environmentally friendly. He visits a showroom and picks out the model that he wants to purchase. As he begins to fill out the necessary paperwork, he is amazed by the sheer quantity of forms that he has to sign. He skims each form and doesn't notice anything objectionable, so he signs. Twelve months later, he discovers that his car is no longer charging, and returns it to the dealership for maintenance under the service plan he remembered from the sales pitch. He is very disappointed to hear that, given a mistake he made in charging the car, the car cannot be fixed, the dealer and manufacturer have disclaimed all liability, and he must pay back certain incentives he received when buying the car. When he complains that this is unfair, Bert is informed that it was in the contract that he signed. Concerned that he missed something, Bert reviews the documents but still can't figure out what the dealer is talking about. Finally, the dealer shows him the provision in question, on page 51 of the 121-page contract, at the end of a paragraph discussing preferred methods of charging the batteries.

As a preliminary matter, recall that we are all presumed to have read the contracts we sign, so ignorance of terms will not normally save us. In this case, it could be even worse for Bert, because he actually read the whole contract, and could have asked for clarification if he didn't understand any of the terms. However, the length of the contract could make a court nervous that hard terms were intentionally hidden away in a seemingly unrelated term, just so consumers wouldn't notice it. If the language of the clause, itself, is exceptionally vague, that will also make the court nervous, and the court's concerns could be heightened even more if Bert is an unsophisticated party. Every additional bit of evidence that points towards Bert not really having a shot at understanding the terms will increase the likelihood that the court will decide that Bert had no meaningful choice and that the clause is unconscionable. Courts address the procedural unconscionability prong within the context of the transaction, and so factors such as Bert's age, education and relative sophistication may all be relevant considerations.

2. Unequal bargaining power

Related to the absence of meaningful choice, a contract might be procured in an unconscionable manner if one of the parties has unfair bargaining power. It is not enough to say that one party had *more* bargaining power, because most transactions have some imbalance of power, and very few of them can really be considered to be unfair. The imbalance must be so unequal that the relationship cannot be seen as fair. One scenario where there might be unequal bargaining power is when there is a monopolist or monopsonist, economics terms for a single seller or a single buyer, respectively. If there is only one person the buyer can buy from, then a monopoly exists and that monopolist can get away with shenanigans that a regular seller couldn't (because the buyer can't take its business elsewhere). Similarly, if there is only one person who can buy from a seller, then a monopsony exists and the monopsonist can abuse sellers because they have no other options. In either case—or in other cases where there is unfair bargaining power—the court will consider relative bargaining positions in addition to the factors surrounding the complaining party's ability to understand and appreciate the terms.

For example, imagine that while Bert is dealing with the electric car situation, things go from bad to worse, because a hurricane comes ashore near the coastal city where Bert lives. Power is out all over the city and Bert, who is diabetic, is worried because he needs a working refrigerator to store the insulin he needs to survive. He is able to find only one supplier of portable generators, who is not only charging extra for the unit but is also requiring buyers to sign a contract waiving all sorts of liability. He purchases the generator and hopes for the best, but given the extreme bargaining power exerted by the seller, a court might not enforce those waivers if it finds them fundamentally unfair and, as a result, unconscionable.

3. Contracts of adhesion

One question that often comes up in any discussion of unconscionability is what to do with contracts of adhesion. Also known as standard form contracts, contracts of adhesion are contracts that are presented in a take-it-or-leave-it scenario. Essentially, one party to the contract offers a pre-printed contract for the other party to accept or reject. There is no bargaining to be done, because the party who brought the standard form contract will only do business according to the terms of the contract. Anyone who wants different terms will have to find a different counterparty. At first glance, this may seem like textbook procedural unconscionability, since one party has no choice as to the terms of the contract, but these contracts aren't some sinister plot. Instead, they are nothing more than businesses responding to the commercial realities of a modern, global marketplace. A company that has access to the internet has access to billions of potential customers worldwide, and it cannot realistically bargain with each of them. The only way to make modern e-commerce work is to standardize contracts so that the cost of doing business stays low. Also, even if the contract is a contract of adhesion, there can still be meaningful choice if there are lots of competitors in the market, so you can still say no to one contract and sign a different standard form contract. All of this means that, while courts will certainly consider the existence of a contract of adhesion, that will not be sufficient for the court to find procedural unconscionability.

C. Substantive Unconscionability

A contract that is procured without the type of flaws described above might still be found to be unconscionable if the substance of the contract is inherently unjust. The normal case where substantive unconscionability is found will be a contract that appears to benefit one party too strongly. To illustrate the point, imagine the extreme case, where every term in the contract benefitted one party at the expense of another. It is very difficult to imagine that contract as being the result of bargaining by free, rational individuals. Instead, it looks like one party was coerced into giving the other party a gift, or set of gifts. It would be quite strange to find a contract that fits that extreme example, but courts may be faced with a contract that is weighted heavily in favor of one party. When that happens, the court has to decide whether it is so bad that it loses the appearance of a voluntary transaction.

One standard that courts have come up with to describe the point at which the contract crosses the line is when it "shocks the conscience." While not exactly a model of precision, this standard at least illustrates that it takes a significant amount of imbalance for the courts to decide that a contract is substantively unconscionable. The task of the courts is complicated by the fact that, according to section 2-302, a court can find that only certain parts of the contract are unconscionable, and many terms only benefit one party. Of course, in the context of the whole bargain, those terms are likely balanced against other terms that benefit primarily the second party. So, if the court looks at a single clause, it might look so unbalanced that it shocks the conscience, but it is part of a larger tradeoff in which both parties get what they want. It is for that reason that section 2-302(2) expressly requires the court to allow the parties to present evidence of the larger context.

It is perhaps because of these difficulties that courts rarely seem to rely on substantive unconscionability. They may reference an unfair imbalance in the terms of the contract, but usually only after they have explained why the contract is procedurally unconscionable. In fact, it is difficult to untangle at least part of procedural unconscionability—unequal bargaining power—from the question of an unfair imbalance. Why would someone agree to a contract that unfairly advantages the other party? The answer would seem to be that the first party had no real choice because the second party was holding all the cards. The end result is that unconscionability analysis tends to rest far more on procedural analysis than on substantive analysis.

D. Unconscionability Is Rarely a Successful Claim

In the end, unconscionability almost always loses. There are a number of reasons for this, although a large part almost certainly rests on the fact that even the U.C.C. does not require a court to do anything about an unconscionable contract; section 2-302 merely says that a court *can* say no to those contracts or clauses. Note that the power to decide whether a contract or clause is unconscionable is left to the court, not a jury, to decide. The reason for this is the drafters of Article 2 feared a jury might too easily find a contract unconscionable when faced with a sympathetic claimant—which may be another reason such claims fail. However, once a court finds a contract or clause to be unconscionable, section 2-302 grants the court broad powers to act as it feels is most equitable. Though this can mean voiding the entire contract, section 2-302 also permits the court to "enforce the remainder of the contract without the unconscionable clause, or . . . so limit the application of any unconscionable clause as to avoid any unconscionable result." Thus, even when there is evidence of unconscionability, a court might still enforce the contract. And if the court decides to act on the evidence of unconscionability, it might stop short of refusing to enforce the contract and either strike certain provisions of the contract or modify them in a way that makes them "conscionable."

Why would a court be reluctant to invoke unconscionability? The lack of precision in the standards for unconscionability analysis—"meaningful" choice, "unequal" bargaining power, "unfair" terms that "shock the conscience"—makes unconscionability a powerful tool, but one that could do more damage than good, if used too often. If the courts regularly refuse to enforce contracts because they think the contracts are bad contracts, or even because they think that the parties entering the contracts are bad people, it will reduce the certainty that contracts of any sort will be enforced. That will lead fewer people to enter into contracts, which would strike at the heart of contract law, which is to facilitate *more* voluntary bargains. Knowing this, most courts are extremely reluctant to declare a contract unconscionable, reserving it for those contracts that would seem to garner almost unanimity for the proposition that they are outlandishly bad.

Checkpoints

- A court can refuse to enforce a contract it deems unconscionable.
- Unconscionability analysis is foundationally a question of fairness.
- Most courts require a contract to be both procedurally and substantively unconscionable before granting relief.
- A contract can be procedurally unconscionable if one of the parties is denied a meaningful choice because unfair terms were hidden in the contract.
- A contract can be procedurally unconscionable if one of the parties' bargaining power was so unequal that it borders on duress.
- A standard form contract, or contract of adhesion, may be evidence of procedural unconscionability, but is not per se unconscionable.
- A contract can be substantively unconscionable if the terms of the contract are so heavily weighted to the benefit of one party that it is shockingly unfair.
- Unconscionability is decided by a judge rather than a jury.
- If a contract or clause is found to be unconscionable, a court may void the entire contract, or excise the offending clause, or reform the contract to avoid the unconscionable effect.
- Due to the effect the doctrine has on commercial contracting, courts rarely invoke it.

Chapter 16

Rejection and Revocation

Roadmap

- Rejecting non-conforming goods
- Must be seasonable
- Must give notice
- Revoking acceptance
- Nonconformity must substantially impair the value
- Believed nonconformity would be cured
- Burden of proof shifts

A. Rejecting Non-Conforming Goods

Rejection was first discussed back in Chapter 12, but the devil, as they say, is often in the details, so we now return to a more precise explanation of what happens when non-conforming goods show up and the buyer wishes to exercise her right to refuse them. Before we do, however, recall that the U.C.C. requires perfect tender, which means that what is delivered must be exactly what was promised, including the method of delivery. The only time exact compliance won't be required is in the case of an installment contract, as those contracts have their own set of standards. Another important reminder from Chapter 12 is that application of certain interpretive rules—usage of trade, course of dealing, and course of performance—may mean that there is some wiggle room in determining what the contract language means.

With those concepts in mind, we can turn to an analysis of rejection. The first question you should always ask yourself when it comes to rejection is whether the goods were exactly as promised. If they are, then the buyer is not allowed to reject, and doing so will subject the buyer to damages for breach of contract. If, however, the goods that show up are not as promised, then the buyer has the right to reject, but must do so in accordance with a few simple rules. First, section 2-602 requires the buyer to reject within a reasonable time and "seasonably" notify the seller. Section 1-205 defines seasonable as being within a reasonable time, so the buyer has to reject and notify within a reasonable time after the goods are tendered. As with most applications of a reasonableness standard, that means that the buyer's rejection will be judged contextually.

1. Must reject in a reasonable time

If a buyer has determined that the goods are nonconforming and wants to reject, it must do so in a reasonable time. Exactly how long that is will depend a lot on the type of goods being sold, as well as other details about the transaction. For example, if the goods are freshly-baked goods, they begin to lose value very quickly, potentially becoming stale within hours, rather than days. For freshly-baked goods, then, a reasonable rejection might have to happen within minutes, allowing the seller to find another buyer who will take not-quite-as-fresh baked goods. On the other end of the spectrum, durable goods like refrigerators and dishwashers will not spoil, so a reasonable rejection might still occur days later.

Other factors may impact the reasonableness of rejection, such as geography. Consider a set of large tents being delivered to a summer camp in the remote mountains of Wyoming. Getting to the goods and inspecting them could take a while, and a court's analysis of reasonableness must take this into consideration. Along the same lines, if a delivery is made early—say five days early—the buyer might not be available to inspect the goods right away, so what would have been a reasonable time period under normal circumstances might need to be extended. In theory, because reasonableness isn't something that can be precisely measured, many different factors might be relevant.

The requirement to reject within a reasonable time serves multiple purposes, including at least one significant benefit to the buyer who is rejecting the goods. Because the duty to mitigate kicks in, the buyer has strong incentives to reject in a timely manner and begin looking for substitute goods. Since the seller may have a right to attempt a cure—also covered in Chapter 12— giving notice within a reasonable time might allow the seller to provide conforming goods. If seller can do that, the buyer will not have to expend any time or money trying to find a substitute provider. In a larger sense, requiring rejection within a reasonable time keeps commerce flowing, which benefits us all.

2. Must give seasonable notice

In addition to rejecting within a reasonable time, the buyer must provide seasonable notification to the seller of the rejection. Since the U.C.C. defines seasonable as being within a reasonable time, the two requirements for rejection have significant overlap. The decision to reject must come within a reasonable time and notice to the seller must also come within a reasonable time. In most cases, the two will happen at almost the same time, with the buyer rejecting and either calling or e-mailing the seller to let it know of the rejection. The terms are not completely redundant, however, because there may be times when notice cannot be provided in such a rapid manner.

For example, returning to an example from Chapter 12, ShoeCorp receives a shipment of athletic shoelaces that are not quite the right shade of blue. ShoeCorp determines that the shoelaces are not conforming and decides to reject them. That decision must be made in a reasonable time and, given the non-perishable nature of the goods, ShoeCorp will likely have hours or maybe a day to decide. Normally, ShoeCorp would simply send an e-mail to its supplier, Laces-R-Us, but Laces-R-Us is based on the coast of the Gulf of Mexico and a sizeable hurricane has just come ashore, knocking out power and telephone lines across the region. It is therefore impossible to contact Laces-R-Us through the normal means, and ShoeCorp must decide whether to wait for power and phone service to be restored or send a rejection notice by courier or mail. In either case, ShoeCorp's rejection within a reasonable time will occur a significant period of time prior to ShoeCorp's "seasonable" notice to Laces-R-Us.

B. Revoking Acceptance

Up to this point, we have been talking about how to reject nonconforming goods that are delivered, but what if the buyer doesn't reject? Sometimes, it will make more sense to accept non-conforming goods and sue for damages. In that case, the buyer's choice determines its available remedies, and revocation is not available. However, there are times when the buyer might be entitled to revoke its acceptance, reversing its earlier decision and returning the goods. Section 2-608, which covers revocation of acceptance, states:

> (1) the buyer may revoke his acceptance of a lot or commercial unit whose non-conformity substantially impairs its value to him if he has accepted it

(a) on the reasonable assumption that its non-conformity would be cured and it has not been seasonably cured; or

(b) without discovery of such non-conformity if his acceptance was reasonably induced either by the difficulty of discovery before acceptance or by the seller's assurances.

(2) Revocation of acceptance must occur within a reasonable time after the buyer discovers or should have discovered the ground for it and before any substantial change in condition of the goods which is not caused by their own defects. It is not effective until the buyer notifies the seller of it.

(3) A buyer who so revokes has the same rights and duties with regard to goods involved as if he had rejected them.

U.C.C. § 2-608.* According to section 2-608(3), revocation places the buyer in the same position as if it had rejected, so it preserves all of the buyer's remedies for breach. In simpler terms, sometimes the buyer made a mistake in accepting the goods and wants to effectively turn back the clock and reject the goods. Section 2-608 gives the buyer that opportunity, under certain circumstances.

The first scenario in which the buyer will be allowed to revoke is if it accepted because it wasn't aware of the nonconformity, either because it was very difficult to find or because the seller assured buyer that everything was fine. The buyer always has the right and responsibility to inspect the goods for nonconformities, and in most circumstances, if the buyer missed something, it doesn't get a second chance to reject. In case you think this sounds terribly unfair, remember that the buyer will still have the right to sue for damages, so it will be made whole, just not through perfect tender. However, if it wasn't the buyer's fault — perhaps because the defects were not reasonably apparent, or because seller's assurances that there weren't any defects short-circuited the inspection — the buyer might still have a chance to revoke.

The second scenario where acceptance can be revoked is when the buyer knew the goods had some defect, but the seller offered to cure. In that case, the buyer was planning on rejecting but was willing to give the seller a chance to make it right. If the seller doesn't make it right, then the acceptance was, in effect, induced by false promises of cure by the seller. In a case like that, it makes sense to allow the buyer to return to its original decision to reject by allowing it to revoke its acceptance. In either case, the buyer must revoke within a reasonable time after the nonconformity is found or should have been found.

With revocation, there will be some costs associated with the fact that the goods were initially accepted, and now they must be returned. The U.C.C. is designed to minimize these types of costs, so we don't want revocation to happen too often. Therefore, section 2-608 only allows revocation when the nonconformity is so serious that it impairs the value of the goods and only before any substantial change in the condition of the goods occurs. And the burden of proof shifts, requiring a buyer that has accepted and wishes to revoke to prove these two factors.

1. Nonconformity must substantially impair the value

Revocation will only be available for goods that have defects that substantially impair their value. You should be thinking, right about now, that you've heard that standard somewhere before, and you have. It is also the standard for installment contracts. It is rare that the U.C.C. diverges from the perfect tender standard, and there is always a reason. In the case of installment contracts, you'll remember, the reason was that the contract and the relationship it represents is presumed to be more important to the parties than any given shipment, so more leeway is given to the seller in providing the goods. When it comes to revocation, the requirement that the nonconformity substantially impair the value is a way of making sure that the costs of revocation are not imposed when the benefits of revocation—curing a minor defect— are relatively low. If the defects are minor, the buyer's remedy is to sue for damages, not revocation. If the defects are substantial, and the other criteria are met, then the buyer will be allowed to revoke acceptance and return the goods.

2. No substantial change in condition

Section 2-608 imposes one other requirement for revocation. It is that revocation must occur "before any substantial change in condition of the goods which is not caused by their own defects." This requirement is an attempt to speed the return of the goods before they are made even worse. The seller has no way of protecting the goods once accepted because the goods belong to the buyer. The seller is responsible for the original defect but shouldn't be forced to bear the cost of additional defects that it did not cause. If the original defect gets worse just through the passage of time, and the buyer acts within a reasonable time, then it is fair to hold the seller responsible for any worsening of the defect. If there are new defects present in the goods, they arose because of the buyer's actions and are, therefore, the buyer's responsibility.

Section 2-608 says that, in cases such as this, buyer loses the right to revoke. If that seems unfair, just imagine the alternative rule, where buyer still has the right to revoke. The buyer would return the goods, leaving seller with goods even more damaged than when delivered to the buyer. The buyer is responsible for the loss, so seller must have the right to sue. In the end, the alternative rule would impose costs associated with returning the goods plus the legal costs to sort out damages. The rule established by section 2-608, on the other hand, leaves the goods in buyer's hands, with buyer being entitled to sue for damages caused by the original defect. The buyer is made whole in either scenario, but section 2-608 saves the cost of returning the goods, in keeping with the U.C.C.'s goals of making sales of goods more efficient.

3. Burden of proof shifts

When it comes to the burden of proof, the fact that it shifts is a natural result of the nature of the claims brought after a rejection, and after a revocation. If the buyer has rejected goods, the buyer is asserting that the goods are nonconforming. A seller who disputes that will bring a lawsuit claiming that the goods were conforming and that the buyer breached by rejecting them. Of course, the seller is the plaintiff, so the seller will bear the burden of proof and will have to establish that the goods were, in fact, conforming. Now consider a buyer who accepts but later revokes. The seller has likely received payment for the goods and will not be interested in accepting return of the goods and returning buyer's payment. The buyer who wishes to revoke, therefore, will have to file a lawsuit, and as the plaintiff, will bear the burden of proof. That will include showing that the goods were accepted either without knowledge of the defect or with the seller's assurance that the defect would be cured.

Checkpoints

- Goods that do not conform in every way to the contract may be rejected under the U.C.C.'s perfect tender rule.

- Rejection must be made in a reasonable time, given the context of the transaction.

- The seller must be notified in a reasonable time, which will often be, but need not necessarily be, contemporaneous to the rejection.

- If defective goods are accepted, the buyer's normal course of action is to sue for damages, but revocation may be possible.

- If the buyer knows of the defects, revocation is allowed only if the goods were accepted with a promise of cure that never materialized.

- If the buyer doesn't know of the defects, revocation is allowed only if the defect was difficult to discover or the seller's reassurances dissuaded buyer from inspecting.

- Revocation is only allowed if the defects are substantial.

- Revocation must occur within a reasonable time, and before any new defects are created.

- If seller disputes buyer's right to revoke, buyer will bear the burden of proving that revocation was appropriate.

Chapter 17

Privity

Roadmap

- Who has privity?
- Intended beneficiaries
- Creditor beneficiaries
- Donee beneficiaries
- Other intended beneficiaries
- Incidental beneficiaries
- Privity and warranties under the U.C.C.

A. Who Has Privity?

The word "privity" is used in a number of areas of the law, and it doesn't always have the same meaning, except that it usually means that two or more people have a relationship with legal significance. In the context of contract law, privity describes the relationship between the parties that have bargained for mutual promises from each other. The legal significance of their relationship is that their promises are legally binding, so the courts can step in if one party decides not to fulfill its promise. So, anyone who has agreed to an oral contract or has signed a written contract is in privity with all other parties to the contract and has the right to ask the courts to enforce the promises in the contract.

The foundations of privity considerations come from the common law, with the U.C.C. adding a layer of specialization for the application of express or implied warranties. Originally, the rule was that *only* parties to the contract could enforce the contract because *only* parties to the contract were in privity. Today, it is still the case that only parties to the contract have privity, but the law has evolved to allow some exceptions to that rule, so that third parties can, in some limited circumstances, enforce contractual promises.

The name almost certainly gives it away, but a third-party beneficiary is someone who was not a party to the contract but who benefits, in some way,

161

from the promises made in the contract. To be clear, just being interested in the outcome of the contract does not make someone a third-party beneficiary. In order to be a third-party beneficiary of the contract, fulfillment of the promises has to yield a direct benefit. If there will be a direct benefit to a third party, that party will be very interested in making sure the promises are kept. Occasionally, the third party will be disappointed and will want to file a lawsuit to enforce the promise that would have benefited it. The question then becomes whether the law allows that type of lawsuit to proceed, and the answer is that an *intended* beneficiary may enforce the promises that benefit it, while an *incidental* beneficiary may not.

B. Intended Beneficiaries

In contract law, one of the primary goals is to effectuate and enforce the intent of the parties, and so it is with beneficiaries. In order to decide whether a third party should be allowed to enforce the contract, we ask whether the actual parties to the contract intended that the third party should be allowed to do so. Hence, the name "intended beneficiary." It might seem strange that the parties would intentionally insert another party into the contract, allowing them to bring a lawsuit. After all, who wants more lawsuits in their life? In the end, courts are reluctant to allow third parties to sue, but they will do so when the context of the contract makes it clear that allowing a third party the right to sue was, in fact, what the parties wanted.

When will this be the case? Let's take a step back for a moment and remember that not all contracts are entirely selfish, so it is conceivable that the parties would be okay if someone else also gained something from their contract. Of course, just knowing—or even desiring—that someone else will be better off once the contract is complete isn't enough. The parties need to have anticipated and intended that the third party would also be allowed to enforce the contract. That is a little harder to imagine, although not impossible. The common law has developed two specific categories of beneficiaries that are *intended* beneficiaries. The first is *creditor* beneficiaries and the second is *donee* beneficiaries. The common law also recognizes a possibility of other intended beneficiaries that do not fit within these categories.

1. Creditor beneficiaries

In keeping with this Chapter's trend of terms that mean what they sound like, a creditor beneficiary is a third party who is also a creditor of one of the parties to the contract. In a typical scenario, the creditor needs to get paid, and the debtor is a party to a contract that requires the debtor's counterparty to pay the creditor, satisfying at least part of the debtor's obligation. The case of a creditor beneficiary is usually the easy case; the parties have made it clear that the creditor is to benefit from the contract — it will get paid — and there is a very believable story as to why the parties intended the creditor to be able to enforce the contract. Consider two simple examples:

Example 1: Bank has loaned Dan some money for a business venture. Every month, Dan (debtor) owes Bank (creditor) $500 in payment on the loan. Charley hires Dan to do some work, and pays Dan $500. Dan turns around and pays the $500 to Bank, which fulfills Dan's obligation for the month.

Example 2: Bank has loaned Dan some money for a business venture. Charley hires Dan to do some work, agreeing to pay the $500 directly to Bank, fulfilling Dan's obligation for the month.

In Example 2, Dan and Charley have made the payment process simpler and more efficient by cutting out Dan. Instead of Charley paying Dan and Dan paying Bank, Charley just pays Bank directly, making it faster and saving Dan some time and effort. We like efficiency in contract law, but efficiency isn't enough to enforce the contract here; we also need to inquire whether the parties intended to give Bank the right to enforce the contract. The rule on creditor beneficiaries answers that question in the affirmative, which shortcuts any analysis of why the parties might have agreed to give Bank that right. Consider a more nuanced example that better illustrates where the presumption of intent comes from.

Example 3: Bank has loaned Dan some money for a business venture. The day for the monthly payment is due, but Dan doesn't have the $500. He informs Bank that he does not have the money but that he is preparing to sign a contract with Charley in which he'll be entitled to $500. Dan promises to pay Bank when Charley pays. Bank agrees not to exercise its rights under the loan, but only if Charley pays Bank directly. Dan and Charley agree to include that clause in the contract. Dan performs the work, but Charley refuses to pay.

When Bank files a lawsuit to collect from Charley (Bank will probably also be enforcing its rights under the loan to Dan, but that's a separate question), it will win, because it is a creditor beneficiary. Even if there were not a specific category for creditor beneficiaries, though, Bank would still win, because the contract directly benefits Bank, and because Dan and Charley both knew and intended that Bank would have the right to sue. Dan needed Charley to pay Bank to satisfy the existing debt to Bank and Charley expressly agreed to make the payment. It's hard to imagine a scenario where Dan and Charley *didn't* intend for Bank to have a right to sue, but the case is even stronger because of this relationship. Bank had a preexisting right to get paid and would never have accepted a promise by Charley—a complete stranger—to pay unless it can enforce that promise, as well. Knowing that, Dan is now highly motivated to make sure that Charley understands the obligation, including that Bank can enforce it.

2. Donee beneficiaries

The second type of intended beneficiary is the donee beneficiary. These are individuals who have a special relationship with one of the parties to the contract; special enough that it makes sense that there was intent to let the beneficiary enforce the contract. Unlike a creditor beneficiary, however, there is no bright line test for when a third party becomes a donee beneficiary. The requirement of a direct benefit still applies, of course, since only then is a third party a beneficiary of the contract, but there is no clear distinction between someone who just happened to benefit from the contract and someone who benefitted due to the express intent of the parties to benefit the third party and bestow a right to enforce.

Part of the difficulty is that there is no general story—outside of the creditor context—for why the parties would have intended a third party to have the right to enforce. The relationship must be close *enough*, though it is not clear just how close. For example, family members often have close relationships, but does it need to be an immediate family member, or could it be part of an extended family? Also, it is often not difficult to think of friends who are more important than some family members, so even the family distinction does not seem capable of truly differentiating between intended beneficiaries and incidental beneficiaries. In the end, the courts are tasked with identifying whether the relationship is close enough that the court can envision the parties being willing to make the promise to the donee enforceable.

3. Other intended beneficiaries

Outside of creditors and donees, there is room for other individuals to be declared intended beneficiaries. The Restatement's general test for an intended beneficiary is that "the circumstances indicate that the promisee intends to give the beneficiary the benefit of the promised performance." From a practical standpoint, if a client's only hope of winning is to convince the court that "the circumstances" indicate that it was intended to have the right to enforce the contract, the likelihood of winning is probably pretty small.

C. Incidental Beneficiaries

If someone benefits from a contract, but does not fall into one of the categories of intended beneficiaries — creditor, donee, "other" — the beneficiary is designated as an incidental beneficiary. Incidental beneficiaries have zero rights under the contract, and may not enforce it, because the parties who put the contract together did not intend to grant them the right to sue. In most cases, their benefit is literally incidental, in that the parties didn't even anticipate that a benefit would be bestowed. In other cases, the benefit will be an anticipated side-effect of the contract, or it may even be a desired outcome, but unless the parties to the contract *intended* the third party to have the right to enforce, that third party is an incidental beneficiary.

D. Privity and Warranties Under the U.C.C.

Section 2-318 establishes an express category of intended beneficiaries, but only as it pertains to the warranties established by the contract. Section 2-318 is also unique in Article 2, in that it provides states with three alternatives for extending warranties beyond the buyer:

Alternative A

A seller's warranty whether express or implied extends to any natural person who is in the family or household of his buyer or who is a guest in his home if it is reasonable to expect that such a person may use, consume or be affected by the goods and who is injured in person by breach of the warranty. A seller may not exclude or limit the operation of this section.

Alternative B

A seller's warranty whether express or implied extends to any natural person who may reasonably be expected to use, consume or be affected by the goods and who is injured in person by breach of the warranty. A seller may not exclude or limit the operation of this section.

Alternative C

A seller's warranty whether express or implied extends to any person who may reasonably be expected to use, consume or be affected by the goods and who is injured by breach of the warranty. A seller may not exclude or limit the operation of this section with respect to injury to the person of an individual to whom the warranty extends.

U.C.C. § 2-318.* The three alternatives make slight changes to the class of individuals who are included as intended beneficiaries. Alternative A, which has become the majority rule, includes only those who are part of the buyer's household, while Alternatives B and C make no such qualification. Importantly, however, all three Alternatives have two common elements. First, the class of intended beneficiaries includes only those who would be reasonably expected "to use, consume or be affected by the goods." U.C.C. § 2-318. Second, sellers are restricted from attempting to exclude anyone from this statutorily created class of intended beneficiaries.

Careful consideration of section 2-318 should make it clear that this is not some dramatic expansion of privity. After all, whether the new intended beneficiaries are members of the buyer's household or any person who uses, consumes, or is affected by the goods, the requirement still exists that they had to be people that the parties should have reasonably expected to interact with the goods in question. If the goods are covered by an express warranty, it is reasonable to presume that the buyer considered not only its own use of the goods but also all others who might reasonably use the goods. Likewise, implied warranties of merchantability and fitness for a particular purpose offer some reassurance to the buyer, and the value of those reassurances includes the fact that others who might reasonably use the goods will also be protected. While these new intended beneficiaries might not easily fit into the category of creditor or donee beneficiary, the circumstances surrounding purchase of goods makes warranties the type of benefit that the buyer might easily have intended to pass to those covered by section 2-318, and the U.C.C. merely codifies that category.

One last discussion is important with regard to the last phrase of each Alternative, that "[a] seller may not exclude or limit the operation of this section." Comment 1 makes it clear that this language is not intended to limit the ability of the seller to control which warranties have been offered. Instead, the language was intended to make sure that, whatever warranties cover the goods extend to all those within the defined class of intended beneficiaries. In other words, a careful seller can still avoid express warranties by making sure no additional affirmations of fact become part of the basis of the bargain.

---

* Uniform Commercial Code, copyright © by the American Law Institute and the National Conference of Commissioners on Uniform State Laws. Reproduced with the permission of the Permanent Editorial Board for the Uniform Commercial Code. All rights reserved.

A careful seller can also follow the prescriptions of section 2-316 in limiting or excluding each or both implied warranties. Whatever warranties remain after those efforts by the seller, however, extend not only to the buyer but to the rest of the defined class of intended beneficiaries.

Checkpoints

- Those who sign their name to a contract—or who verbally agree to a binding contract—are in privity, and that privity includes the right to enforce promises.

- A third party who is not in privity may not enforce the contract *unless* it shows that the actual parties to the contract intended to give it the right to enforce.

- Intended beneficiaries may enforce; incidental beneficiaries may not.

- A third-party beneficiary who is also a creditor of one of the parties to the contract can be an intended beneficiary.

- A donee who has a special relationship with one of the parties might be able to enforce, if the relationship is close enough that the court can conclude that the parties intended to grant the right to enforce.

- Any other third party who wishes to enforce must show that the circumstances of the contract indicate that the parties intended to grant the right to enforce.

- Any third-party beneficiary that is not an intended beneficiary is an incidental beneficiary, and may not enforce.

- Each state can adopt one of three alternatives to establish a statutory class of intended beneficiaries of express and intended warranties.

- Sellers remain free to limit or exclude warranties but any warranties offered to the buyer extend to this statutory class of intended beneficiaries.

Chapter 18

Risk of Loss

Roadmap

- Why risk of loss is important
- When does it pass
- When goods are shipped
- The case of breach
- Least cost avoider

A. Why Risk of Loss Is Important

Parties to a contract usually feel very optimistic about their prospects, and how the contract will make them better off. Unfortunately, the world is an uncertain place, and things can happen that will make the contract less advantageous to one or both parties. In a contract for goods, one thing that will certainly ruin someone's day is loss or destruction of the goods. Someone is going to be poorer after everything gets sorted out, because either the buyer will have to pay for goods that it never got to use, or else the seller will not get paid for goods that were actually produced. The fact that valuable resources were used to make the goods guarantees that someone will lose, so the only question will be who bears the loss, and the answer will depend on who bore the risk of loss when the goods were lost or destroyed.

B. When Does It Pass?

As soon as the contract is signed, there is a risk of loss, because the seller has promised to deliver goods to the buyer. Until those goods have been provided to the buyer, seller's obligation persists, so for most of the duration of a contract, the risk of loss stays with the seller. A failure to deliver the goods as promised will subject the seller to liability for breach, even if the cause of the breach was not something under the seller's control. Something could go wrong with the production process, making the sale of goods unprofitable—such as would occur with a shortage of some important input. Or the goods could be completed but then destroyed in a fire. Short of something that meets the standards for commercial impracticability, no event will eliminate seller's obligation to deliver goods. All the time and money that seller put into procuring or producing the goods will yield zero benefits, since the seller will have to do it all again to meet its contractual obligations. Loss means twice the expense but only a single payment from buyer.

The U.C.C. establishes some basic ground rules for determining who bears the risk of loss, based in part on the understanding that a sale of goods is a "passing of title from the seller to the buyer." Anyone who has sat through a property law class should recognize that title is a representation of ownership, so a contract for the sale of goods is a contract for the transfer of ownership from the seller to the buyer. As a general rule, each individual is responsible for its own property, and bears the loss if something happens to that property. At some point during the contractual relationship between seller and buyer, title will pass from the former to the latter. According to section 2-401(1), the parties are allowed to pass title "in any manner and on any conditions explicitly agreed on by the parties."

Given the flexibility of this language, it would be impossible to list every way that title can be transferred, and to some extent, the job of a lawyer is to advise the client on how to structure the contract to minimize the risk of loss. There are a few general scenarios where the outcome is pretty well assured. For example, if the goods have been tendered by seller and accepted by buyer, then title to the goods will have transferred to the buyer, and the buyer, as the owner of the goods, will bear the entire risk of loss. On the other extreme, if the goods have been procured or produced, but are sitting in seller's warehouse, they still belong to the seller and seller will bear all the risk of loss. In some cases, the seller transfers possession to a third party, who holds the goods until the buyer comes to get them. In a case like that, section 2-509(2) states that risk of loss passes to the buyer either when the buyer receives a document of title or the third party acknowledges the buyer's right to possession of the goods.

1. When goods are shipped

More difficult than these two extremes are those cases where the goods have left the seller's physical possession but have not yet been delivered to—and accepted by—the buyer. Section 2-401(2) covers the default rules for when seller has completed its performance and title passes to the buyer:

(2) Unless otherwise explicitly agreed title passes to the buyer at the time and place at which the seller completes his performance with reference to the physical delivery of the goods, despite any reservation of a security interest and even though a document of title is to be delivered at a different time or place; and, in particular and despite any reservation of a security interest by the bill of lading

(a) if the contract requires or authorizes the seller to send the goods to the buyer but does not require him to deliver them at destination, title passes to the buyer at the time and place of shipment; but

(b) if the contract requires delivery at destination, title passes on tender there.

U.C.C. § 2-401(2).* Section 2-509(1) works in tandem with section 2-410(2), covering when risk of loss is passed:

(1) Where the contract requires or authorizes the seller to ship the goods by carrier

(a) if it does not require him to deliver them at a particular destination, the risk of loss passes to the buyer when the goods are duly delivered to the carrier even though the shipment is under reservation (Section 2-505); but

(b) if it does require him to deliver them at a particular destination and the goods are there duly tendered while in the possession of the carrier, the risk of loss passes to the buyer when the goods are there duly so tendered as to enable the buyer to take delivery.

U.C.C. § 2-509(1).** Putting the two together, and in simpler terms, this means that title (and, consequently, risk of loss) does not pass to buyer until seller completes performance, however that is defined in the contract. A contract may define a specific location for the seller's tendering the goods, but a contract can also direct the seller to ship the goods to buyer without specifying a location. In the first case—a specific location for tender—section 2-401(2)(b) says that title passes only when the goods are tendered at that location and section 2-509(1)(b) says that the risk of loss passes to the buyer when the carrier—whoever was hired to ship the goods—makes the goods available for buyer to take possession.

In the second case—where the seller has a general obligation to deliver goods but without a specific destination—section 2-401(2)(a) says that title passes when the goods are shipped. Section 2-509(1)(a) likewise says that the risk of loss passes to the buyer as soon as seller delivers the goods to the carrier. To understand why title and risk transfer earlier in this second case, consider that if there is no specified location for delivery, the buyer must have contracted with the carrier for a specific delivery. After all, *someone* has to know where to drop off the goods, and if the contract says only that they have to be shipped, but not where, then the buyer is reserving that information for itself, and presumably the carrier. In other words, the carrier is acting as the agent of the buyer, so as soon as the seller hands over the goods to the carrier, they are in the buyer's possession. This is backed up by section 2-319(3), which requires buyer to "seasonably give any needed instructions for making delivery."

The buyer and seller are free to work out any other method for transferring title and risk, but the distinction described in section 2-509(1) represents an intuitive place to draw the line for passing risk of loss from seller to buyer. Once out of the control of the seller or the carrier that seller has hired—seller's agent—title and risk will transfer. Notice that sections 2-401(1) and 2-509(1) provide an outline of when title and risk pass, but do not say much about the actual duties the parties bear during shipment. For that, we turn to section 2-319(1), which says:

(1) Unless otherwise agreed the term F.O.B. (which means "free on board") at a named place, even though used only in connection with the stated price, is a delivery term under which

(a) when the term is F.O.B. the place of shipment, the seller must at that place ship the goods in the manner provided in this Article (Section 2-504) and bear the expense and risk of putting them into the possession of the carrier; or

(b) when the term is F.O.B. the place of destination, the seller must at his own expense and risk transport the goods to that place and there tender delivery of them in the manner provided in this Article (Section 2-503);

(c) when under either (a) or (b) the term is also F.O.B. vessel, car or other vehicle, the seller must in addition at his own expense and risk load the goods on board. If the term is F.O.B. vessel the buyer must name the vessel and in an appropriate case the seller must comply with the provisions of this Article on the form of bill of lading (Section 2-323).

U.C.C. § 2-319(1).* When the parties specify delivery options with the terms F.O.B., those delivery instructions establish how far the goods must travel before the buyer assumes the risk of loss. As usual, these are default terms and the parties are free to contract around them.

When the contract specifies F.O.B., and a location on the buyer's side of the transaction (more or less, the "place of destination" from subsection 1(b)), the seller bears the risk and expense of delivering the goods to that location by whatever means the seller chooses. An F.O.B. term of this sort is one way of describing a specific location for tender, as we saw in sections 2-401(2)(b) and 2-509(1)(b). Alternatively, the contract could specify F.O.B. and a location on the seller's side of the transaction (the "place of shipment" from subsection 1(a)), indicating that the seller bears the risk and expense of getting the goods to that location and delivering the goods to the carrier. In either case, the seller has the responsibility to make the arrangements for shipping and provide the necessary documents—a bill of lading. Remember that the buyer is required to provide instructions for delivery, but the obligation remains on seller to contact the shipping agent to make the actual arrangements.

Two additional caveats are important to mention at this point. First, if buyer fails to provide instructions for delivery, there is no breach by buyer but seller is free to "move the goods in any reasonable manner preparatory to delivery or shipment." U.C.C. § 2-319(3). Second, section 2-319(1)(c) allows the buyer to specify a *particular* "vessel, car or other vehicle" for shipment, which then imposes an additional risk on seller—that of actually loading the goods into the vehicle. After that point, the risk and expense is on the buyer, and the carrier will effectively serve as the buyer's agent to deliver the goods. This is obviously the same outcome as the more general provisions of sections 2-401(2)(a) and 2-509(1)(a).

As but one example of how this would work, GrainCo—based in Kansas— has agreed to sell 10 tons of flax seed to HalfFoods, a health food store based in New Hampshire. The contract describes the shipment as "Ten (10) tons of USDA certified premium flax seed, F.O.B. Kansas City railyard, Great

---

Western Railroad, car 1,054,864, May 21, 2020, 5:00 pm." GrainCo knows that it will need to get the grain to Kansas City by May 21, 2020. According to section 2-319(3), GrainCo is free to use any reasonable means to get the grain there on time, but a fixed location has been provided, and GrainCo knows when the risk of loss will pass to HalfFoods. Because HalfFoods has identified the specific car, GrainCo bears the risk until the goods are loaded onto the car. If the precise car had not been mentioned, GrainCo would have been responsible for providing the goods to Great Western Railroad at the Kansas City railyard by the date and time in the contract, but would not have automatically born the risk of loading.

Section 2-319 has another term, "free alongside," or "F.A.S," that is used a lot in international shipping. Free alongside specifies a maritime vessel that will transport the goods and the port at which the vessel will be located. A contract that specifies F.A.S. requires the seller to bear the risk and expense of transporting the goods to the port and arranging for the goods to be delivered alongside the vessel in whatever procedure is used at that port. You can probably imagine that, two hundred years ago, bringing the goods alongside would have required seller to use boats to get the goods out into the harbor near the shipping vessel. If you've seen a modern port, you know that the modern version is to get the goods in large shipping containers on the dock next to the vessel, at which time a crane will set each container onto the vessel.

Once the goods have been delivered "alongside" the vessel, seller is required to tender a receipt for the goods, which will obligate the shipping company to issue a bill of lading. Without getting too technical, a bill of lading is a receipt for shipment and an acknowledgement that the goods have been loaded onto the vessel. When the seller has received the bill of lading — or when the goods have been delivered to the F.O.B. location — seller has complied with the terms of the contract, and the risk of loss passes to the buyer in most cases.

The contract could, of course, describe a completely different point at which risk of loss passes, but these rules govern in most cases because the U.C.C. rules should function as useful default rules that will cover what most bargainers would want. One additional contract term that pertains to risk in an indirect way is the C.I.F. term, which stands for cost of insurance and freight and stands in contrast to a C.F. term, which stands for cost of freight. C.I.F. is used in reference to the contract price, and a C.I.F. price includes the payment for insurance, which the seller is obligated to purchase. Obviously, if an insurance policy was provided for, but not purchased, the seller will have breached its obligations and will bear any loss suffered due to the lack of insurance.

2. The case of breach

Up to now, we have been dealing with the risk of loss in the normal course of performance under a contract. As every student of contract law knows, sometimes the parties don't comply with their contractual obligations. How do we deal with the risk of loss in those situations? Section 2-510, Effect of Breach on Risk of Loss, says:

> (1) Where a tender or delivery of goods so fails to conform to the contract as to give a right of rejection the risk of their loss remains on the seller until cure or acceptance.
>
> (2) Where the buyer rightfully revokes acceptance he may to the extent of any deficiency in his effective insurance coverage treat the risk of loss as having rested on the seller from the beginning.
>
> (3) Where the buyer as to conforming goods already identified to the contract for sale repudiates or is otherwise in breach before risk of their loss has passed to him, the seller may to the extent of any deficiency in his effective insurance coverage treat the risk of loss as resting on the buyer for a commercially reasonable time.

U.C.C. § 2-510.* Subsection (1) functions as a basic default rule, that when the seller tenders goods but they do not meet the perfect tender standard, the risk of loss remains on the seller. This should make sense, because the seller has an obligation to provide goods that conform exactly to the contract. If seller delivers non-conforming goods instead, the seller has, in essence, dropped a pile of random goods on the buyer's (figurative) doorstep. The goods don't belong to buyer, so risk of loss cannot have passed to buyer. Seller will need to either arrange to have the goods picked up before something happens to them, convince the buyer to accept the goods — probably by offering some sort of discount — or cure the defect.

What if the buyer accepts the goods but later revokes that acceptance? At the moment of acceptance, it looked like title and risk would have shifted to the buyer, but revocation turns back the clock and the goods are no longer accepted. Section 2-510(2) states that, in such a case, not only does risk of loss pass back to the seller, but the buyer is allowed to treat risk of loss as if it had remained with the seller the entire time.

Some breaches by buyer will involve a failure to pay for the goods or a refusal to accept the goods. In those cases, it is possible that the risk of loss will have already passed. After all, risk of loss typically passes when the goods are tendered, not when they are accepted. If buyer repudiates the contract, or otherwise breaches the contract before that moment where the risk would have passed to buyer, section 2-510(3) states that seller can treat the risk of loss as having passed to the buyer for a commercially reasonable time. This provision might seem a little strange, but as we'll discuss in Chapter 19, the seller's remedies are tied to the idea of a commercially reasonable time. To give you a brief preview of the next Chapter, when a buyer breaches, a seller will either try to sell the goods to someone else or will be allowed to recover the difference between the contract price and a market price identified within a commercially reasonable time. So, in essence, 2-510(3) places the risk of loss on the breaching buyer while the seller explores its options for remedies.

One last important point about section 2-510 is the effect of insurance. Notice that subsection (2) passes risk of loss back to the seller if acceptance is revoked. The exact measure of loss, however, is "any deficiency in [buyer's] effective insurance coverage." U.C.C. § 2-510(2). In other words, if acceptance is revoked after the goods have been harmed or destroyed, buyer's insurance should cover the loss to the extent allowed by the policy. If there is any excess loss not covered by the policy, that loss passes back to the seller. Similarly, subsection (3) measures the loss which passes to the buyer as "any deficiency in [seller's] effective insurance coverage." U.C.C. § 2-510(3). So, if the goods are harmed while seller is seeking its remedies, seller's insurance should cover the loss and buyer will bear only that amount of loss which is not covered by insurance. It may seem strange to place the risk of loss on the party not at fault, but in each case, the party bearing the risk of loss is the least cost avoider.

C. Least Cost Avoider

As we finish up this discussion of risk of loss principles in the U.C.C., it may be helpful for some to think about the U.C.C. rules in the context of the least-cost-avoider rule. The least-cost-avoider rule is that the party who can avoid or mitigate the risk most cheaply should bear the cost if something should happen. Under the common law, default rules developed based on this rule because it helps to maximize the total value of contracts by minimizing costly prevention efforts, and those rules have carried over to the U.C.C.

For example, imagine what would happen if the U.C.C. always assigned the risk of loss to the buyer of goods. As soon as the contract was signed, the buyer would need to have someone present at the production facilities, to make sure nothing happened to the goods, and a representative of the buyer would have to accompany the goods anytime they were transported. Paying the representative for all of that time would cost buyer a lot of money, so buyer would be willing to pay far less for the goods. Perhaps even more important, from the beginning of the contract to its completion, the buyer's representative would need to have pretty significant authority in order to make sure that the goods were not lost or destroyed. Seller would not appreciate having to cede that much control to an outsider, and would insist on a higher price for the goods as compensation for the loss of control.

Clearly that rule wouldn't work; it's overly complicated and it makes a lot of contracts far less likely to occur at all. The important thing is why it wouldn't work—because it is very costly for the buyer to avoid or mitigate the loss. Instead, we have a rule where the seller bears the risk of loss while the goods are in seller's possession. Until the goods are tendered to buyer or buyer's agent (including buyer's preferred carrier), seller bears the risk of loss because seller is in the best position to keep the goods out of danger, or if danger arises, to mitigate any loss. Once the goods have been tendered, buyer is in the best position to avoid or mitigate the loss. By keeping prevention efforts as low as possible, the buyer pays a lower price, seller receives a higher price, and both parties realize far greater value from the contract.

Checkpoints

- Risk of loss rules govern who loses out if the goods are lost or destroyed.
- Seller bears the risk of loss during production or procurement, and retains the risk until the goods are tendered.
- If the contract requires tender without delivery, buyer bears risk as soon as goods are tendered.
- If the contract requires seller to deliver to a specific location, seller bears the expense and risk of getting goods to that location.
- If the contract specifies a particular vessel or vehicle for transport, seller bears the expense and risk of loading the goods into that vessel or vehicle.
- If the contract requires only general delivery to the buyer, seller bears the risk until goods have been provided to the carrier for transport.
- If the contract is breached, the breaching party bears the risk of loss until cure or cover occurs.
- Risk of loss rules impose the risk on the least cost avoider of loss.

Chapter 19

Seller's Remedies

Roadmap

- Wrongful rejection of goods
- Cover
- Hypothetical cover
- Lost volume sellers
- Recover price
- Scrap and salvage or finish?

A. Wrongful Rejection of Goods

Before we can discuss *what* the seller's remedies are, we must first determine *if* the seller has *any* remedies. Legal remedies under contract law are available only when the contract has been breached, so seller has remedies only if the buyer has breached. And how does a buyer breach the contract? By not accepting goods when those goods are as promised in the contract. As we discussed in Chapter 12, section 2-601 entitles the buyer to perfect tender. If the seller fails to provide the goods exactly as promised in the contract, then the buyer can reject the goods, although usage of trade, course of dealing, and course of performance might give the seller some small amount of leeway when it comes to determining whether the goods are conforming.

If the goods conform to the contract, the buyer must accept them or breach. A breach by buyer gives the seller a few choices, all listed in section 2-703.

> Where the buyer wrongfully rejects or revokes acceptance of goods or fails to make a payment due on or before delivery or repudiates with respect to a part or the whole, then with respect to any goods directly affected and, if the breach is of the whole contract (Section 2-612), then also with respect to the whole undelivered balance, the aggrieved seller may

(a) withhold delivery of such goods;

(b) stop delivery by any bailee as hereafter provided (Section 2-705);

(c) proceed under the next section respecting goods still unidentified to the contract;

(d) resell and recover damages as hereafter provided (Section 2-706);

(e) recover damages for non-acceptance (Section 2-708) or in a proper case the price (Section 2-709);

(f) cancel.

U.C.C. § 2-703.* First of all, section 2-703 allows the seller to stop delivery on any portion of the contract that hasn't yet been delivered, either by withholding delivery of goods not yet shipped or recalling goods that are in transit. This should make sense since, if the buyer has already repudiated the contract or refused a portion of the goods, the seller shouldn't have to go through the expense of shipping the goods, only to pay to recover them so that other remedies can be pursued. Beyond withholding the remaining goods, what can the seller do? First, the seller can sell the goods to someone else and recover damages. Second, the seller can recover the difference between the contract price and the market price at the time of breach. Under certain specific circumstances, the seller might be able to do both—recover the difference between market price and contract price and resell the goods—or even just recover the contract price. Finally, if a seller finds out about the breach while still making the goods, seller can salvage or finish the goods in order to mitigate damages.

The thing to keep in mind as we talk about seller's remedies—and buyer's remedies, too—is that the baseline is expectation damages. In other words, we want to make the non-breaching party as well off as it would have been if the other side had not breached. When it comes to a seller, what is the expectation? Typically, it is to hand over the goods and receive payment in return. Because the goods cost something to make, the real expectation of the seller is to make a profit, to have more money after the sale than it took to make and deliver the goods. If the buyer refuses to pay for the goods, the seller has expended resources but received nothing in return. Seller's remedies are

* Uniform Commercial Code, copyright © by the American Law Institute and the National Conference of Commissioners on Uniform State Laws. Reproduced with the permission of the Permanent Editorial Board for the Uniform Commercial Code. All rights reserved.

designed to correct that divergence from expectations by giving the seller different ways to get paid for the goods it has already produced.

B. Cover

The first remedy for the seller is "cover," the U.C.C.'s term for finding a substitute for the original counterparty. For the seller, that means finding another buyer that wants the goods. After the seller receives payment from the *new* buyer, it can recover from the *original* buyer the difference between what it would have had if the contract had been honored and what it actually has. Although this sounds easy, section 2-706 establishes a number of requirements that a seller has to meet before it can avail itself of this option. First of all, the new sale has to be made in good faith and in a commercially reasonable manner, which means that the seller can't engage in any shady dealings, perhaps acting out of spite and trying to harm the original buyer by arranging to sell the goods at a really low price (so that the buyer has to pay more).

The seller can sell the goods at a public or private sale. If the seller chooses a public sale, the seller must hold the sale at a place typically used for public sales or auctions and the seller may participate as a buyer. The seller must give the buyer reasonable notice of the sale unless the goods are perishable and will go bad or lose value if not sold quickly. The seller also has to make the goods available for potential buyers to inspect. If the seller chooses a private sale, the seller must give the buyer reasonable notice of intent to resell the goods.

These requirements serve the same purpose as the requirements of good faith and a commercially reasonable manner of sale—to protect the buyer while making sure the seller receives its expectation damages. By mandating proper notice and advertising, the U.C.C. makes sure that there are more people at the sale, and the right of potential buyers to inspect the goods makes sure that everyone knows exactly what they are bidding on. Ideally, a large enough number of buyers and good information about the goods will result in the sale price being as high as possible. In that case, the seller walks away from the sale with almost as much money as it had expected to receive from the original buyer. The seller can then sue the original buyer for the difference between the contract price and the sale price, plus whatever expenses were incurred getting ready for and putting on the sale. These latter costs are called "incidental costs." Once those damages are recovered, the seller has rid itself of the goods and is holding onto the purchase price that the original buyer promised to pay—the seller's expectations have been met.

C. Hypothetical Cover

The rules for carrying on a section 2-706 sale are not insurmountable, but neither are they simple. A seller who does not want to—or cannot, for whatever reason—jump through those hoops needs some other way to recover expectation damages. Section 2-708(1) provides an alternative, often referred to as "hypothetical cover." Under this option, the seller doesn't actually have to sell the goods to any other buyer, keeping the goods and recovering what it likely would have received by selling the goods on the open market. Again, the seller doesn't actually cover by finding a substitute buyer, but recovers what the court presumes the seller would have recovered if, hypothetically, the seller had done so.

Section 2-708(1) has a small phrase at the end that can be a little confusing at first glance. After describing the damages for hypothetical cover and allowing for incidental damages to be recovered, the section requires a deduction from damages for "expenses saved in consequences of the buyer's breach." This provision exists because, at times, the contract was bound to be a money loser for the seller. As a result, the buyer did the seller a favor by breaching, and the total calculation of damages should account for the fact that the seller would have been poorer after the contract—that the expected damages were negative.

To see how this works in practice, consider the following example: CompuCorp makes computer processors and has signed a contract to provide Laptops, Inc. with 10,000 microprocessors at $10 each. CompuCorp has just started production when Laptops sends a notice that it is having cash flow problems and cannot buy the processors. From section 2-703, we know that CompuCorp does not have to ship any finished goods, but can hold on to them while it determines what to do. CompuCorp decides that it would be too costly to hold a sale under 2-706, so it looks at the market price for processors like the ones it produces. That price is $9, so it intends to send Laptops a demand for $10,000—the $1 difference between contract price and market price, multiplied by the number of units—when the lawyers notice a problem. It turns out that the price of platinum has just doubled. This is a problem, because the processors use a lot of platinum. In fact, it turns out that, given the increase in the price of platinum, it would have cost CompuCorp $10.50 to make each processor. Since it would have cost $0.50 more to make each processor than it would receive from Laptops, CompuCorp would have lost a total of $5,000 on the contract. As a result, we take the $10,000 that Laptops owes for its breach and subtract off the $5,000 that CompuCorp *would have lost* if Laptops had not breached.

D. Lost Volume Sellers

Section 2-708(2) begins with the phrase: "If the measure of damages provided in subsection (1) is inadequate to put the seller in as good a position as performance would have done. . . ." This concedes that there are times when a seller will not be made whole through hypothetical cover but the section is silent as to when and why this might occur. After all, if a seller expected to make a certain amount of profit off of the transaction, and hypothetical cover is supposed to approximate that profit, why would a seller not be made whole? The answer has to do with the fact that, once the seller has recovered damages for hypothetical cover, it still has the goods in its inventory. The seller is presumably not in the business of just storing goods for the fun of it, so it will want to sell those goods. Doing so, however, will mess up the court's calculation of the seller's expectation damages, and seller will likely have to pay back some amount to the original buyer.

To see why, remember that, for a normal seller, the buyer's breach has left them with a pile of goods when what the seller expected from the contract was a pile of profits. Either through cover or hypothetical cover, the pile of goods is disposed of and money is recovered from the original buyer. With hypothetical cover, the goods are still around; if the seller sells them, then the seller has no pile of goods, the original profits recovered from the buyer, and now a second pile of money received from the new buyer. Again, the seller's expectation was that the pile of goods would be gone, replaced by a single pile of money (profits). If the court allows the seller to recover profits from the original buyer *and* sell to the new buyer and keep the profits, the seller will have double its expectations. The court will not allow that, and will likely require the seller to pay some or all of the windfall profits from the resale to the original buyer. The seller will have its expectations met, and the buyer will pay only the difference between resale and expectations, just like with a sale under 2-706.

At this point, you should be curious as to how long the seller has to hold onto the goods. After all, the seller can't immediately resell the goods, but surely they can't be required to hold on to the goods indefinitely. Inventories cost money, after all, and that would be punishing the seller for exercising one of its stated remedies. The U.C.C. offers no express guidance on this question, and the courts have not provided much assistance, but it seems reasonable to presume that the seller can sell the goods as soon as enough time has passed that the new sale looks like a new sale, and not just an attempt to offload the goods after buyer breached. How long will that be? It depends on just how frequently the seller sells goods of these sorts, and in what quantities. If a seller sells large quantities of goods on a regular basis, it might even be possible for the seller to resell the goods immediately and keep the profits from the resale. In other words, a seller that had the capacity to make multiple sales at the same time might be able to keep its lost profits and resell, as a "lost volume seller."

Subsection (2) says that the measure of damages for a lost volume seller is "the profit (including reasonable overhead) which the seller would have made from full performance by the buyer, together with any incidental damages provided in this Article (Section 2-710), due allowance for costs reasonably incurred and due credit for payments or proceeds of resale." U.C.C. §2-708(2). Although not entirely clear from the language of the section, the profits that a lost volume seller would have made from full performance include both the profits from the hypothetical resale covered by 2-708(1) plus any revenues that the lost volume seller gets from actually selling the goods in question. The key to understanding this particular remedy is to remember that a lost volume seller is different, usually in that the lost volume seller sells a higher volume, all of it profitably, so that the real profits lost go beyond the single sale.

As an example, assume Abe owns apple orchards and sells apples to grocers across the nation. Bart owns a small grocery that buys apples from Abe. Bart breaches a contract to buy 10 bushels of apples for $100 ($10 per bushel). The market rate for apples is $10 per bushel. If Abe were to try and sue for a market differential, he would get nothing. Further, it is likely that Abe has sold many bushels since the breach, but if he were to seek cover, assuming he sells at the same price, he would get nothing. But from Abe's point of view, he is out money as he is still sitting on a large inventory of apples that would have been smaller had Bart not breached. Yes, he has since sold the 10 bushels and many more, but Abe will assert he would have made those sales anyway. Abe would be a classic lost volume seller in such an instance. As such, he would be entitled to his profit off of the lost apple sales. So if he pays laborers $3 per bushel picked, and those are his only costs, then Abe would be entitled to $7 per bushel, or $70.[1]

The lack of clarity in section 2-708(2) leaves open the possibility for other circumstances where a seller could obtain lost-profits damages from the

---

1. At this point you may be saying, "But Abe surely has more costs than that. What about the cost to irrigate the land and other utility bills? What about all the other overhead costs he may incur?" The calculation for damages, however, allows Abe to keep these as he gets "the profit (including reasonable overhead)." U.C.C. §2-708(2).

original buyer, and also resell the goods immediately. For now, however, only lost volume sellers are allowed to do so. A seller who wants the opportunity must prove that it: (1) had the capacity to produce enough goods for the original sale *and* the resale; (2) that both sales would have been profitable; and (3) that it would have made both sales if not for the original buyer's breach. The first part of the test is pretty easy—the court just asks whether the seller had excess productive capacity. The second part may seem easy but can get complicated given the dynamic nature of markets. For example, it is possible that the second sale would have required finding an entirely new supply of some important input. If so, costs to produce goods for the second sale would have been much higher, making the sale unprofitable.

The third part is the source of the term "lost volume seller." It is never entirely certain whether sales would have occurred, but a seller that produces a significant volume of goods will be doing so because the demand for goods is high. In that situation, each sale makes up a relatively small part of the total volume of goods being produced and sold. When the original buyer breached the contract, all that happened was that some of that total *volume* was *lost* to the seller. The only way to compensate the seller is to let it continue to sell in high volumes to everyone else and recover lost profits for the amount of volume that it lost to the breach.

It is important to make one final point with regard to section 2-708, specifically the last phrase. By its express terms, subsection (2) requires that the damages for a lost volume seller be offset by "credit for payments or proceeds of resale." U.C.C. § 2-708(2). Of course, if the lost volume seller is required to subtract the amount of payments received from resale of the goods, then there is no difference between the damages awarded in subsection (1) and those awarded in subsection (2) and subsection (2) would be irrelevant. Because taking subsection (2) at face value would render it obsolete and contradict its purpose of making up inadequacies in the damages award under subsection (1), courts ignore this final phrase in most cases. The last phrase was likely intended to apply only to a small class of specialty component manufacturers (the result of which results in the same damage award as the scrap provisions addressed in F below).

E. Recover Price

One of the primary purposes of the U.C.C., as discussed in previous chapters, is to facilitate the flow of commerce in goods. The remedies available to the seller, therefore, are primarily designed to make sure that goods are sold to someone, even if it isn't to the original buyer. So long as the goods have value, there should be a willing buyer somewhere. Selling to a willing buyer provides some value to the seller, lessening the amount that the original buyer has to pay in damages. It's a win-win scenario for everyone involved, including society, which benefits because valuable goods are still flowing to people who want them. There are some rare occasions where resale is not an option. For example, if the buyer has taken possession of the goods, or if the goods have been lost or destroyed on the buyer's watch. It may also be that the seller still has possession of the goods and has tried to resell them but can find no willing buyer at a reasonable price. In any of these cases, the seller is left with no money and either a pile of value-less goods or no goods at all.

Section 2-709 allows the seller to seek expectation damages by suing buyer for the purchase price in these three situations. This is, in effect, the seller's form of specific performance, making the buyer do exactly what it promised to do under the contract — hand over a pile of money. As with other forms of specific performance, this remedy is disfavored, so it is available in no other circumstances. Section 2-709 also provides that, if buyer pays the contract price, it is entitled to possession of the goods and seller must hold onto the goods to allow buyer to claim them. Also, if an opportunity arises for the seller to resell the goods, it must do so and repay the original buyer any amount received for the goods. These provisions protect against overcompensation of the seller. Once buyer has paid damages, seller has a pile of money, and potentially a pile of goods; if buyer wants the goods, removing them from seller's possession will further the buyer's and seller's expectations. If the seller is later able to resell the goods, its pile of money will be too high, and the buyer should be refunded that amount.

F. Scrap and Salvage or Finish?

If seller is in the process of making the goods and buyer repudiates the contract, what should the seller do with them? Depending on where seller was in the manufacturing process, the goods might not be in a state that would allow them to be resold, so that option is out unless the seller is allowed to finish production. Section 2-704(2) allows seller to choose between finishing the goods and reselling them or stopping production and scrapping and/or salvaging the goods. Whatever choice the seller makes will help determine the amount of damages that the buyer has to pay, since the value of the goods as resold — or as salvaged — will be subtracted off the amount that the seller would need in order to be made whole. Because this is, in essence, a part of the seller's duty to mitigate, the decision must be done "in the exercise of reasonable commercial judgment for the purposes of avoiding loss and of effective realization." U.C.C. § 2-704(2). In other words, the seller has to make the decision from the perspective of an accountant, just trying to make sure the outcome is better for everyone.

In order to make the decision, the seller will have to determine what price the goods would bring if completed, the cost of completing them, and the value of the goods if they were just scrapped or salvaged. Salvage value is the value that can be obtained by removing components that have some independent value. Scrap value is the value of the base materials, if they can be reclaimed for some purpose. To restate the seller's task, it is to determine whether the value of the unfinished goods is greater that the net profit from completing and selling the goods. For example, Bill has agreed to sell Gertrude 100 widgets at $4 per widget. Gertrude later repudiates the contract, but the widgets are only partially complete. If Bill shuts down production today, he could sell the unfinished widgets to recyclers for $1 per widget. It would only cost Bill $0.20 per widget to complete the widgets, at which point he could sell them each for $3. If Bill takes the first path, he could recover damages of $3 per widget— the difference between the contract price of $4 and the scrap value of $1. If Bill takes the second path, he could recover $1—the difference between the contract price of $4 and the sale price of $3. Either way, Bill will be made whole, but taking the second path will limit his loss, benefit Gertrude by reducing the amount of damages she has to pay, and benefit society by yielding a net positive return on investment (investing $0.20 to yield an additional $2 in value).

Checkpoints

- If buyer rejects or refuses to pay for conforming goods, it has breached, and seller can choose its remedy.

- If buyer repudiates, seller can cancel shipment for any goods not yet shipped, or recall any goods still in transit.

- Seller can "cover"—reselling the goods to a new buyer—and recover the difference between the sale price and the contract price, but only if seller acts in good faith and in a commercially reasonable manner.

- If seller uses a public sale to cover, it must be done at a place normally used for such sales, buyer must be given notice, and potential buyers must be given the opportunity to inspect the goods.

- If seller uses a private sale to cover, buyer must be given adequate notice.

- Seller can use "hypothetical cover"—keeping the goods for its own inventory—to receive the difference between the contract price and the market price at the time of the breach.

- Seller cannot immediately resell the goods after hypothetical cover unless it is a lost volume seller, meaning that it had the capacity to make both the contractual sale and the resale, both sales would have been profitable, and the new sale would have happened anyway.

- A lost volume seller is allowed to recover the profits from a hypothetical resale *and* resell the goods, because doing so is the only way to compensate a lost volume seller for the particular loss occasioned by buyer's breach.

- Courts ignore—as a drafting error—the final phrase of section 2-708(2) requiring offset for any resale proceeds.

- Seller can recover the contract price *only* if the buyer has already taken possession of the goods or if seller has tried and failed to resell the goods.

- If buyer breaches during the production process, seller can either scrap and salvage the unfinished goods—or finish the goods if doing so is commercially reasonable—and recover the difference between the contract amount and the resale value of the goods.

Chapter 20

Buyer's Remedies

Roadmap

- Rejection of imperfect tender
- Cover
- Hypothetical cover
- Specific performance
- Damages after acceptance
- Scrap and salvage
- Incidental and consequential damages
- Limitations on damages

A. Rejection of Imperfect Tender

When a buyer signs a contract, it has the right to receive goods that are exactly as described in the contract. Recall from Chapter 12 that the U.C.C. uses the perfect tender standard, and that the standard is very strict. It may be helpful to review Chapter 12 to remind yourself of both the strictness of the standard and the doctrines that mitigate the potential severity of the standard's application. That review will remind you that the buyer is entitled to reject any imperfect tender — goods that fail to comply in every way with the contract. A buyer can, of course, choose to accept imperfect tender and sue for damages, as described in Chapter 12 and again in Chapter 16. A buyer who accepts might also, under certain circumstances, revoke that acceptance, as described in Chapter 16. These remedies are also available if the seller refuses to deliver any goods or otherwise repudiates the contract.

In any event, a buyer has the right to have its expectations met. Recall that a seller's expectations are to have one less pile of goods and a new pile of profits. The buyer's expectations are the converse — a new pile of goods and a much smaller pile of cash. The buyer's remedies, listed in section 2-711, are designed to meet the buyer's reasonable expectations. Specifically, the buyer can "cover" by buying on the open market and recovering the extra money paid from the seller, can engage in "hypothetical cover" by recovering the difference between market price and contract price, or can — under specific circumstances — force the seller to provide the goods as described. Finally, if a buyer has accepted non-conforming goods, the buyer can sue for damages but will have to account for scrap and salvage value.

B. Cover

Recall from Chapter 19 that the seller has the right to "cover" when a buyer breaches. We use the same term to describe the buyer's right in finding a substitute seller to provide the goods. Some find this term to be confusing, but the term is used in a similar way in various other areas of our lives. In an employment context, for example, a co-worker might ask you to "cover" their shift if they cannot make it. By doing so, the employer's need for someone to work is filled, the harm is minimized, and your co-worker will then owe you a favor. Similarly, a friend might ask you to "cover" for her if she has to be in two places at once. By covering for your friend, you will minimize the loss to both your friend and those who were relying on her. In a contract relationship, the non-breaching party is allowed to "cover" for the breaching party by finding a substitute to fill the gap and minimize the harm caused by the breach. Just as cover for friends and coworkers is not required in your personal life, cover is not required by contract law, but it is often the best way for the non-breaching party to maximize expectation damages.

A buyer who elects to cover just needs to find substitute goods. For many goods, this will be quite easy, as there are many "thick" markets — markets with lots of buyers and sellers. In a thick market, the failure of one seller to provide you with goods is a minor inconvenience, since there will be many other sellers ready and willing to provide you with what you need. If the market doesn't have as many sellers, it might take longer and cost more to find a substitute seller, but the process is essentially the same. Section 2-712, subsection (1) requires the buyer to look for a substitute in good faith and without unreasonable delay, so the buyer can't wait to see whether the price will go up or down. Subsection (2) then establishes the remedy, that buyer can then recover the difference between the price that was paid and the contract price, plus any incidental costs associated with finding a substitute seller.

As mentioned, cover is usually the best way to make sure the buyer receives all its expectation damages. For example, if RetailMart had contracted to buy 10,000 computers from Laptop, Inc. at $100 per computer, RetailMart's post-contract expectations were to have 10,000 computers and $1 million less in its bank account. If Laptop doesn't deliver the computers, RetailMart still has money in its bank account but no computers. It makes a few phone calls and finds a substitute supplier, Desktop Co., to provide similar computers, but for $120 per computer. In order to get the computers in time for Black Friday, RetailMart will also need to pay $5 extra per computer for expedited delivery. When RetailMart has "covered," it will have paid out a total of $125 per computer ($1,250,000 total) when it had expected to pay only $100 per computer ($1,000,000) under the contract. Section 2-712 allows RetailMart to recover $25 per computer—$20 difference in price plus $5 in incidental damages—for a total of $250,000. After recovering that amount, RetailMart will have exactly its expectations, a pile of 10,000 computers and $1 million less in its bank account.

C. Hypothetical Cover

Section 2-712 contains a final provision, subsection (3), that says that a buyer that does not exercise its right to cover is not precluded from other remedies. This is important because there are times when the buyer will not want to cover. Section 2-713 allows for "hypothetical cover," or the ability of the buyer to recover the difference between the market price and the contract price. You can think of this as the profits the buyer would have made if it had received the goods from seller as promised and immediately resold them in the market for a profit. The buyer might take this option if, for any reason, it does not want the actual goods.

For example, if RetailMart had contracted with TreeCorp for the purchase of 5,000 Christmas trees, at $20 per tree, to be delivered on November 30. On November 29, TreeCorp repudiates the contract, and RetailMart begins looking for a substitute. It discovers that most local tree farms have already sold out; if it wants trees, it will have to pay $30 per tree. RetailMart knows that its customers will not be willing to pay more than $30 per tree, so it could not make a profit on the trees. Buying the trees would not make sense for RetailMart, so it can sue for the $10-per-tree difference between the contract price ($20 per tree) and the market price ($30 per tree). Alternatively, imagine that RetailMart could get trees for $25 per tree but delivery would be delayed until December 20. RetailMart decides that it could not sell enough Christmas trees in the five days before December 25 to make the purchase worthwhile. RetailMart could recover $5 per tree in damages.

There are a few technical provisions related to section 2-713 that deserve mentioning. First, the U.C.C. contains provisions about how "market price" is to be determined. Section 2-723 specifies that market price is the prevailing price for the same type of goods "at the time when the aggrieved party learned of the repudiation." Notwithstanding this language, courts have construed section 2-713 to award damages based on the market price a commercially reasonable time after repudiation. The justification for this interpretation is that section 2-610 gives the non-breaching party a commercially reasonable time to seek remedies, and that guarantee would be illusory if a buyer could only recover based on the market price *at the precise moment of repudiation*, which is what the text of section 2-713 seems to require. If there are no goods available at the time and place of the contract when repudiation occurs, market price can be determined a reasonable time before or after, or at another location, taking into consideration the cost of transporting the goods.

D. Specific Performance

Under certain circumstances, a buyer might be entitled to the goods that are described in the contract. It may seem redundant to say that, since we've already discussed that the buyer's general right is to the goods described in the contract. However, the fact that perfect tender establishes a breach of contract if seller does not provide goods exactly as described does not mean that the buyer can literally insist that the seller provide the goods, only that remedies are available if that standard is not met. A full description of specific performance will wait for Chapter 21, but it is worth mentioning at this point that the buyer *might* be able to insist that the seller actually deliver the precise goods described, if the criteria of section 2-716 are met.

E. Damages After Acceptance

In those cases where the buyer has accepted non-conforming goods and has not later revoked that acceptance, it is making due with goods that are not as they were described. That means that the buyer is worse off than it expected to be when it signed the contract. Whatever flaw the goods possess, it is something that reduces the value of the goods, which leaves the buyer with a pile of goods that are not worth the full price the buyer paid for them. In order to fulfill the buyer's expectations, section 2-714 provides that the buyer can recover damages for the nonconformity, stating:

> (1) Where the buyer has accepted goods and given notification (subsection (3) of Section 2-607) he may recover as damages for any

non-conformity of tender the loss resulting in the ordinary course of events from the seller's breach as determined in any manner which is reasonable.

(2) The measure of damages for breach of warranty is the difference at the time and place of acceptance between the value of goods accepted and the value they would have had if they had been as warranted, unless special circumstances show proximate damages of a different amount.

(3) In a proper case any incidental and consequential damages under the next section may also be recovered.*

Subsection (1) establishes that the failure to deliver the goods as promised gives rise to a cause of action for damages. Subsection (2) establishes how those damages are to be measured, as the difference between the value they have as delivered and the value they would have had as promised. There are two important things to remember here: first, that damages are to be measured at the time and place of acceptance; and second, that there is always opportunity to establish damages of a different amount. Comment 3 makes clear that subsection (2) is merely the "standard and reasonable method of ascertaining damages," but it is not exclusive. For example, comment 3 describes a situation where the buyer accepts but also has the option to revoke; the appropriate time and place to affix damages could be where and when the buyer indicates its decision not to revoke.

One final difficulty remains—how to determine the difference between the value as delivered and the value as promised. While section 2-714 does not specify, courts will typically make a determination based on either the cost of repair or cost of replacement. The first measure is straightforward, the amount the buyer would need to pay a repair service to bring the goods into conformity with the contract description. The second measure can be understood by imagining that the buyer sold the defective goods on the market and purchased conforming goods. Because defective goods will be worth less, the buyer will have less money, and the seller can be required to write a check for that amount.

Section 2-714 does not specify which method is preferred, but there are some circumstances in which cost of repair will not be appropriate because the good simply cannot be made to look like the good that was promised in the contract. For example, ShoeCo contracts to buy a computer from RetailMart but the computer that shows up has less RAM, a slower processor, and a number of other problems. ShoeCo has clearly been harmed by receiving defective goods, and is entitled to damages under section 2-714. ShoeCo takes the computer to CompuCorp, a local computer repair shop, and asks for an estimate on the cost to bring the computer into conformity with the contract. CompuCorp says that it can fix the motherboard, the software glitches, and the hard drive for $200, but that the computer has been assembled in a way that makes it impossible to upgrade the RAM to the amount promised by RetailMart. Because there is simply no way for anyone to repair the computer and turn it into the computer promised in the contract, cost of replacement will be the appropriate measure of damages.

If the court decides that cost of repair is the appropriate measure of damages, the evidence presented will be the actual or proposed repair bills. If the court decides that cost of replacement is the appropriate measure of damages, the evidence presented will have to establish the market value of the goods as delivered and the value of goods as promised, with damages being the difference between the two. To establish the value of goods promised, the court will start with the contract price but will let the buyer attempt to establish a higher value. This should make some sense, since the buyer might have struck a really good bargain. To establish the value of goods delivered, the court will expect evidence of the market value of goods similar to what was delivered. So, for example, ShoeCo will need to provide the court with evidence of what inferior goods are worth. If the computer ShoeCo ordered is worth $500 and the one that arrived sells for $250 online, ShoeCo will be able to recover $250.

F. Scrap and Salvage

There are some circumstances when the goods as delivered are so defective that they have no real market value as a combined unit. In that case, the court will look to scrap and salvage value to determine the value of goods delivered. Salvage value refers to the value of those items that can be removed and sold separately from the goods. Scrap refers to the value of any remaining raw materials that make up the goods. For example, ShoeCo's computer will have certain components that can be sold separately on the open market. The processor, the hard drive, any optical drive, perhaps the wireless card, and so on. Once those have been removed from the computer and sold, the remaining value is scrap value—the value of any platinum or gold used in the components, for example. Obviously, a new computer is going to have some independent market value, but for those goods that do not, scrap and salvage value may be the only way to assign any value to the goods as delivered. Damages can then be assessed as the difference between that value and the market value of the good described in the contract.

G. Incidental and Consequential Damages

Expectation damages often include incidental damages, those extra expenses that are incurred as the non-breaching party tries to preserve and pursue its remedies. There is another type of damage that might be recoverable — consequential damages. Consequential damages are those damages that arise as a secondary effect of the initial breach. Recall an example from Chapter 12: ShoeCo receives non-conforming laces from its supplier LaceCo and has to decide whether to accept them. In Chapter 12, we assumed ShoeCo accepted the goods in order to avoid defaulting on its contractual obligation to ship 500 shoes to RetailMart. Now, let us consider what happens if ShoeCo rejects the non-conforming goods, and as a result, breaches its contract with RetailMart. ShoeCo will have to pay damages to RetailMart, and those damages are a consequence of LaceCo's breach. As a result, ShoeCo will be able to choose one of the options listed above and *may* also be allowed to recover the amount paid to RetailMart as consequential damages.

Section 2-715(1) says that incidental damages can be recovered by the buyer so long as they are "reasonably incurred in inspection, receipt, transportation and care and custody of goods rightfully rejected." In other words, when seller delivers non-conforming goods, buyer may have to expend some time, effort, and money trying to deal with those goods. As long as buyer acts like a reasonable person would in dealing with the mess that seller's breach has caused, buyer will be able to recover those extra costs. Buyer can also recover "commercially reasonable charges, expenses, and commissions" that it incurs while exercising its rights to cover, or any other reasonable expenses.

Section 2-715(2) describes consequential damages in two types of instances: pure economic harm, or harm to person or property.

> (2) Consequential damages resulting from the seller's breach include
> (a) any loss resulting from general or particular requirements and needs of which the seller at the time of contracting had reason to know and which could not reasonably be prevented by cover or otherwise; and

    (b) injury to person or property proximately resulting from any
breach of warranty.*

Subsection (2)(a) addresses pure economic consequential damages as those
that arise from the needs of the buyer that the seller "had reason to know."
The needs that give rise to consequential damages can be general—those that
are common to everyone—or they can be more particular to the unique circumstances of the buyer. Notice, however, that only those needs that the seller
has reason to know can give rise to consequential damages. When the needs
are general, almost any seller will have reason to know because they are common to everyone. When the needs are specific, on the other hand, a seller won't
necessarily know anything about them unless the buyer says something that
would tip the seller off. At its most basic, the idea of consequential damages
boils down to whether the seller should have known that buyer was going to
suffer a lot more than just standard buyer's damages if seller were to breach.
A seller who knows that is the case will almost certainly demand a higher price
for the goods, since the risk if something goes wrong is much higher. Note also
that subsection (2)(a) also provides a limitation in that consequential damages that could have been prevented by the buyer making reasonable mitigation efforts are not recoverable.

    Subsection (2)(b) addresses consequential damages that include personal
injuries and injuries to property. This provision is broader than the previous
subsection in that there is no foreseeability standard nor is there a duty to mitigate. However, the causation standard is higher, requiring that the breach be
the proximate cause of the injury, unlike pure economic injuries, which are
governed by a "but for" standard.

    The U.C.C. does not contain a specific provision for consequential dam-
ages in the case of the seller, but a minimal amount of reflection should make
it clear why that is. A seller's expectations are to have a pile of money and no
goods after the contract. If the buyer breaches, seller has a pile of goods and
less money. The relative lack of money is certainly a problem, but there are a
number of places that the seller can go for money to fill the gap until the
goods are resold and damages are paid. For example, seller could get a loan
from a bank; doing so would require paying interest, but that would seem to
fall more into the category of incidental damages. Conversely, a buyer's
expectations are to have a pile of goods, and it is much more difficult—if not

---

impossible—to procure a replacement pile of goods. Whatever the buyer's plans for the goods, those plans can easily be thwarted, leading to even more harms downstream, from those who relied on the buyer's providing the goods. That stream of consequences can continue, disrupting many more people, and consequential damages are designed to make the seller take that into consideration before deciding whether to repudiate or breach. It is worth noting that section 2-719(3) permits contracts to limit consequential damages unless doing so would be unconscionable, but provides that it is prima facia unconscionable to limit consequential damages for personal injuries in a consumer contract.

H. Limitations on Damages

Section 2-719 provides a number of opportunities for the parties to limit or modify remedies if their contract ever results in a legal dispute. It states:

(1) Subject to the provisions of subsections (2) and (3) of this section and of the preceding section on liquidation and limitation of damages,

(a) the agreement may provide for remedies in addition to or in substitution for those provided in this Article and may limit or alter the measure of damages recoverable under this Article, as by limiting the buyer's remedies to return of the goods and repayment of the price or to repair and replacement of non-conforming goods or parts; and

(b) resort to a remedy as provided is optional unless the remedy is expressly agreed to be exclusive, in which case it is the sole remedy.

(2) Where circumstances cause an exclusive or limited remedy to fail of its essential purpose, remedy may be had as provided in this Act.

(3) Consequential damages may be limited or excluded unless the limitation or exclusion is unconscionable. Limitation of consequential damages for injury to the person in the case of consumer goods is prima facie unconscionable but limitation of damages where the loss is commercial is not.*

Subsection (3) and its provisions on limiting consequential damages were discussed above. Subsection (1) allows the parties to modify remedies, either

---

limiting them or augmenting them. Of particular note is that the parties can expressly limit buyer's right to return the goods and get its money back or the buyer's right to demand that defective goods or parts be repaired or replaced. So, if the contract so stipulates, buyer may not be able to demand a replacement for a defective good, but may only be able to get a refund. Alternatively, the contract might specify that refunds are not allowed and the buyer has to make do with a replacement or a repair.

This may seem particularly harsh to the buyer, but remember that this is an example the authors used, and similarly harsh modifications of remedy could be fashioned to the disadvantage of the seller, as well. Another question is often raised: what if the seller tried to limit the buyer's right to a refund *and* to repair or replacement? That would be truly harsh, and comment 1 states that "it is of the very essence of a sales contract that at least minimum adequate remedies be available." In other words, if the parties go too far and limit one party's remedies in an unconscionable fashion, the court will act as if the limitations and modifications were deleted from the text of the contract. So, there is a limit to how much you can limit damages, as it were. Subsection (2) does the same with even apparently fair or reasonable provisions — if they fail of their essential purpose, the courts will refuse to enforce them and will apply the traditional remedies included in Article 2 of the U.C.C.

Subsection 1 also contains an important provision regarding the default rule for interpreting modifications of remedies. Modifications and limitations on remedies included under the authority of 2-719 are presumed to be optional, not exclusive, and if the parties intend for a particular remedy to be the exclusive remedy, they must express that intent clearly in the contract.

One last note on damages limitations; under the common law, all damages must be calculable with reasonable certainty, making any future damages problematic. Past damages aren't a precise science — people's perception of the consequences of a breach will differ — but the regular evidentiary problems associated with establishing damages are relatively easy when compared to predicting the future. Section 1-305 requires that damages be "liberally administered," and Comment 1 adds that the U.C.C. rejects "any doctrine that damages must be calculable with mathematical accuracy." Of course, that doesn't mean that the court won't closely scrutinize a damages calculation for some certainty, but it does recognize that there is some uncertainty in everything and provides some flexibility in measuring and proving damages.

Checkpoints

- A buyer's remedies are triggered by seller's repudiation or delivery of non-conforming goods.

- Buyer can accept the goods and sue for damages or it can reject and pursue cover, hypothetical cover, or specific performance.

- If buyer chooses to cover, it buys substitute goods and can recover from seller the difference between what it paid and what it would have paid under the contract.

- If buyer chooses hypothetical cover, it recovers from the seller the difference between the market price of the goods and what it would have paid under the contract.

- Under certain circumstances, buyer might be able to force seller to provide the goods exactly as described in the contract.

- If buyer accepts the goods, buyer can recover from seller the difference between the value of goods as promised and the value of goods as delivered.

- If the goods can be repaired, buyer can recover the cost of having someone repair them.

- If the goods cannot be repaired, buyer can salvage and scrap the goods and recover the difference between the price of substitute goods and the salvage and scrap value.

- Salvage value is the value of components that can be sold separately.

- Scrap value is the value of raw materials that can be recovered from the non-conforming goods.

- Reasonable incidental damages are recoverable by buyer as part of the cost of cover.

- Damages to persons or property can be recovered as consequential damages if it can be shown that a breach of warranty was the proximate cause.

- Economic damages to the buyer can be recovered as consequential damages if the seller has reason to know of the buyer's needs.

- If buyer's needs are general, no special evidence need be shown but, if buyer's needs are specific to buyer, evidence of seller's knowledge will be required.

- Limitations on consequential damages are allowed unless unconscionable, and limitations on personal injuries in a consumer contract are prima facie unconscionable.

- Buyer and seller can agree to modify or limit remedies to the contract, but may not reduce a party's remedies below a minimum adequate remedy.

- Listed remedies will be not be considered as exclusive remedies unless the parties are clear and express in their intent.

- If a remedy fails in its primary purpose, traditional remedies will be applied.

- All contract remedies are subject to a requirement of reasonable certainty.

Chapter 21

Specific Performance and Liquidated Damages

Roadmap

- Specific performance
- Default is no specific performance
- Unique goods
- "Other circumstances"
- Replevin
- Liquidated damages
- Reasonableness
- No penalties

A. Specific Performance

As we discussed in Chapter 20, there are certain circumstance when it is possible to obtain specific performance, which is just a way of saying that the court can, under those circumstances, force the other party to do exactly what they promised. The seller's version of specific performance is a recovery of the contract price under section 2-709, as described in Chapter 19. For the buyer, specific performance is a recovery of the actual goods promised under section 2-716. The most important thing to know about specific performance is that it is strongly disfavored, and only available in very narrow circumstances. Section 2-716 allows for specific performance only when the goods are unique or "in other proper circumstances," although if goods have been identified to the contract, the buyer might have an action in replevin for those goods. Notice also that section 2-716(2) gives the court significant flexibility to adjust the order for specific performance in order to make sure the outcome is just.

1. Default is no specific performance

Courts will always be reluctant to order specific performance. There are two reasons for this reluctance. The first is a question of individual autonomy and liberty, that each individual should be free to act independently, including the decision to breach a contract. Forcing seller to make and deliver goods to the buyer when seller has refused to do so is an infringement on seller's autonomy. This is highlighted when you consider that the alternative is to make the seller pay damages. So long as damages will make the buyer whole, there is no need to infringe seller's autonomy by forcing seller to make and deliver goods.

Specific performance may also be inefficient, in that it would be a very tempting tool for buyers to use to strongarm sellers. If the seller wants out of the contract, seller can do so, provided it pays an amount in damages equivalent to its performance. A moment of reflection will make clear that a seller who knows this will only breach the contract if it believes that the buyer is in a better position to find a substitute seller. Unless the seller doesn't like money, it will fulfill the contract every time doing so will be cheaper than paying damages for breach. Likewise, if seller knows it is in a better position to find a substitute seller than buyer, seller will buy the goods from someone else, and deliver those because doing so will minimize the incidental damages it has to pay to buyer. In each of these cases, buyer gets what it bargained for, and the goods are provided in the cheapest way possible.

Imagine now that the buyer knows it can force specific performance. Seller contacts buyer and indicates that seller will be unable to fulfill the contract. Rather than begin mitigating, buyer threatens to go to court to force seller to make and deliver the goods. When seller says that it cannot provide the goods without driving itself almost into bankruptcy, buyer says: "That would be a terrible shame . . . maybe I'd be willing to let it go if you hand over $5,000." Doing so might make economic sense to the seller — it is better than bankruptcy — but this type of behavior is not appropriate in contract, which is supposed to be about voluntary transactions. Admittedly, this is an over-dramatic example, but the same idea — that the buyer can coerce a little extra out of a seller in exchange for not demanding specific performance — is an important justification for the default rule *against* specific performance.

2. Unique goods

Section 2-716(1) says that specific performance is available for goods that are unique. When that is the case, the buyer will obviously not be able to cover. For example, imagine that buyer has agreed to purchase the famous painting, Starry Night, by Vincent van Gough. Seller later tells buyer that the painting is no longer for sale. There is literally nowhere in the world buyer can procure a second Starry Night, and it would not be the same thing to buy a replica of the painting. Just as cover is impossible, hypothetical cover will be problematic, as there is no "market price" for a unique painting like this one. It might be possible to find an expert who could offer an opinion as to how much it is worth, but remember that section 2-723 states that market price is the price of goods of the same type. With unique goods, there are no goods of the same type, so market price cannot be determined. Specific performance might be disfavored, but in the case of unique goods, no other remedy is available.

With unique goods, there is also the danger of both over-compensation and under-compensation. Since there is no market for the goods, one way of judging how much the buyer was damaged by non-delivery is to ask buyer how much the goods were worth to it. Unfortunately, that creates a strong incentive for the buyer to lie and overestimate the value, leading to overcompensation. Alternatively, we could ignore buyer's subjective value and attempt to identify an objective value for the goods, but those who purchase unique goods are usually those who place subjective value on the goods. If we ignore their subjective value, we will undercompensate them and they will not be made whole. The only thing we truly know in this situation is that the parties bargained for an exchange of unique goods for a pile of cash. If we want to avoid the risk of over- or under-compensation, our best option is specific performance—make the parties effectuate the bargained-for exchange.

3. "Other circumstances"

Section 2-716(1) allows for specific performance outside of unique goods if there are other circumstances that are "proper" for specific performance. The U.C.C. does not define what those circumstances are, but courts will consider whether the same general conditions are present. Specifically, courts will consider whether the other remedies—cover or hypothetical cover—are available to the buyer in a meaningful sense. In other words, while buyer might be able to take these options, will either one make the buyer whole? If not, then the courts might allow specific performance. Of course, that just raises a new question: under what circumstances will cover and hypothetical cover not be effective to make the buyer whole?

In some cases, the goods might not be unique—one of a kind—but might be close enough that the same conditions apply. Finding a replacement may be difficult if not impossible, simply because the current owners of alternatives might not be willing to sell. If the goods are not bought and sold regularly, there may not be a reliable "market price," so hypothetical cover might be difficult. If there is reason to suspect that goods have subjective value, either over- or under-compensation is possible. At some point, the number of substitute goods gets high enough that cover or hypothetical cover become meaningful options, but it's not clear exactly how many have to exist before that happens. Even if there is a larger number, there might still be situations where over- and under-compensation are still a concern. Of course, if seller can prove that cover was possible and not overly-expensive, specific performance is probably off the table.

4. Replevin

Section 2-716(3) provides one other specific performance option, in the form of a cause of action for replevin, but only if cover is not possible. Replevin, if you remember your torts terms, is a cause of action to recover specific items. Replevin is allowed here only when the goods have been identified to the contract, which requires that the goods have already been created and were intended for the buyer. In other words, if the seller has the goods in its possession and it was the parties' intention that they be delivered, the buyer can sue to force their delivery.

B. Liquidated Damages

Contracts will often have a liquidated damages clause, which is a clause that defines exactly what damages will be in the case of a breach, or at the very least, the formula for calculating damages. Rather than leave calculation of damages to the courts, the parties have bargained for the level of damages up-front. One or both parties might insist on a liquidated damages clause if they believe that they will have difficulty proving damages in the wake of a breach. Perhaps the damages calculations are likely to be complex, for example, which might make it hard to persuade a jury that the damages have been proved with certainty. And if buyer knows that seller will have a hard time proving damages (or vice versa), buyer will have an incentive to act strategically, possibly even breaching because buyer knows that seller's damages will be limited. A liquidated damages clause can avoid that problem.

Including a liquidated damages clause bypasses all of the damages calculations—including all discussions of mitigation—and shifts any discussion of damages to whether the clause is enforceable. Section 2-718 says that damages can be liquidated if the amount is reasonable but not if it is so large that it acts as a penalty.

1. Reasonableness

For a liquidated damages clause to be enforceable, it must be reasonable. Section 2-718 elaborates on the meaning of reasonableness; specifically, damages can be liquidated if the amount is a reasonable approximation of the anticipated or actual loss, if it will be difficult to prove loss, and if there is doubt regarding the ability of the parties to obtain "an adequate remedy." There is a substantive element, a procedural element, and an overall justice element.

Substantively, a liquidated damages clause must be reasonable in terms of the amount of damages defined by the clause. Interestingly, section 2-718 says that the clause must have a reasonable approximation of the *anticipated* or *actual* harm, indicating that substantive reasonableness can be determined at either the time the contract was signed or at the time damages would be assessed. If, at the time the contract was signed and the parties agreed to the contract, the clause defined damages in a way that looked like what the parties could have expected the damages to eventually be, then the clause will be okay. Surprisingly, however, a clause that would have seemed outlandishly high at the time the contract was signed might still be reasonable if, once breach has occurred, the actual damages are in-line with what the clause defines.

Procedurally, a liquidated damages clause is reasonable if calculation of damages will be very difficult. One way that might be true is if the loss one or both parties would suffer is lost future profits. All calculations of future damages are going to be looked at skeptically, but it can be much worse if the party claiming damages is a new business. An old business might have years of sales and profit data, and could call an expert witness to testify about general market trends, past profits, etc., and make a good case for what profits would have been made in the future. If the business is new, there is no historical data to rely on, so almost everything will be speculative, considering market trends only, rather than things specific to the business. A liquidated damages clause in a contract involving a new business would be more likely to be enforced than one in a contract with an older business, because of the increased difficulty in proving damages.

The final way that a liquidated damages clause must be reasonable is with regard to the ability of the parties to obtain an adequate remedy. This is a concern about the overall justice of the contract. If a contract will leave a party uncompensated or significantly undercompensated, then a court is far more likely to enforce the liquidated damages clause.

2. No penalties

Liquidated damages clauses are often challenged as being unenforceable penalties. Section 2-718 expressly states that a clause that fixes an unreasonably large amount of damages will be "void as a penalty." This is tied to the substantive element of liquidated damages regulation under the U.C.C., that the amount must be reasonable. It is also part of a general prohibition on punitive damages in contract law. Punitive damages are somewhat common in tort law, although subject to some limitations, but they have no place in contract law for two reasons. First, because contracts are voluntary agreements, and the parties need some certainty regarding their risks and obligations. Punitive damages are, by their nature, unpredictable ex ante, as they depend on many factors, including how outraged the judge or jury are on the day the verdict is rendered. If the parties cannot know how much they will pay if they breach the contract, they might continue to perform when breach and contract damages would make all parties better off. Even worse, some parties might never be willing to contract because the risk of punitive damages is just too high.

Second, contract damages are designed to precisely compensate the non-breaching party so that they are indifferent between breach and non-breach. Regular under-compensation will lead all parties to consider breaching, since they will pay less for a breach than they would by performing. Regular over-compensation, on the other hand, creates an incentive for the parties to act strategically, trying to get the other party to breach because performance is second-best to the damages it would receive as the non-breaching party. Either way, deviating from exact compensation skews the relationship between the parties and makes all contracts less stable. Punitive damages, by their nature, are over-compensatory, so they are incompatible with contract law.

There is one way in which punitive damages might be awarded in a contract *case*, but not for a contract *claim*. If the plaintiff is able to prove—during the process of proving the necessary elements of a contract claim—actions by the defendant that constitute an independent tort, punitive damages might be recoverable, but only to the extent that the tort, itself, justifies the punitive damages.

Checkpoints

- Specific performance is disfavored, available only in limited circumstances.

- For the seller, specific performance is an action for the sales price under section 2-709.

- For the buyer, specific performance is available for goods that are unique because other buyers' remedies are unavailable.

- For the buyer, specific performance might also be available in cases where other remedies are not meaningfully available, such as when the number of substitute goods are very few or where cover would be particularly difficult.

- If the goods have been identified to the contract, buyer has a right in replevin to force delivery of those goods.

- Liquidated damages clauses establish a clear method of calculating damages, bypassing all other testimony regarding damages.

- Liquidated damages clauses are enforceable if they are substantively and procedurally reasonable, or if necessary to avoid the non-breaching party's being deprived of a remedy.

- Liquidated damages clauses are substantively reasonable if the amount of damages is a reasonable approximation of the damages as expected at the time the contract was signed, or as actually realized after the breach.

- Liquidated damages clauses are procedurally reasonable if there was reason to believe, at the time the contract was signed, that damages would be difficult or impossible to prove at trial.

- A liquidated damages clause is void if the amount of damages fixed by the clause is high enough that it constitutes a penalty.

- Penalties are disallowed in contract law because they overcompensate and because they destroy the parties' ability to anticipate the cost of breach.

Mastering Sales Checklist

Chapter 1 • The Scope of Article 2

❏ Article 2 of the U.C.C. displaces the common law for contracts.

❏ Where Article 2 does not address a matter, it is supplemented by the common law.

❏ Article 2 covers "transactions in goods" which includes sales.

❏ Though the term "transactions" is broader than just sales, it **does not** include leases.

❏ "Goods" are all things that are movable and identifiable.

❏ "Goods" do not include money used to buy things or securities.

❏ "Hybrid" or "mixed" transactions involve services and goods.

❏ The majority approach to "hybrid" transactions is the predominant purpose test.

❏ The minority approach to "hybrid" transactions is the gravamen test.

❏ Software is a gray area, and application of Article 2 may depend on the manner in which the software is marketed.

❏ Article 2 applies to merchants and non-merchants alike, but there are special provisions for merchants.

❏ The term merchant applies more broadly to some provisions, such as the statute of frauds, but narrowly to others, such as the implied warranty of merchantability.

Chapter 2 • Distinguishing Sales from Leases

❏ A transaction involving a secured sale of goods can be structured to look like a lease.

❑ Leases of goods are governed by Article 2A, while secured sales are governed by Articles 2 and 9.

❑ Characterization of a lease as a sale can negatively affect the lessor/seller's rights under Article 9 and bankruptcy if the interest is not perfected.

❑ Characterization of a lease as a sale may also affect tax deductions.

❑ To determine whether a lease is a disguised secured sale, courts use two tests: the "bright-line" test and the "economic realities" test.

❑ The "bright-line" test has 2 elements: 1) lessee has no right to realistically terminate the lease; and 2) one of the "residual value" factors are met.

❑ If the "bright-line" test is not met, courts move on to the "economic realities" test, which looks to see if the lessor is retaining a meaningful reversionary interest in the goods.

Chapter 3 • Contract Formation Under the U.C.C.

❑ Article 2 endorses a broad approach to contract formation, looking to the intent of the parties to be bound.

❑ Ads are presumptively not offers but can become offers if clear and definite as to how to accept, and if they leave nothing open for negotiation.

❑ With regard to acceptance, Article 2 differs from the common law only when the offer calls for prompt shipment, in which case the offeree can accept by shipping nonconforming goods, thus accepting and breaching the contract.

❑ In output/requirements contracts, the U.C.C. excuses a definite quantity, obligating the parties to rely upon good faith needs.

❑ Output/requirements contracts must be exclusive-dealings contracts to be enforceable.

❑ Firm offers are distinct from option contracts in that there is no need for consideration, so long as the offeror is a merchant and the period is no longer than three months.

❏ Online terms and conditions are governed by the same rules as other contracts, but the key inquiry is whether the design of the website puts the purchaser on reasonable notice of the terms' existence.

Chapter 4 • Battle of the Forms—Offer and Acceptance

❏ Section 2-207 applies to two situations: contracts on the forms, and confirmations of prior oral agreements.

❏ If an acceptance is definite and seasonable, there will be a contract on the forms, unless the acceptance is expressly conditional on imposition of its own terms.

❏ Definite terms are non-boilerplate, core transactional terms.

❏ For contracts on the forms, additional terms in the acceptance are proposals that can be ignored by the offeror if **a non-merchant is involved**.

❏ For contracts on the forms, **as between merchants**, additional terms in the acceptance are proposals that become a part of the contract unless: the original offer expressly limits acceptance to the terms in the offer; the offeror objects to the terms in a reasonable amount of time; or the additional terms materially alter the contract.

❏ Material alteration turns on whether the new terms would impose **surprise or hardship** on the party upon whom enforcement is sought.

❏ For contracts on the forms, **as between merchants**, different terms in the acceptance are subject to one of three jurisdictional approaches: the treat as additional approach, the ignore the proposed change approach, and the "knock-out rule" approach.

❏ Under the majority "knock-out rule" approach, differing terms knock each other out and the court gap-fills.

❏ If there is no contract on the forms, but the parties nonetheless proceed as if they have a contract, then there is a contract, but only on the terms upon which the offer and acceptance agree—other terms fall away and the court may gap-fill where needed.

Chapter 5 • Battle of the Forms — Confirmations

❏ Section 2-207 applies to two situations: contracts on the forms, and confirmations of prior oral agreements.

❏ Different terms in the confirmation are ignored, unless expressly agreed to by the other party, as a party cannot unilaterally amend a previously formed contract.

❏ Additional terms in a confirmation are proposals for addition. If a non-merchant is involved, the proposed additions are ignored unless expressly agreed upon.

❏ As between merchants, additional terms in a confirmation will become a part of the contract subject to the caveats listed in section 2-207(2)(a)-(c) (as discussed in the previous Chapter).

❏ Particularly in situations involving shrink-wrap terms, some courts have adopted a "rolling" (or "layered") contract approach.

❏ The rolling contract approach considers the later form to be the offer (rather than a confirmation) which can be accepted or rejected by the recipient.

❏ Under the rolling contract approach, the later form must still conspicuously give the recipient the right to reject the offer, and explain how to do so.

❏ The rolling contract approach may result in terms becoming a part of the contract that would not survive an analysis under section 2-207(2).

Chapter 6 • Statute of Frauds

❏ Writings and signatures may be in electronic form.

❏ A signature may consist of any symbol intended to be adopted by a party, including letterheads of businesses and email addresses.

❏ Section 2-201(1) requires a writing indicating a contract, with a signature by the party against whom enforcement is sought, and a quantity.

❏ Section 2-201(1) has four exceptions: a "between merchants" exception, a "specially manufactured goods" exception, a payment/acceptance exception, and an admission exception.

❑ The between merchants exception allows a confirmation that would be enforceable against the sender, to be enforceable against the recipient if there is no written objection within 10 days.

❑ The "specially manufactured goods" exception only applies to sellers who have made a substantial beginning or commitments for procurement.

❑ The payment/acceptance exception allows enforcement of a contract but only in proportion to what has been paid or accepted.

❑ Under the admission exception, most courts permit some discovery before granting a motion to dismiss, to permit a plaintiff to solicit an admission.

❑ Section 2-201(1) may implicate other sections, in particular section 2-207 with regard to confirmations and section 2-209(3) when a modification brings a contract within section 2-201.

Chapter 7 • Contract Interpretation and the Parol Evidence Rule

❑ Contracts are to be interpreted within the context in which they are made.

❑ When interpreting contracts, the following hierarchy is to be followed: express terms, followed by course of performance, course of dealing, and finally usage of trade.

❑ Course of performance is how the parties have acted under the contract in dispute.

❑ Course of dealing is how the same two parties have acted in similar previous contracts with each other.

❑ Usage of trade is how other parties in the industry act in similar circumstances.

❑ Courts determine, as a matter of law, whether contract terms are ambiguous, and whether contracts are fully or partially integrated.

❑ The U.C.C. generally rejects a "plain meaning" approach to ambiguity.

❑ Under the U.C.C., if a contract is partially integrated, then extrinsic evidence may be introduced so long as it does not contradict the writing.

❏ Under the U.C.C., if a contract is fully integrated, then extrinsic evidence may not be introduced, except for course of performance, course of dealing, and usage of trade, so long as it is not used to contradict the writing.

❏ The parol evidence rule does not apply to subsequent agreements, nor to writings **not** intended as a final expression of the parties' agreement.

❏ The parol evidence rule generally does not apply when a voidability defense is at issue.

❏ The presence of a merger clause may call into question the availability of a fraud defense in some jurisdictions.

Chapter 8 • Express Warranties

❏ Express warranties can be created by promises, affirmations of fact, descriptions, samples, or models.

❏ The word "warranty" or "guarantee" need not be used for a statement to be actionable as an express warranty.

❏ Affirmations of value and opinions are **not** actionable as express warranties.

❏ All express warranties must be viewed within the context that they are made.

❏ Express warranties may be based on pre-sale negotiations and statements that do not end up in the final sale contract.

❏ Aggrieved buyers need not show reliance on the statement, only that the statement became some part of the basis of the bargain.

❏ Post-sale warranties, though subject to a basis of the bargain defense, may be enforceable under a number of theories.

❏ Puffery, or seller's talk, is not actionable, as such statements could not become the basis of the bargain for any reasonable buyer.

❏ Puffery includes both exaggerated boasts which would be unreasonable to believe and vague or highly subjective claims of product superiority.

Chapter 9 • Implied Warranties

❏ Article 2 contains default implied warranties of merchantability and fitness for a particular purpose.

❏ The warranty of merchantability only applies to contracts for the sale of goods in which the seller is a merchant with regard to goods of the type at issue.

❏ Whether a good is merchantable depends heavily on what passes without objection in the trade.

❏ Merchantable goods must also be fit for their ordinary purpose — an inquiry that will often require expert testimony.

❏ To be merchantable, goods must also be adequately packaged and labelled.

❏ Merchantability also requires that goods live up to any express promises made on the container or label, regardless of whether such statements were the basis of the bargain.

❏ The fitness warranty applies to merchants and non-merchants alike.

❏ The fitness warranty has three elements: 1) the seller must have reason to know of the buyer's particular purpose; 2) have reason to know the buyer is relying on the seller's skill or judgment; and 3) the buyer must, in fact, rely upon the seller's judgment.

Chapter 10 • Disclaiming and Limiting Warranties

❏ Express warranties may be reasonably modified, but not negated, through other contractual language.

❏ Express warranties are still subject to the parol evidence rule and merger clauses.

❏ Implied warranties of merchantability and fitness may be excluded through the use of safe harbor language found in section 2-316(2), but must be conspicuous.

❏ Implied warranties of merchantability and fitness can also be disclaimed through "as is" clauses or clauses of similar import.

❑ Implied warranties may be negated by an examination, if the examination ought to have revealed the defect, taking into consideration the buyer's expertise.

❑ A refusal to examine may also be the basis of a disclaimer, but the seller must essentially demand that the buyer conduct such an examination.

❑ Disclaimers may also be found through course of performance, course of dealing and trade usage.

❑ Apart from disclaiming warranties, sellers may also limit the buyer's remedies so long as the limitation does not "fail of its essential purpose."

❑ Sellers may limit a buyer's remedies to repair or replace.

❑ Sellers may also exclude consequential damages, but such limitations for personal injuries involving consumer goods are prima facie unconscionable.

Chapter 11 • Warranty of Title

❑ Sellers generally can convey no more title than they themselves have, subject to voidability and entrustment exceptions.

❑ If the seller has voidable title, the seller may convey good title to a good faith purchaser for value.

❑ If a merchant seller has been entrusted with goods, the seller may convey good title upon a buyer in the ordinary course of business.

❑ Every sale of goods comes with a warranty that title is good, rightful, and free of all liens.

❑ The warranty of title may be disclaimed by either specific language or by the circumstances.

❑ To disclaim by specific language, the language must be clear and unequivocal, and should probably be conspicuous.

❑ The circumstances that will give rise to a disclaimer of title are ones outside the normal commercial practices, in which it is known that the seller is selling an unknown or limited right, such as a sheriff's sale.

❏ Every sale by a merchant also comes with a warranty against infringement, which covers subsequent claims against the buyer such as for patent, trademark, or copyright infringement.

Chapter 12 • Breach and Cure

❏ Article 2 adopts the perfect tender standard for a seller's contract performance.

❏ The perfect tender rule requires performance in exact compliance with contract terms.

❏ The perfect tender rule also opens the door to extortionary pressures, which can lead to forfeiture.

❏ Article 2 mitigates the risk of forfeiture through interpretive rules, the duty to mitigate, the opportunity to cure, and the nature of markets for goods.

❏ If non-conforming goods are received, the buyer can reject the whole shipment, accept the whole shipment (and sue for damages), or accept one or more commercial units and reject the rest.

❏ If the buyer wishes to reject non-conforming goods, it must notify the seller of the specific nature of the non-conformity.

❏ The duty to mitigate requires the non-breaching party to take reasonable actions to lessen the harm caused by the breach.

❏ If a seller sends non-conforming goods, but can get a shipment of conforming goods to the buyer before the time of performance, the buyer must allow it.

❏ If a seller had reasonable grounds to believe non-conforming goods would be accepted, the seller may send conforming goods within a reasonable time after the time of performance.

❏ Article 2 adopts an exception to the perfect tender rule for installment contracts.

❏ An installment can be rejected only if the non-conformity substantially impairs the value of the shipment.

❏ An installment contract can only be terminated if one or more faulty shipments substantially impair the value of the whole contract.

Chapter 13 • Anticipatory Repudiation and Adequate Assurances

❑ A party can repudiate a contract either expressly or impliedly.

❑ Express repudiation must be unambiguous.

❑ Implied repudiation occurs when actions make it plainly impossible to perform.

❑ The non-breaching party can wait a commercially reasonable time after repudiation, but must then start mitigation efforts.

❑ The breaching party can retract the repudiation at any time before the next deadline for performance or until the non-breaching party accepts the repudiation.

❑ If the non-breaching party is uncertain regarding repudiation, or the capacity of the other party to perform, it can demand reasonable assurances.

❑ If assurances don't come, aren't adequate, or aren't given in a commercially reasonable time, the uncertain party can consider the contract repudiated.

Chapter 14 • Impracticability

❑ Under the right circumstances, an unexpected occurrence can excuse performance.

❑ Excuse is available only if the occurrence is something that the parties assumed would not happen.

❑ Excuse is available only if neither party accepted the risk of the occurrence happening.

❑ Assumption of risk can be found implicitly, as through the least-cost-avoider doctrine.

❑ Excuse is available only if performance would be commercially impracticable, or so expensive as to make it unjust to require performance.

❑ If goods identified to the contract are harmed, the contract will be partially or completely avoided due to the impracticability of delivering the identified goods.

❏ If performance is excused for one party, the entire contract is excused and both parties can walk away.

❏ If either party has partially performed, it might recover the value of the benefit bestowed, based on equitable claims for unjust enrichment.

❏ If impracticability only affects part of the seller's ability to perform, the seller must allocate the goods to its customers in a fair and reasonable manner, usually on a pro rata basis.

Chapter 15 • Unconscionability

❏ A court can refuse to enforce a contract it deems unconscionable.

❏ Unconscionability analysis is foundationally a question of fairness.

❏ Most courts require a contract to be both procedurally and substantively unconscionable before granting relief.

❏ A contract can be procedurally unconscionable if one of the parties is denied a meaningful choice because unfair terms were hidden in the contract.

❏ A contract can be procedurally unconscionable if one of the parties' bargaining power was so unequal that it borders on duress.

❏ A standard form contract, or contract of adhesion, may be evidence of procedural unconscionability, but is not per se unconscionable.

❏ A contract can be substantively unconscionable if the terms of the contract are so heavily weighted to the benefit of one party that it is shockingly unfair.

❏ Unconscionability is decided by a judge rather than a jury.

❏ If a contract or clause is found to be unconscionable, a court may void the entire contract, or excise the offending clause, or reform the contract to avoid the unconscionable effect.

❏ Due to the effect the doctrine has on commercial contracting, courts rarely invoke it.

Chapter 16 • Rejection and Revocation

❏ Goods that do not conform in every way to the contract may be rejected under the U.C.C.'s perfect tender rule.

❏ Rejection must be made in a reasonable time, given the context of the transaction.

❏ The seller must be notified in a reasonable time, which will often be, but need not necessarily be, contemporaneous to the rejection.

❏ If defective goods are accepted, the buyer's normal course of action is to sue for damages, but revocation may be possible.

❏ If the buyer knows of the defects, revocation is allowed only if the goods were accepted with a promise of cure that never materialized.

❏ If the buyer doesn't know of the defects, revocation is allowed only if the defect was difficult to discover or the seller's reassurances dissuaded buyer from inspecting.

❏ Revocation is only allowed if the defects are substantial.

❏ Revocation must occur within a reasonable time, and before any new defects are created.

❏ If seller disputes buyer's right to revoke, buyer will bear the burden of proving that revocation was appropriate.

Chapter 17 • Privity

❏ Those who sign their name to a contract—or who verbally agree to a binding contract—are in privity, and that privity includes the right to enforce promises.

❏ A third party who is not in privity may not enforce the contract *unless* it shows that the actual parties to the contract intended to give it the right to enforce.

❏ Intended beneficiaries may enforce; incidental beneficiaries may not.

❏ A third-party beneficiary who is also a creditor of one of the parties to the contract can be an intended beneficiary.

❏ A donee who has a special relationship with one of the parties might be able to enforce, if the relationship is close enough that the court can conclude that the parties intended to grant the right to enforce.

❏ Any other third party who wishes to enforce must show that the circumstances of the contract indicate that the parties intended to grant the right to enforce.

❏ Any third-party beneficiary that is not an intended beneficiary is an incidental beneficiary, and may not enforce.

❏ Each state can adopt one of three alternatives to establish a statutory class of intended beneficiaries of express and intended warranties.

❏ Sellers remain free to limit or exclude warranties, but any warranties offered to the buyer extend to this statutory class of intended beneficiaries.

Chapter 18 • Risk of Loss

❏ Risk of loss rules govern who loses out if the goods are lost or destroyed.

❏ Seller bears the risk of loss during production or procurement, and retains the risk until the goods are tendered.

❏ If the contract requires tender without delivery, buyer bears risk as soon as goods are tendered.

❏ If the contract requires seller to deliver to a specific location, seller bears the expense and risk of getting goods to that location.

❏ If the contract specifies a particular vessel or vehicle for transport, seller bears the expense and risk of loading the goods into that vessel or vehicle.

❏ If the contract requires only general delivery to the buyer, seller bears the risk until goods have been provided to the carrier for transport.

❏ If the contract is breached, the breaching party bears the risk of loss until cure or cover occurs.

❏ Risk of loss rules impose the risk on the least cost avoider of loss.

Chapter 19 • Seller's Remedies

❏ If buyer rejects or refuses to pay for conforming goods, it has breached, and seller can choose its remedy.

❏ If buyer repudiates, seller can cancel shipment for any goods not yet shipped, or recall any goods still in transit.

❏ Seller can "cover" — reselling the goods to a new buyer — and recover the difference between the sale price and the contract price, but only if seller acts in good faith and in a commercially reasonable manner.

❏ If seller uses a public sale to cover, it must be done at a place normally used for such sales, buyer must be given notice, and potential buyers must be given the opportunity to inspect the goods.

❏ If seller uses a private sale to cover, buyer must be given adequate notice.

❏ Seller can use "hypothetical cover" — keeping the goods for its own inventory — to receive the difference between the contract price and the market price at the time of the breach.

❏ Seller cannot immediately resell the goods after hypothetical cover unless it is a lost volume seller, meaning that it had the capacity to make both the contractual sale and the resale, both sales would have been profitable, and the new sale would have happened anyway.

❏ A lost volume seller is allowed to recover the profits from a hypothetical resale *and* resell the goods, because doing so is the only way to compensate a lost volume seller for the particular loss occasioned by buyer's breach.

❏ Courts ignore — as a drafting error — the final phrase of section 2-708(2) requiring offset for any resale proceeds.

❏ Seller can recover the contract price *only* if the buyer has already taken possession of the goods or if seller has tried and failed to resell the goods.

❏ If buyer breaches during the production process, seller can either scrap and salvage the unfinished goods — or finish the goods if doing so is commercially reasonable — and recover the difference between the contract amount and the resale value of the goods.

Chapter 20 • Buyer's Remedies

❏ A buyer's remedies are triggered by seller's repudiation or delivery of non-conforming goods.

❏ Buyer can accept the goods and sue for damages or it can reject and pursue cover, hypothetical cover, or specific performance.

❏ If buyer chooses to cover, it buys substitute goods and can recover from seller the difference between what it paid and what it would have paid under the contract.

❏ If buyer chooses hypothetical cover, it recovers from the seller the difference between the market price of the goods and what it would have paid under the contract.

❏ Under certain circumstances, buyer might be able to force seller to provide the goods exactly as described in the contract.

❏ If buyer accepts the goods, buyer can recover from seller the difference between the value of goods as promised and the value of goods as delivered.

❏ If the goods can be repaired, buyer can recover the cost of having someone repair them.

❏ If the goods cannot be repaired, buyer can salvage and scrap the goods and recover the difference between the price of substitute goods and the salvage and scrap value.

❏ Salvage value is the value of components that can be sold separately.

❏ Scrap value is the value of raw materials that can be recovered from the non-conforming goods.

❏ Reasonable incidental damages are recoverable by buyer as part of the cost of cover.

❏ Damages to persons or property can be recovered as consequential damages if it can be shown that a breach of warranty was the proximate cause.

❏ Economic damages to the buyer can be recovered as consequential damages if the seller has reason to know of the buyer's needs.

❏ If buyer's needs are general, no special evidence need be shown but, if buyer's needs are specific to buyer, evidence of seller's knowledge will be required.

❏ Limitations on consequential damages are allowed unless unconscionable, and limitations on personal injuries in a consumer contract are prima facie unconscionable.

❏ Buyer and seller can agree to modify or limit remedies to the contract, but may not reduce a party's remedies below a minimum adequate remedy.

❏ Listed remedies will be not be considered as exclusive remedies unless the parties are clear and express in their intent.

❏ If a remedy fails in its primary purpose, traditional remedies will be applied.

❏ All contract remedies are subject to a requirement of reasonable certainty.

Chapter 21 • Specific Performance and Liquidated Damages

❏ Specific performance is disfavored, available only in limited circumstances.

❏ For the seller, specific performance is an action for the sales price under section 2-709.

❏ For the buyer, specific performance is available for goods that are unique because other buyers' remedies are unavailable.

❏ For the buyer, specific performance might also be available in cases where other remedies are not meaningfully available, such as when the number of substitute goods are very few or where cover would be particularly difficult.

❏ If the goods have been identified to the contract, buyer has a right in replevin to force delivery of those goods.

❏ Liquidated damages clauses establish a clear method of calculating damages, bypassing all other testimony regarding damages.

❏ Liquidated damages clauses are enforceable if they are substantively and procedurally reasonable, or if necessary to avoid the nonbreaching party's being deprived of a remedy.

❏ Liquidated damages clauses are substantively reasonable if the amount of damages is a reasonable approximation of the damages as expected at the time the contract was signed, or as actually realized after the breach.

❏ Liquidated damages clauses are procedurally reasonable if there was reason to believe, at the time the contract was signed, that damages would be difficult or impossible to prove at trial.

❏ A liquidated damages clause is void if the amount of damages fixed by the clause is high enough that it constitutes a penalty.

❏ Penalties are disallowed in contract law because they overcompensate and because they destroy the parties' ability to anticipate the cost of breach.

Index

A

Acceptance, 26–28, 31, 34–38, 45, 46, 60, 64, 87, 153, 189, 210–213
  breach, 175, 176
  confirmation, 47, 48
  contract formation, 23, 24, 32, 33
    as between merchants, 39, 41
    as between non-merchants, 39
  damages, 192, 193
  different terms, 42–44
  of non-conforming goods, 119, 120, 157
  part performance exceptions, 59
    payment/acceptance exception, 61
  rejection of the whole, 118
  revocation, 155–157
  rolling contract, 50–52
  wrongful rejection, 179, 180
Advertisements, 23, 25
Agent, 4
  least cost avoider, 177
  merchant status, 12
  rejection of the whole, 118
  shipped goods, 172, 173
  threshold requirements of U.C.C. §2-201(1), 56
  warranty, 93–95
Ambiguous, 73, 213
  disclaiming implied warranty of title, 109
  judicial approaches, 67, 68

Arbitration, 45, 51
  additional terms, 38
  "knock-out" rule, 43, 44
  U.C.C. §2-207, 52
Assurances, 129, 135, 218
  adequate assurance, 132–134
  installment contracts, 126
  repudiation, 132
  revocation, 156

B

Bankruptcy, 22, 210
  commercial law, 4
  impracticable performance, 141
  sales, 16, 17
  specific performance, 202
Battle of the Forms, 35, 36, 47, 211, 212
  merchant, 13
Breach, 27, 82, 126, 128, 188, 192, 199, 207, 217, 222, 223, 225
  adequate assurance, 132–134
  cover, 190
  damages, 193
    incidental and consequential, 195–197
    limitations on, 198
  disclaiming implied warranties, 95
  duty to mitigate, 122, 123
  excuse by impracticability, 137, 138
  hypothetical cover, 182

of installment contracts, 125
limiting remedies, 100
liquidated damages, 204
    unenforceable penalties, 206
lost volume sellers, 183–185
perfect tender rule, 113–116
reasonableness, 205
rejection of non-conforming
    goods, 153
repudiation, 129–132
revocation, 156
risk of loss, 169, 173–176
specific performance, 202
unallocated risk, 140
void title, 105
of warranty, 165
wrongful rejection of goods, 179,
    180

C
Common Law, 14, 34, 37, 55, 60, 65,
    140, 209, 210
acceptance, 26, 27
commercial law and, 4
contract formation, 24
contract modification, 28, 29
damage limitations, 198
duty to mitigate, 123
firm offer, 30, 31
hybrid transactions, 7–9
intended beneficiaries, 162
judicial approaches to contract
    interpretation, 68
    parol evidence rule, 69
least cost avoider, 176
"mirror image" rule, 35, 36
perfect tender rule, 116
performance exceptions, 59
privity, 161

repudiation under, 129, 132
threshold requirements of U.C.C.
    §2-201(1), 57
unconscionability, 146
Confirmation, 12, 46, 53, 57, 64,
    133, 211, 212, 213
"between merchants" exception,
    58
changed terms, 48
follow-up confirmations, 47, 48
rolling contract, 49, 52
U.C.C. §2-201(1), 63
U.C.C. §2-207, 36, 37, 50, 51, 62
Consequential Damages, 95, 97, 122,
    189, 193, 195–197, 199, 216,
    223, 224
remedy limitations, 100, 102
Consideration, 23, 34, 78, 102, 210,
    216
"bright line" test, 18, 19
"economic realities" test, 20
firm offers, 30, 31
modification, 48, 63, 81
in requirements and exclusive
    dealings contracts, 28–30
Course of Dealing, 43, 73, 102, 115,
    213, 214, 216
contract interpretation and
    construction, 65–68
implied warranties, 87
    disclaiming of, 99, 100
    merchantability, 88
parol evidence rule, 69
    fully integrated contracts, 71
    partially integrated contracts,
    70
rejection, 153
    wrongful rejection, 179

Course of Performance, 43, 73, 102, 115, 132, 175, 203, 213, 214, 216
  contract interpretation and construction, 65–68
  disclaiming implied warranties, 99, 100
  parol evidence rule, 69
    fully integrated contracts, 71
    partially integrated contracts, 70
  rejection, 153, 179
Cover, 177, 179, 181, 188, 199, 207, 221–224
  adequate assurance, 134
  breach, 176
  consequential damages, 195
  hypothetical cover, 182, 191
  imperfect tender, 189, 190
  lost volume seller, 183, 184
  shipped goods, 174
  specific performance, 202–204
    replevin, 204
    unique goods, 202, 203
Crops, 7, 142
Cure, 113, 116, 128, 159, 177, 217, 220, 221
  breach, 175, 176
  duty to mitigate, 121
  installment contracts, 125, 126
  opportunity to, 124
  perfect tender rule, 116
  rejection, 154
  revocation of acceptance, 156, 157

D
Disclaim, 41, 86, 93, 111, 126, 216
  express warranties, 94
  implied warranties, 95–100, 109

Disclaimer, 85, 109, 111, 216
  additional and different terms, 36, 38, 41, 45
  express warranties, 94
  implied warranties, 95, 96, 98, 100
  of title, 108
  remedy limitations, 100–102
Duty, 10, 13, 113, 128, 217
  adequate assurance, 132, 133
  after rejection, 117, 118
  excuse by impracticability, 137
  to mitigate, 121–123, 125, 131, 132
    consequential damages, 196
    under installment contracts, 125
    under repudiation, 130, 187
    under rejection, 154
      anticipatory repudiation, 131, 132
  to read, 32

E
Exclusive Dealings Contract, 23, 28, 34, 210
Excuse(s)(d), 34, 41, 99, 130, 132, 141, 143, 144, 210, 218, 219
  by impracticability, 137
    commercial impracticability, 140, 142
    unallocated risk, 139, 140
    unexpected contingency, 138, 139
  requirements and output contracts, 30

F
Firm Offer(s), 23, 29, 30, 31, 34, 210

G

Good Faith, 34, 111, 115, 132, 188,
    210, 216, 222
    after repudiation, 118
    cover, 181, 190
    descriptions, 78
    entrustment, 106, 107
    excuse by impracticability, 137,
        138
    merchant status, 13
    requirements and output con-
        tracts, 29, 30
    voidable title, 104, 105
    void title, 105

I

Impracticability, 142–144, 170, 218,
    219
    excuse by, 137
        unexpected contingency, 138,
            139
    impracticable performance, 140,
        141
Incidental Damages, 199, 223
    cover, 191
    expectation damages, 195, 196
    hypothetical cover, 182
    lost volume sellers, 184
    substitute seller, 202
Inspection, 41, 93
    basis of the bargain, 80
    disclaiming implied warranties
        by, 98
    harmed goods, 141
    incidental damages, 195
    revocation of acceptance, 156
    sample/model, 79
Insurance, 20, 141
    breach, 175, 176
    shipped goods, 174

Interpretation, 29, 67, 99, 192, 213
    parol evidence rule, 72
    under the U.C.C., 65, 66

L

Lease(s), 4, 14, 22, 209, 210
    "bright-line" test, 18–20
    "economic realities" test, 20, 21
    sales and, 15–18
    transactions, 6
Least Cost Avoider, 169, 177, 221
    risk of loss, 176
    unallocated risk, 140
Liquidated Damages, 201, 207, 224,
    225
    liquidated damages clause, 204
    penalties, 206
    reasonableness, 205, 206
Lost Volume Seller, 179, 183–185,
    188, 222

M

Market Price, 188, 199, 222, 223
    breach, 176
    hypothetical cover, 182, 191, 192
    imperfect tender rejection, 190
    U.C.C. § 2-716(1), 204
    unique goods, 203
    wrongful rejection, 180
Merchant, 3, 4, 9, 14, 30, 34, 36, 46,
    53, 55, 57, 62, 64, 79, 92, 98,
    108–111, 118, 122, 209–213,
    215–217
    additional terms between mer-
        chants, 39, 41
    adequate assurance, 133
    "between merchants" exception,
        58
    controlling terms, 42, 48
    disclaiming implied warranties, 95

entrustment, 106, 107
  firm offers, 31
  merchantable, 85–88, 99
merchant status, 11–13
  non-merchant, 39, 90
  rolling contract, 49, 52
Merger Clause(s), 68, 73, 102, 214,
  215
  avoiding parol evidence rule, 72
  disclaiming express warranties, 94
Mitigate, 113, 128, 217
  adequate assurance, 132
  contract repudiation, 130
  damages, 196
  duty to, 121–123
  imperfect tender rejection, 189
  installment contracts, 125
  least cost avoider, 176, 177
  mitigation/breach, 131, 132
  reasonable rejection time, 154
  scrap/salvage, 187
  unallocated risk, 140
  wrongful rejection of goods, 180
Modification, 64, 213
  avoiding parol evidence rule, 72
  bargain, 81
  consideration, 29
  controlling terms, 48
  damages limitations, 198
  interaction of § 2-201 with §§
    2-207 and 2-209 and, 63
  limiting remedies, 100
  merchant status, 13

O
Option Contract, 23, 34
  firm offers, 30, 31
Output Contract, 29

P
Parol Evidence Rule, 65, 73, 102,
  213–215
  ambiguity and interpretation, 68
  avoiding application of, 71, 72
  bargain basis, 80
  disclaiming express warranties, 94
  fully integrated contracts, 71
  partially integrated contracts, 69,
    70
Privity, 161, 167, 220
  U.C.C. warranties, 165, 166
Property, 15–17, 141, 199, 223
  damages, 195, 196
  risk of loss, 170
  software, 9

R
Rejection, 115, 158, 220
  acceptance of non-conforming
    goods, 119, 120
  additional terms between mer-
    chants, 41
  breach, 175
  imperfect tender, 189
  installment contracts, 126
  of non-conforming goods, 153,
    154
  reasonable notice, 155
  reasonable time, 154
    rejection of the whole, 117, 118
    wrongful rejection, 179
Reliance, 83, 214
  affirmations, 76
  avoiding parol evidence rule, 72
  bargain, 79–81
  implied warranty of fitness, 90, 91
  part performance exceptions, 59

Remedies, 102, 199, 207, 221, 222, 224
  acceptance, 27
  adequate assurance, 133
  breach, 176
  damages limitations, 197, 198
  disclaim or limit warranty, 93, 94
  hypothetical cover, 191, 192
  imperfect tender, 189
  incidental and consequential, 195
  limiting remedies, 100, 101
  lost volume sellers, 183
  non-conforming goods, 119
  U.C.C. §2-716(1), 203
  recover price, 185
  rejection of the whole, 117
  repudiation, 130
  revoking acceptance, 155, 156
  specific performance, 192
  wrongful rejection, 179, 180
Replevin, 204, 207, 224
  specific performance, 201
Repudiation, 129, 130, 133, 135, 199, 218, 222
  adequate assurance, 132
  hypothetical cover, 192
  mitigation/breach, 131, 132
  specially manufactured goods exception, 59, 60
Requirement(s) Contract, 34, 210
  consideration in, 29, 30
Revocation, 153, 159, 220
  acceptance and, 155–157
  breach and, 175
  burden of proof, 158
  nonconformity, 157
  substantial change, 157
Risk of Loss, 20, 89, 141, 221
  breach, 175, 176
    importance of, 169
    least cost avoider, 176, 177
    when goods are shipped, 171–174
    when it passes, 169, 170

S
Salvage, 179, 188, 189, 199, 222, 223
  imperfect tender, 190
  sale/lease distinction, 19
  scrap and, 186, 187, 194, 195
  wrongful rejection of goods, 180
Scope, 15, 25, 66, 88, 93, 209
  Article 2, 4, 5
  commercial law, 3, 4
Scrap, 123, 179, 185, 188, 189, 199, 222, 223
  imperfect tender, 190
  salvage, 186, 187, 194, 195
Seasonable, 46, 153, 211
  acceptance, 28
  contract formation when writings fail, 44
  contract formation with a written offer, 37
  non-conforming goods, 120, 154
  notice, 155
  rejection of the whole, 117, 118
  U.C.C., 36
Software, 3, 9, 11, 14, 52, 194, 209
  disclaiming implied warranties, 96, 97
  distinguishing ads from offers, 25
  rolling contract, 49
  transactions, 6
  Zeidenberg, ProCD, Inc. v., 49, 50
Specific Performance, 189, 199, 201, 207, 223, 224
  default, 202
  recover price, 186

replevin, 204
U.C.C. 2-716(1), 203, 204
unique goods, 202, 203
Statute of Frauds, 14, 48, 55, 64, 209, 212
admission exception, 61
"between merchants" exception, 57, 59
consideration, 29
contract formation and U.C.C., 24
hybrid transactions, 9
interaction of § 2-201 with §§ 2-207 and 2-209 and, 63
merchant status, 12
part performance exceptions, 59
payment/acceptance exception, 61
threshold requirements of U.C.C. §2-201(1), 56

T
Tender, 128, 159, 217, 220, 221
breach, 175, 176
imperfect tender rejection, 189
installment contracts, 125–127
least cost avoider, 177
limiting remedies, 101
non-conforming goods acceptance, 119
non-conforming goods rejection, 153
opportunity to cure, 124, 125
perfect tender rule, 113–116
rejection of the whole, 116, 117
revoking acceptance, 156
shipped goods, 171–174
specific performance, 192, 193
substantial impairment, 157
wrongful rejection of goods, 179

Third-Party Beneficiaries, 167, 220, 221
privity, 161, 162
Tort, 89, 204
implied warranty of merchantability, 87
penalties, 206
software, 10
Trade Usage, 79, 102, 216
ambiguity and interpretation, 68
"knock-out rule", 43
merchantable meaning, 88
U.C.C. tools, 65, 67

U
Unambiguous, 135, 218
ambiguity and interpretation, 67
payment/acceptance exception, 61
repudiation, 129
Unconscionability, 145, 151, 219
absence of meaningful choice, 147
adhesion contracts, 148, 149
avoiding parol evidence rule, 72
limiting remedies, 102
procedural, 146
rolling contract limitations, 51
substantive, 149, 150
success of claim, 150

W
Warranty, 10, 36, 40, 90–94, 96, 98–100, 165, 166, 193, 196, 199, 223
express warranty, 75–83, 214
affirmations of fact, promises, and descriptions, 76
bargain, 80, 81
express warranties, 75–76
role of puffery, 82

implied warranty of merchant-
    ability, 14, 85, 87, 209, 215
    affirmations of fact, 78
    contract formation when
        writings fail, 45
    disclaiming, 108
    disclaiming implied warranties,
        95
    disclaiming implied warranty
        of title, 108

hybrid transactions, 8
implied warranty of title, 86,
    103–111, 216
merchant status, 11, 13
software, 11
warranty against infringement,
    103, 109, 111, 217
warranty of fitness, 85, 89, 215
    disclaiming implied warranties,
        95